MW01645020

Norwegians in America, Some Records of the Norwegian Emigration to America:

A transcribed and translated version of the 1888 Nordmændene i Amerika, Nogle Optegnelser om De Norskes Udvandring til Amerika

Written by Knud Langeland

Translated into English by Odd-Steinar Dybvad Raneng

Transcribed from Dano-Norwegian Gothic script by Benjamin Keith Huntrods

Edited by Odd S. Lovoll

Indexed and Published by Deb Nelson Gourley

Astri My Astri Publishing

Norwegians in America, Some Records of the Norwegian Emigration to America:
A transcribed and translated version of the 1888 Nordmændene i Amerika, Nogle Optegnelser om De Norskes Udvandring til Amerika

Library of Congress Control Number: 2011944584

ISBN: 978-0-9760541-8-4

Written by Knud Langeland
Translated into English by Odd-Steinar Dybvad Raneng
Transcribed from Dano-Norwegian gothic script by Benjamin Keith Huntrods
Edited by Odd S. Lovoll
Foreword, biographical sketch and back cover written by Odd S. Lovoll
Indexed by Deb Nelson Gourley
Cover layout by Chris Shelton
Website distribution by Anundsen Publishing Company, Decorah, IA

Published and marketed by:
Astri My Astri Publishing
Deb Nelson Gourley
602 3rd Ave SW
Waukon, IA 52172 USA
Phone: 563-568-6229
gourleydeb@gmail.com
http://www.astrimyastri.com

First printing 2012, Made in USA

Table of Contents/Indholdsfortegnelse.

Page/*Side*

English — Part 1:

English — Part 2:

Norsk — 1ste Del:

Norsk — Anden Del:

Foreword.

In *Nordmændene i Amerika*, published in 1888, only a few weeks before his death on February 8, Knud Langeland reflected on his memories from life in Norway and in America, offering a striking social and political portrait of the time in which he lived. *Skandinaven,* whose first editor he was, explains in his obituary the great uncertainty associated with its completion because of Langeland's declining health. *Skandinaven* hailed his book as a new saga and predicted that "In it his memory will be preserved for posterity, and from it will a future author get the key to evaluate the time and the work in which Langeland took part."

Langeland divided the book into two sections, the first one treating immigration and his activities in the United States and the second his life in Norway before his departure for America in 1843 at the age of thirty. (See biographical sketch.) It is a strongly autobiographical account, emphasizing Langeland's own life experience, intellectual growth, and activities in the old and the new world; he expands the account by adding factual information and insights about his surroundings and the people with whom he interacted. Yet, the reader might wonder why there is no reference to his marriage in 1849 to Anna Jensdatter Hatlestad and their eight children. His family life in America is not covered. An explanation might be found, as he himself explains, that he initially had in mind a much larger work, but time and poor health prevented him from realizing his initial ambition.

In a brief foreword, it will only be possible to make a few references to and observations about the content of *Nordmændene i Amerika*. Langeland considers migratory forces and reviews the early overseas movement from Norway, beginning with the departure of the sloop *Restauration* in 1825; he chronicles the founding of the early settlements in Illinois and Wisconsin, places of renown like the two mother colonies Fox River in Illinois and Muskego in Wisconsin, as well as the tragic outcome of the Beaver Creek settlement. Langeland dwells on the process that led to his own decision to emigrate. In 1836 he paid a visit to Knud Slogvig, one of the Sloopers of 1825 on a return visit to Norway, and received assurance of the accuracy of what he had read about America in a German book, *Travels in America*, which he had found in a friend's library in Bergen. George Flom, a student of the early migration, considers Langeland's description of how his interest in America was aroused a significant document in immigration history. Langeland did not, however, emigrate until 1843. He offers a vivid portrayal of the hardship and tragic incidents, including sickness and death, during the nearly eight-week-long crossing on the brig *Lucy Marie* the spring and summer of 1843, carrying 52 passengers, nearly all from the municipality of Voss.

In his account of pioneer life and adjustment to unfamiliar circumstances, Langeland takes on the role of a personal and observant guide. His own story is reflective of a broader historical narrative of the westward movement of the American nation. Norwegian pioneer farmers and town dwellers are integrated into this history of drama and courage. Langeland relates his own arrival at Yorkville Prairie, Racine County, his purchase of 80 acres of land, his sojourn in Columbia County, and his exploration into unsettled areas. He reminisces about Cleng Peerson, the pathfinder of Norwegian emigration, and his death in Texas; he underscores the influence on the overseas movement of the America guide written by Ole Rynning, an emigrant of 1837, and its circulation "by the thousands" in the Norwegian countryside.

The Norwegian pioneer press is the final topic covered in the first section. Langeland was engaged in immigrant journalism nearly from its start in 1847 with the launching of the small four-page weekly *Nordlyset*. It was the fall of 1849, he committed, as he claims, the folly of becoming co-owner of the paper with his brother-in-law O. J. Hatlestad. Changing the title to *Democraten* did not improve the weekly's prospect by much, and it folded in October 1851. Langeland strove in these pioneer journals to educate his compatriots to America's political landscape, but, as he surmised, they had come too early as political organs. His list of subscribers, described by Langeland as "a list of enlightened and liberal progressive men," held positive visions for the future of Norwegian immigrant journalism. A separate study of the men behind these names would surely add significantly to our understanding of the Norwegian pioneer community.

Langeland introduces *Skandinaven*, defining its beginning in 1866 as "a new era in our newspaper literature," but only in the book's concluding chapter does he enlarge upon his own editorial role in the growth of the paper. He, like his fellow pressmen, engaged in a personal journalism, dominant in America at that time. It was evident from the start of Langeland's journalistic career in his grasp of American public affairs, his antislavery agitation, his championship of the American common school, and in his prolonged clashes with the high-church Norwegian Synod's clergy.

The class distinction and social discrimination he suffered in his childhood and youth in Norway might certainly have influenced his argument and outlook. His spirit of independence and his belief in human equality and social justice are much in evidence in the second half of *Nordmændene i Amerika*. He notes the vast difference between himself and members of the upper classes in his home community of Samnanger; he was ridiculed and laughed at because of his ragged clothing. "What have I done?" he asks,

"And what have they done, so that there should be such a great difference between us?"

Langeland's strained relations in youth with the authoritarian Lutheran parish clerics deepened his egalitarian convictions. He encountered the class discrimination of his day directly in his confirmation preparation. Langeland's account makes evident the social standing and dominion of the parish pastor in his dealings with his parishioners. Perhaps the most disturbing, as well as intriguing, incident for the modern reader is Langeland's efforts after becoming an itinerant teacher to establish a reading society. The severe criticism of the selection of books and the members of the society by both lay people and the Lutheran establishment reveals the ignorance and prejudice of the day. Langeland was encouraged by the support of younger enlightened men who closed formation around the society.

What resonates throughout Langeland's narrative is a striving for education and love of reading. The influence of his father's brother - a public school teacher - in encouraging Langeland's intellectual curiosity illuminates the broader social advances that were being achieved by the less privileged classes. The accusations against his uncle, when seeking a precentor position, of harboring heresy instead of "the pure doctrine" gave on the other hand evidence of existing social barriers. Langeland encountered the conflict over pure doctrine and the disharmony between high-church and low-church persuasions among his compatriots in America. Langeland clearly sided with the laity and the low-church movement. His portrayal of what he deems to be the first controversy between a pastor and the Norwegians in America, affirms his faith in the greater equality and social justice in the new land. He furthermore believed that the advancement of American civilization lay in the common man.

The final chapter is titled "Life in America," and it is here Langeland expands on the Norwegian American press and his association with *Skandinven*. He describes himself as an avid Republican. Historians have credited him with doing more than any other person to attach his compatriots to the Republican Party. Nevertheless, as Langeland makes clear in his final commentary, by the time he wrote *Nordmændene i Amerika* he had become disillusioned by party politics and how the large Republican majorities had brought ruthless politicians to the forefront. He himself had shown great independence of thought and belief throughout his life, and he encouraged his fellow Norwegians to act more independently in their political activities. Langeland had consistently worked to secure greater political visibility and election to public office for Norwegians and other Scandinavians. His final advice to his nationality when being ignored by the political leadership was to hit back at the ballot box rather than complain.

The book is dedicated to the memory of Clarence A. Clausen (May 30, 1896 – May 10, 1991), long-time friend and active supporter of the work of the Norwegian-American Historical Association. He became a member in 1926, one year after the Association's founding, and had a major impact on its publications. As the Association's editor, I worked together with Clausen to publish *Nordmændene i Amerika* in English translation. We were unfortunately not able to complete the project. It would have pleased him greatly to see our plans come to fruition in the present volume. Clausen had a distinguished career as a professor of history at several institutions, his longest tenure at St. Olaf College; he was a talented writer and translator. Clausen responded to government call to service during World War II and later, 1951-53 serving as cultural attaché at the United States Embassy in Sweden.

Forord.

I *Nordmændene i Amerika*, utgitt i 1888, bare noen få uker før hans død 8. februar, reflekterte Knud Langeland på sine minner fra sitt liv i Norge og i Amerika, og ga et slående sosialt og politisk portrett av sin egen tid. *Skandinaven*, hvis første redaktør han var, forklarer i hans nekrolog den store uvisshet vedrørende bokas fullførelse på grunn av Langelands skrantende helse. *Skandinaven* hyllet hans bok som en ny saga og spådde at "I den vil hans Minde bevares for Efterslægten, og af den vil en fremtidig Forfatter faa Nøglen til at bedømme den Tid og det Arbeide hvori Langeland tog Del".

Langeland inndelte boka i to deler. I den første behandler han immigrasjon og sitt virke i USA og i det andre sitt liv i Norge før sin avreise til Amerika i 1843 30 år gammel. (Se den biografiske skissen.) Det er en sterkt selvbiografisk fortelling som legger vekt på Langelands egne livserfaringer, intellektuelle vekst og virke i den gamle og den nye verden; han utvider fortellingen ved å ta med faktiske opplysninger og innsikt om sine omgivelser og de mennenskene han har omgang med. Likevel, kan kanskje leseren forundre seg over hvorfor det er ingen referanse til hans ekteskap i 1849 til Anna Jensdatter Hatlestad og deres åtte barn. Hans familie i Amerika er ikke kommet med. En forklaring kan kanskje finnes i, som han selv forklarer, at han i utgangspunktet hadde i tankene et mye større arbeide, men tid og dårlig helse hindret ham fra å fullføre sine opprinnelige ambisjoner.

I et kort forord vil det bare bli mulig å gjøre noen få referanser til og kommentarer om innholdet i *Nordmændene i Amerika*. Langeland behandler migrasjonsårsaker og gir en oversikt over den tidlige oversjøiske utvandringen fra Norge, hvor han begynner med avreisen til sluppen *Restauration* i 1825;

han opptegner grunnleggelsen av de to moderkoloniene Fox River i Illinois og Muskego i Wisconsin, og også det tragiske utfallet til Beaver Creek-settlementet. Langeland dveler ved prosessen som førte til hans egen bestemmelse om å utvandre. I 1836 avla han besøk hos Knud Slogvig, en av Sluppefolket i 1825 på gjenbesøk til Norge, og fikk bekreftet riktigheten i det han hadde lest om Amerika i en tysk bok, *Reiser i Amerika*, som han hadde funnet i en venns bibliotek i Bergen. George Flom, som forsket på den tidlige utvandringgen, anser Langelands beskrivelse av hvordan hans interesse for Amerika ble vekket et betydelig dokument i immigrasjonshistorie. Langeland utvandret imidlertid ikke før i 1843. Han gir en levende beskrivelse av trengsler og tragiske hendinger, inkludert sykdom og dodsfall, under den nærmere åtte-ukers lange overfarten på briggen *Lucy Marie* våren og sommerem 1843, med 52 passasjerer, nesten alle fra Voss.

I sin framstilling av pionérliv og tilpasning til ukjente forhold, tar Langeland på seg rollen som en privat og observant guide. Hans egen livshistorie avspeiler et større historisk narrativ om den amerikanske nasjons vandring mot vest. Norske pionérfarmere og småbyinnbyggere er integrert i denne historien full av dramatikk og pågangsmot. Langeland beretter om sin egen ankomst til Yorkville Prairie i Racine *county*, kjøp av 80 *acre* (vel 320 mål) jord, sitt opphold i Columbia *county*. og sin utforsking av ubebodde områder. Han erindrer Cleng Peerson, stifinneren i norsk utvandring, og hans død i Texas; han understreker innflytelsen på den oversjøiske vandringen til amerikaveilederen skrevet av Ole Rynning, en utvandrer i 1837, og dens utbredelse “i tusenvis” utover i norske bygder.

Den norske pionérpressen er det siste emne dekket i første del. Langeland engasjerte seg i immigrantjournalistikkk nesten fra dens start i 1847 med lanseringen av det lille firesiders ukebladet *Nordlyset*. Det var høsten 1849 han begikk, som han hevder, den dumhet å bli medeier i avisen sammen med sin svoger O. J. Hatlestad. Å forandre tittelen til *Democraten* gjorde ikke avisens framtidsuksikter mye bedre, og den opphørte i oktober 1851. Langeland anstrengte seg i disse to pionéravisene for å lære sine landsmenn om Amerikas politiske landskap, men, som han formodet, de hadde kommet for tidlig som politiske organer. Hans liste over abonnenter, beskrevet av Langeland som “en Liste over oplyste og frisindede Fremskridtsmænd”, rommet positive visjoner om den norske immigrantpresses framtid. En egen studie om mennene bak disse navnene ville opplagt øke betraktelig vår forståelse av det norske pionérsamfunnet.

Langeland bringer *Skandinaven* på bane og presiserer at dens begynnelse i 1866 var “en ny Æra i vor Avisliteratur”, men først i bokas avsluttende kapittel utbrer han seg om sin egen redaktørrolle i avisens vekst. Han, i likhet med sine journalistkolleger, engasjerte seg i personlig journalistikk, framherskende i Amerika på den tid. Forholdet var åpenbart fra starten i Langelands journalistiske karriere i hans beherskelse av amerikanske offentlige anliggender, hans antislaveri agitasjon, hans forsvar for den amerikanske *common-* eller grunnskole, og i hans langvarige sammenstøt med det høykirkelige norske Synodes presteskap.

Den klasseforskjell og sosial diskriminering han led under i sin barndom og ungdom i Norge kunne opplagt ha påvirket hans utvikling og livssyn. Hans selvstendighetsånd og hans tro på menneskelig likestilling og sosial rettferdighet kommer sterkt til syne i den andre halvdelen av *Nordmændene i Amerika*. Han merker seg den store ulikheten mellom seg selv og medlemmer av overklassen i sitt hjemsted Samnanger; han ble latterliggjort på grunn av sine fillete klær. "Hvad har jeg gjort?" spør han, "Og hvad har disse gjort, at der skal være saa stor en Forskjel mellem os?"

Langelands anstrengte forhold i sin ungdom til de autoritære lutherske sogneprester styrket hans egalitære overbevisninger. Han opplevde den tids klassediskriminering i konfirmasjonsforberedelsen. Langelands beretning klargjør den sosiale stilling og dominans til sognepresten i hans befatning med sine sognefolk. Kanskje det mest urovekkende, men også fengslende, tilfelle for den moderne leser er Langelands forsøk etter at han ble omgangsskolelærer på å danne et leseselskap. Den strenge kritikken angående utvalg av bøker og av medlemmene i selskapet av både legfolk og de lutherske myndigheter legger for dagen tidens uvitenhet og fordom. Langeland ble oppmuntret av støtten fra yngre opplyste menn som dannet forsvarsformasjon rundt selskapet.

Det som går igjen gjennom hele Langelands narrativ er bestrebelsen på å få utdannelse og gleden ved lesning. Innflytelsen til hans fars bror – en offentlig skolelærer – i å tilskynde Langelands intellektuelle nysgjerrighet belyser den bredere sosiale framgang som ble oppnådd av de mindre privilegierte klasser. Beskyldningene mot hans onkel, da han søkte en klokkerstilling, at han næret falsk lære istendefor "den rene Lære" beviste på den andre siden en eksisterende klassebarriere. Langeland ble stilt overfor konflikten om ren doktrine og disharmonien mellom høykirkelige og lavkirkelige anskuelser blant sine landsmenn i Amerika. Hans skildreing av det han mener å være den første kontrovers mellom en prest og nordmennene i Amerika, bekrefter hans tro på den større likestilling og sosial rettferdighet i det nye landet. Han trodde enn videre at den amerikanske sivilisasjons framgang lå hos den vanlige mann.

Det siste kapitlet heter "Livet i Amerika", og det er her Langeland går nærmere inn på den norskamerikanske presse og sin forbindelse med *Skan-*

dinaven. Han beskriver seg selv som en ivrig republikaner. Historikere har tillagt ham æren for å ha gjort mer enn noen annen person for å knytte sine landsmenn til det republikanske partiet. Ikke desto mindre, som Langeland gjør klart i sine avsluttende kommentarer, på den tid han skrev *Nordmændene i Ameerika* var han blitt desillusjonert med partipolitikk og hvordan de store republikanske majoritetene hadde brakt hensynsløse politikere til fronten. Han selv hadde vist stor selvstendighet i tanke og tro gjennom hele livet, og han oppmodet sine mednordmenn å oppføre seg mer selvstendig i deres politiske virksomhet. Langeland hadde konsekvent virket for å sikre større politisk synlighet og valg til offentlige embeter for nordmenn og andre skandinaver. Hans avsluttende råd til sin nasjonalitet når ignorert av den politiske ledelse, er å slå tilbake ved valgurnen heller enn å klage.

Boka er tilegnet minnet til Clarence A. Clausen (30. mai 1896 – 10. mai 1991), langtidsvenn og aktiv støttespiller i Det norskamerikanske historielagets virksomhet. Han ble medlem i 1926, et år etter dets grunnleggelse, og hadde en betydelig innvirkning på historielagets publikasjoner. I min egenskap som historielagets redaktør, arbeidet jeg sammen med Clausen for å utgi *Nordmændene i Amerika* i engelsk oversettelse. Vi klarte dessverre ikke å fullføre prosjektet. Det ville ha gledet ham stort å se våre planer bli virkeliggjort i nærværende utgivelse. Clausen hadde en høyt anerkjent karriere som professor i historie ved flere institusjoner, hans lengste tjenestetid ved St. Olaf College; han var en talentfull forfatter og oversetter. Clausen var under andre verdenskrig og senere lydhør overfor styresmaktenes påbud om å stå til tjeneste, 1951-53 tjenestegjorde han som kulturattaché i USAs ambassade i Sverige.

Odd Sverre Lovoll
Professor Emeritus of History, St. Olaf College

Norwegians in America.
Some records of the Norwegian emigration to America.
By Knud Langeland.

Chicago.
John Anderson & Co., Publishers,
183, 185 & 187 N. Peoria Street.
1888.

Skandinavens Boghandel.
Scandinavia Book — and Accident Printers,
Bound at Scandinavia Book Binders,
183, 185 and 187 N. Peoria St., Chicago, Ill.

Introduction.

Our descendants in the western part of the globe after a century's elapse would probably not search in vain for information about their father's first immigration to America, as we now with eagerness, vainly try to lift history's veil from our ancestor's immigration to the Scandinavian countries. Against such an emptiness and complete lack of historical testimony, humanity's future epoch is guaranteed. Even if we assume as a possibility that history with its decline and its dark ages repeats itself in the future as in centuries past, the Scandinavian immigration to America will however hardly disappear from history as long as on the terrestrial orb there is found a trace of our nationality, for whom such historical memories has some interest. It is not such an extreme view of the case that has moved me to commit to paper these memories. However, there is an approaching future, which without doubt will feel the want of such memorandum. And they will rightly complain of our neglect and indifference if we all, either through the lack of confidence in ourselves or through other causes, should wait for more able hands or men with better opportunity to take on the task when all the earlier immigrants, with their personal memories and experiences, lie in their grave from where their memories can no longer be retrieved. To do one's best to remedy such a longing by our closest succeeding generations we should therefore exempt the writer from accusations of conceit and vanity. Let therefore many write such memories even though they — as I have — put to paper a simple everyday act. It is not the intention to deliver any perfect historical work, but on the other hand to bring the timber and the rocks that the simple worker brings to the experienced builder, so that from this he can erect that historical building. Now, for example if a man from every emigration group would deliver such memoirs, one would soon have a rich stockpile that through a proficient hand's processing that could be made into interesting yearbooks. Surely, the time has come to make a start of this, though I wonder if it will not soon be too late to achieve this goal.

It is the author's contribution to this goal that is here submitted.

I.
Migration of a Nation.

Folk migration seems to have happened since the time of man's first appearance. The migration among Noah's earliest descendants are frequently mentioned in the Bible, aye, God even commanded Abraham to emigrate. "Be ye fruitful, multiply thyself and fill the earth," was a Command, which derived the order of nature, as it came from nature's Lord. When the pastures on Bethel's plains became too poor, the shepherds quarreled amongst themselves, and Abraham and Lot went each their own way. Such it is assumed to have gone with people of prehistoric times, and later the history of the world shows us enough evidence of greater and lesser migrations of the human race.

Mighty tribes advanced from different parts of Asia towards the west through the areas of the Black Sea and the countries along the Danube. The Goths thrust in through the great Roman Empire's borders because the Huns intruded on them from the east. According to historians, these people movements were from the old Iranian or the present Indian or Persian empire. Also considered among these migrations are the German and the Norse tribes, which in two parallel lines are drawn from east towards west, until through time they reached the Baltic Sea from where they spread towards the South and North and finally settled in the German and Scandinavian countries. The well-known Norwegian historian [Jakob Rudolf] Keyser holds that our fathers have come to the latter country some 400 to 500 years earlier than our reckoning. That the Norse tribe had partly gone over the Gulf of Bothnia and partly north of the gulf, and that they from there went south. At that time there were already a nomadic people there who were called Finns, Lapps, Celts and Cimbri. These were gradually driven out — the Finns to the far north in Norway, Sweden and Russia, the Celts and Cimbri to the south and west all the way to England, Ireland and Scotland. Finally, the Norse drove the gothic Germans, who had come to southern Sweden, Denmark and Schleswig, further south and west, whereby once more the Angels and Saxons were forced out from their places of residence over to Britain.

II.
The Discovery of America.

Several centuries later, Harald Haarfager's oppressions drove many of our best Nordic fathers over to Iceland and the Faroe Islands, from where they in their travels to the south accidently discovered America. The sagas tell us that the Norwegians made many voyages to the land in the west that they named Vinland, and built a colony on the coast of Massachusetts, which they called *Leifsboder* [? Leif's huts — archaeological remains that may indicate a settlement by Leiv Eiriksson and his followers about the year 1000. However, these have been found and identified at L'Anse aux Meadows, Newfoundland, but not in Massachusetts]. When the Black Death occurred around 1350 [1347-1351], one forgot in Norway and Iceland the way to the New World, and the presumptions are that the Norwegian colonists in *Leifsboder*, when supplies no longer arrived from the mother country, mixed with the country's aboriginal population, — Indians (known as *Skrællinger*). There is a vague suspicion that traces of grave mounds and other antiquities that in many places are found in the United States, and cannot have originated from the Indians, are perhaps of Norwegian origin. Let it be as it may. More likely is it that Christopher Columbus on his famous voyage to Iceland [1477], first heard the story of the westward-lying Vinland, and that this gave rise to his voyage of discovery to the west, which ended with the re-discovery of America in 1492.

III.
Grounds for Emigration.

Grounds for migrations can be different: partly nomadic life and the imperfect hunting tools, which is why large tracts of land were needed to sustain the tribe's ever increasing population; partly the barbaric times when the stronger simply by force drove out the weaker; perhaps also partly through the tribe's free choices and decisions.

The Norwegian's Viking forays must be seen partly as straightforward assaults and plundering of the neighboring countries, and partly as an exercise in campaign and war of that time. We read that on these forays that they frequently visited England's, Ireland's and Scotland's coasts as well as Germany and France; that they in the latter country founded a colony that is still called Normandy and from where the Norwegian invasion army departed and conquered England — and so forth.

The Spaniard's first emigration to America after Columbus' discovery consisted of a band of adventurers who sought thither to find gold and silver, and it was only later that they began to build colonies. During the reign of Queen Elisabeth [I], Englishmen came to the east coast of North America and after some fruitless attempts; they managed to found a colony in Virginia. It seems in particular, to have been commercial interests that had inspired them. While at the same time, the Puritans and the Huguenots traveled to America to seek religious freedom and avoid the hard religious persecutions that they had to endure in their home countries of England and France. In 1624, a few Norwegians founded a colony in the present New Jersey, and a town they called Bergen, which still carries this name. In the same area, the Swedes founded a colony, but the Dutch, who at that time had settled themselves in New York, were so numerous that they absorbed everything around them, until they themselves succumbed to the English element.

Our present Nordic aristocracy does lay claim to have descended from the old ancestral chieftains that immigrated to Norway and Sweden, and that the peasants descended from serfs or thralls. History's testimony does not confirm this supposition. Rather it is beyond all doubt that the current aristocracy of officialdom and the so-called upper social echelon originated from the German nobility, who through the German kings in Denmark, were imported to supply them with income and power whilst in office and be the necessary support for the monarchy.

IV.
The first Norwegian Emigration Party.

There is a sector of the old heroic pioneers' descendants, the Norwegian peasant emigration to America in modern times, we shall discuss here. All, both written and oral stories that the author has been able to consult, concur that Cleng Peerson, from Skjold parish in Stavanger County, was the one who actually gave the first occasion for the Norwegian peasant emigration to America. It was in the year of 1821 that he and a friend, by the name of Knud Eide left the fatherland to investigate conditions in America. Religious constraint was at that time strictly practiced in Norway where there were signs of divergence. In Stavanger County, Hauge's followers were numerous, and subsequently the Quaker devotees were not so few. The latter were greatly persecuted. The author knows that the stories about the Quaker devotees are not of dubious folklore. Through the demand of the pastor, the sheriff arrived with his men, and took the Quaker children by force and brought them to the pastor for baptism and confirmation. If the parents did not come to the alter as the others in the congregation, they were fined — that is to say, they had to pay a fee to the State Church, though they themselves did not use it. It was this situation that was the main reason that the two aforementioned men were sent by the Quakers to investigate the circumstances in America. There are statements from several reliable men that this is what happened, and therefore we also see that after Cleng Peerson's stay of three years in America, he came back in 1824, organized the first Norwegian emigration party in Stavanger, which nearly in its entirety consisted of Quakers from Stavanger and Skjold County. It was the often-discussed *Sloopers*, a party of fifty-two persons who with their own ship sailed from Stavanger on the 4th of July in 1825. Subsequently, the adventurous voyage to America by this party is rendered partly from Ole Rynning's little book about America (printed in Christiania in 1838), and partly by word of mouth from some of the participants themselves.

"In 1821 a person by the name of Cleng Peerson arrived from Stavanger parish in Norway to New York in the United States. In 1824, he took a quick trip back to Norway, and by his stories of America, he aroused the desire in many to journey there. An emigration party of fifty-two people bought a small sloop for 1,800 *speciedaler* [an annual wage for a male teacher in 1825 in Trondhjem was approximately 750 *speciedaler*], which they loaded with iron to go to New York. The skipper and first officer were themselves members of this venture. They passed through the channel [English Channel] and sailed into a small coastal harbor where they began selling spirits, which was a forbidden item there. When they noticed the danger they thereby had exposed themselves to, they had in all haste once more to set sail. Because of the skipper's ignorance or headwind, they came as far south as the Madeira Islands. Here they found a barrel of Madeira [wine] floating on the sea, which they hauled on board and began to drink. When the entire crew was intoxicated, the ship came drifting like a plague ship into the harbor, without command and without hoisting the flag. A coastal guard who was at the ready called out to them that they must immediately hoist the flag if they did not want to be greeted by the fort's cannons, which were already pointed at them, and so finally, one of the passengers found the flag and had it hoisted. After these and other dangers, they eventually reached New York. In all, they had taken fourteen weeks from Stavanger to America. However, no one had died on the journey and everyone was healthy on landing. In New York, there was general astonishment that the Norwegians had dared to venture over the open sea in such a small vessel, which until now was unheard of. Through ignorance or misunderstanding, they had manned the ship with more crew than American laws allowed, which is why the skipper, along with the ship and cargo, was arrested. [The Steerage Act of 1819 stated that a ship could not take more than 2 passengers for each 5 tons of ship.] Now I cannot with certainty say, that the government itself dismissed the charges in regards to our good countrymen's ignorance or childish conduct, or if the Quakers already then had taken care of the matter; as it is, the skipper was set free and the ship and cargo was given back to the owners. They lost however a lot by the sale, which did not earn them more than $400. — With the Quakers' contribution, they had support to trek further into the land. Two from the party settled in Rochester; one of these by the name of Lars Larsen, whose widow still resides there. They bought land five miles northwest of Rochester in Morris County. Here they had to give $5.00 per acre; but as they had no money to pay with, the payment was to be paid by installments over ten years. Each bought about forty acres. The land here was almost overgrown with brush and difficult to clear. The first four or five years were therefore very troublesome for these people. They often suffered great need and wished themselves only to return to Norway; but they saw no possibility to go there without having to sacrifice the last mite of their assets, and they did not want to go back as beggars. Nevertheless — beneficent neighbors helped them and by their own diligence they finally had their land in such a condition that they were able to live on it, aye, live better than in their old native land." — Rendered from Rynning's book.

V.
Rochester-Settlement.

After further information, it should be added that Lars Larsen, who settled in Rochester, was considered the party's leader and was the only one who understood a little English. He now has for many years been dead, but several members of his family are apparently still alive, some in Rochester, others in Chicago. One son studies at the Frankean Synod College and worked as a Lutheran pastor among his countrymen, but died at an early age. Those who bought land in Kendall and Morris Counties moved there in the month of November just when winter began. The land thereabouts was still only a little developed and it was difficult for them to find work and even more difficult to find shelter for the winter. Four and twenty of them joined forces and built a log cabin being just big enough to allow each of the residents one square foot of space. Thrust together in this cramped hut, the newcomers truly needed a good deal of patience, and only an unshakable faith in a better future could under the circumstances maintain their courage and make their position more or less, tolerable. Threshing machines had yet not come into use and by threshing for neighbors by hand, they earned enough for their subsistence. For this work, they actually received every eleventh bushel of the product. The following year they began clearing the land they had bought, but as this was overgrown with dense brush, it only progressed slowly. However, the second summer they were able reap two acres of wheat. This gave them courage to continue their hard work, but it must here be mentioned, that the first four or five years brought many disappointments and sorrows to these people. It was with them as it has since been with so many of their migrating countrymen, they wished themselves back in Norway, and perhaps with good reason. But they could go nowhere because of the lack of funds, and even the few who could find the funds for the return journey knew only too well what it would mean to come home empty handed, and they remained in America irrespective of this unfortunate beginning.

VI.
From 1825 to 1836.

However, through participation of helpful neighbors and by their own diligence, they were able to clear so much of the fertile land as to have enough food for their own consumption. The prospects soon became better and they began to realize that America offers the industrious worker many advantages, and they encouraged many of their countrymen, through letters to their old home, to seek their fortune on this side of the ocean. The consequence was that in the years from 1825 to 1836 not so few emigrated, but they traveled in small groups looking for available shipping accommodation either over Göteborg [Gothenburg] in Sweden, Hamburg in Germany or Le Havre in France, from which places, passage to the United States was often found. From Göteborg the emigrants traveled with American ships that transported Swedish iron to America; but this was a little uncertain and one was often forced to wait several weeks for passage. They therefore began to go to Hamburg where the German emigration had for a long time been in regular operation, with the so-called American packet ships. However, here also the Norwegian emigrants met with the problem that if one had not been registered from one to two weeks in advance, one would lay over until the next packet ship departed. This resulted then in that many made their way over to Le Havre in France, where the influx of emigrants were smaller and the packet traffic was about the same as it was from Hamburg. A friend of the writer by the name of Gjert Hovland, an enlightened and liberal farmer from Hardanger in Bergen Diocese, was one of those who in 1831 journeyed to America through Göteborg and wrote many excellent letters to Norway.*) As he was well know in several parishes in Bergen Diocese, his letters were circulated widely in hundreds of transcripts and aroused great interest among the people. For not so many years ago, he still lived at a great age in Ottawa, Illinois.

\) The author has seen a copy of a letter from Gjert Gregoriussen Hovland, written from Morris County, N. J., in 1835, where he had at that time lived for four years. From here, it is seen that he with his family left Norway on the 24th June 1831; they traveled through Göteborg and departed from there on the 30th of July the same year. They arrived in New York on the 18th of September. He bought fifty acres of forested land that he worked on for four years and then sold for a profit of $500. In 1836, he arrived in Illinois and did not live far from Ottawa in La Salle County, where he died at a great age. In this letter, he wrote much praise about the American legislation, equality and freedom in contradistinction to the social extortionists in Norway. Recommending all who could to come to America, as the Creator nowhere had forbidden man to live where he wanted — and so forth. His letters were copied in the hundreds and distributed in the Norwegian villages, and without doubt had a very decisive influence on the migration.

VII.
Emigrating in 1836.

Finally one of the *Sloopers* [common name of the Norwegians who had earlier migrated to America on the sloop] by the name of Knud Slogvig arrived back in Norway in 1835 after having spent ten years in the New World. He stayed mainly in his home village in Skjold Parish and stories of his homecoming went like a *budstikke* [a message stick used in the Norse times, sent from farm to farm to call people together for defense etc.] from man to man with unbelievable speed. Everywhere, from Bergen Diocese to Stavanger County people traveled long roads to speak with him. Three of the writer's relatives, who traveled from Bergen in 1837, were among those who in the winter of 1836 visited him and came home full with *America fever*. Two brigs in Stavanger, which together could carry a total of 160 passengers, were outfitted by the Kiel Shipping Company in the spring of 1836; they traveled under the leadership of the aforementioned Knud Slogvig to America. They had a lucky crossing, visited their countrymen in Rochester, and continued their journey to Chicago. They settled mainly in La Salle County, seventy miles west of Chicago, in the so-called Fox River Settlement, which through his adventurous wanderings, the relentless Cleng Peerson had proposed. From what he told the author, when he on his third visit to Norway stayed in Bergen during the winter of 1843, he was the first Norwegian emigrant who went west from the great lakes and visited Chicago and other places in Illinois. However, the year and the particular details I can no longer give as the records that were made then are now gone. Whether he personally escorted them or gave instructions on the location, — is however not recalled. But an interesting description that he gave to me about his adventurous journey of discovery over Illinois' grassy and flowery prairies — of how he on a walking excursion the first time from Chicago, came upon high ground from where he could peruse the picturesque and enchanting region where the prosperous Norwegian settlement of Fox River is now found, and where at that time not a house was found without there being several miles between them on the forested edge along the Fox River, and where a few Americans had begun to locate — is still fresh in my memory. Nearly dead from hunger and hardships on his long journey through an uninhabited country, he threw himself on the ground, thanked God who had allowed him to come and see nature's so breathtakingly and richly provided land, and with his soul strengthened and comforted, he forgot his hunger and his sufferings. He thought of Moses when he from Mount Nebo saw the Promised Land that God had promised his people.

VIII.
The Fox River Settlement.

Guided by Cleng Peerson, and encouraged by his description of this region, was this, that the immigrant group from Stavanger in 1836 came to Fox River and established the second Norwegian settlement in America. How much these people as well as the people who later came to this region have to thank him for, which they may have never thought of, will in a more articulate manner describe the succeeding year's Norwegian emigrant's fate in the hapless Beaver Creek Settlement. It happened so, that malaria everywhere out in the west, in a more or lesser degree, attacked the newcomers during the land's first cultivation; but on high land away from marshes and swamps these visitations were relatively quickly over with. This was the case at Fox River.

We have seen in earlier times that the first emigrant ship had left Norway already in 1825 — that is to say sixty-two years ago; also that the next direct emigration from Norway was first held eleven years later when the two Kiel brigantines in 1836 transported 150 emigrants from Stavanger to New York.

It is also briefly mentioned earlier how in the meantime, almost every year, people traveled either individually or in small groups through other European ports to America. Next, we shall bring up the third direct emigration group — that is to say, the one from Bergen in 1837.

IX.
The third Emigration Group.

About this emigration, the author can speak of personal experience as well as what steps preceded this and in a manner prepared the way for it among the Bergen farmers, who were the main reason thereof. Through pure accident the author found in a friend's book collection in Bergen, a German *Reiser i Amerika* [Travels in America]. At the age of sixteen, the influence of imagination is very much alive, and when within the book there were several lifelike pictures of the distant region that the traveler had visited as well as the impressions he had received from the land and the people of the New World, it was read with romantic allurements. Here was detailed information about the German emigration to America. With this travelogue in my pocket one early summer's morning, I headed towards *Solemsviken* and up *Lyderhorn's* sheer sides. Up there, I read and dreamed about the new and wonderful world far away to the west. The fog had descended over the fjords between the islands near Bergen, but up there near the top of the mountain, it was clear and sunny. It was the first time I saw this peculiar and delightful image from the mountain. Had my prosaic nature ever been influenced by poetic inspiration and enlightenment, it was at this moment whilst my eyes perused the mist's sunlit surface, and in the distant west, the North Sea's shining shield that seemed to rise to the same height as the mountain. Oh, why do such moments come so seldom in an ordinary man's life? And far away to the west, thousands of miles away, lies the land of which I read — lies the large but still little known continent with its secrets and its wonders. To this point in my life's early years are attached my first memories of America, of the land that now for nearly a half century has been my second birthplace. As from this time, I searched all the books and writings of travels I was able to acquire regarding America. And together with my uncle we began to gather further information of the new world through other books as well as oral tales from around Stavanger that had now started to spread through the countryside in regards to Cleng Peerson's emigration and return — even though we still had no serious thought of emigration. With a selfless friend's help in 1834, I had the opportunity of a six-month stay in England, at which stage I collected several pamphlets and books about America and the English emigration. In this way, in our group, more definite and reliable information about the conditions in America and the journey thereto was obtained. This made many of the ridiculous and unreasonable stories that now were consistently spread among the people, not find the necessary conviction. Slowly but steadily, the thought of emigration to America spread; more and more people joined the group, who seriously began to speak about selling their farms and leaving. Then the bishop of Bergen wrote his pastoral letter to the Bergen farmers with the text: "Stay in the land, maintain yourself honestly!" Whether he forgot it or did not consider it appropriate for the occasion, is probably why he did not cite the second scripture's bid: "Be ye fruitful, multiply thyself and fill the earth." This last one, [scripture] the farmers had accomplished. Most of them had large families and as the farmland there at home was mostly occupied, and as they heard that there were still large tracts of land vacant in the New World, they decided to go against the bishop's advice and journey to the new Canaan, which flowed with milk and honey.

X.
Reasons for the Journey.

Whilst visiting Knud Slogvig we received safe and sound confirmation on what we had earlier heard and read. This was in the winter of 1836. In the fall of the same year, Behrens the ship's captain from Bergen, arrived home with the bark *Ægir* from a freight voyage to America. And when he heard that more affluent countrymen from different regions of the county had sold their farms and sought passage to America, he decided (he was both the owner and the skipper), to fit out his good *Ægir* (God of the sea) for passenger service, and the contract was ready for the voyage the following spring of 1837. Captain Behrens had in New York's harbor, seen German and English emigrant ships arrive and knew much about shipping arrangements and of the American laws as well as port administration concerning the immigrants. Two German pastors who were on their way home to collect donations for church building, accompanied him to Europe, and through them, he became well informed on the German emigration, which had now for many years clearly gone through Baltimore to Pennsylvania, on a large scale.

The knowledge of conditions in America would however not have led to this first emigration from Bergen. For the majority of people it was hard times, dwindling livelihoods and a huge poor-tax that created heavy demands on their lives. Yet, I know for certain individuals there were other contributing factors. The old, totally self sacrificial folklorist scholar, N. P. Langeland, who had chosen the way of learning, but through lack of funds had been obliged to stop halfway through primary school, had been unfairly judged by the superstitious and ignorant public. The clergy found that this too radical thinker was not a suitable man to direct the public teaching in this very conservative province, and his teaching activity became an all too thankless task. Assisted by a number of faithful and enlightened friends but persecuted by a greater number of ignorant bigots, hampered his beneficial undertakings. He was rewarded with ingratitude for his noble endeavors, and the bond that tied him to the fatherland and the work he loved so dearly, crumbled. For his part, this was likely the main reason for his emigration, and this situation was indeed also a decisive factor for many of his friends and relations. However, through all this it must be maintained that without the better economic prospect, which presented itself for the family in the rich, sparsely populated America, with its mild climate and fertile soil, scarcely any of this group would have gone to America. Besides the abovementioned teacher Langeland, others who belonged to this group we can here mention: Mons Aadland, Nils Frøland, Anders Norvig, Anders Rosseland, Thomas Bauge, Ingebrigt Brudvig, Thorbjørn Veste and others, all of whom had a large family, as well as a number of single persons, among whom were Døvig, Rosseland, Bauge, Frøland, Norvig, Hisdal, Tøsseland and more, many of whom still live in Illinois as prosperous people, which is also the case with many of the elder's offspring. In all, there were eighty-four persons. As far as I remember, they paid 60 *speciedaler* for the voyage over to New York for a grown person and half for children under twelve years of age.

XI.
Ole Rynning.

It was only after the preliminary agreement was completed with Captain Behrens, and after the ship had been prepared for the voyage, that the celebrated student Ole Rynning from Snaasen in Trondhjem Diocese, who became famous through his little book about America, came to Bergen to join the group. He had first received information about the departure of the group through an announcement in the newspapers, whereupon he corresponded with the shipping company in Bergen. He had thus not the smallest part in bringing this emigration to realization. What really drove him to emigrate I cannot with certainty say. After a few statements from Captain Behrens, it seemed that Rynning was more democratically minded and sympathetic towards the farming class than was good, — his more aristocratic minded father, Dean [Jens] Rynning, thought. A betrothal that his father deemed a misalliance should however be the immediate reason for his trip to America.

Such at least was Captain Behrens' conception and it is certain that Rynning's manner gave the impression of deep melancholy, which very easily could be the explanation in such a situation. That his decision at that time to return to Norway after a short stay, at least for a visit, he made no secret of. This is also evident in a verse that appears in a song that he wrote during the voyage, which was sung at sea during a small celebration of America's Independence Day on the 4th of July, and sounds like this:

Nu ligger Norges Klippeland
Saa dybt i Skjul bag salten Vove,
Men Længslen higer til den Strand
Med gamle, dunkle Egeskove,
Hvor Graners Sus og Jøklers Drøn
Er Harmoni for Norges Søn.

Men om end Skjæbnen bød ham der,
Som fordum Bjørn af Leif, at tjelde,
Han vil dog stedse have kjær
Sit gode gamle Norges Fjelde,
Og længes ømt, med sønlig Hu,
At se sit elskte Hjem endnu.

Norway's land of cliffs now lie
Deeply hidden behind salty waves,
But with longing, yearn for the shores
With ancient dark oak forests,
Where the spruce's rustling and the glaciers' roar
Is harmony to the son of Norway.

But although fate bade him there,
Where the old bear by Leif, was hung as a shelter,
He would still have dear
His most precious Norwegian mountains,
And longing with affection and filial desire
To still see his beloved Norway.

It was an eight-week voyage from Bergen to New York and the passengers were all in good standing. Captain Behrens spoke a great deal about the voyage when the author [Langeland] later met him in Bergen. When the farmers who had never seen the ocean before, saw that it was calm, they soon lost their fright of its fury. The violin appeared and one began to dance on the deck; however, the captain soon had to protest when the ballroom (the deck) suffered too much from the ladies' and gentlemen's shoes, which were soled using many nails. On the sea, a large American packet ship came very close to them, so that through an erroneous maneuver they came together. As the sea was heavy and the ships could not immediately come clear of each other, the passengers came with their axes and began chopping at ropes and rigging; they thought their last hour on this earth had come, but they escaped with just a scare. The ships were not badly damaged.

All the reports are correct in that Ole Rynning was a rare and noble philanthropic man who sacrificed much of his time and talents to his travelling companions' service. Because of this, as well as his language skills, they showed him the utmost confidence. He was one of the three travelers who were sent from Chicago to locate a suitable place for them to settle, as most of them intended to be farmers.

The journey from New York at that time was very difficult compared to how it is now and cost these large families much more than they had at first thought. When they arrived in Detroit, Michigan, the aforementioned N. P. Langeland had run out of money and had a family of eight. His other friends in the group had promised to help him through to Chicago; but now they had become discouraged and afraid because of the many unforeseen disbursements, and would not make any further outlays. He therefore went ashore in Detroit with his family. The future did not look good, but he was a strenuous worker as well as a skilled carpenter and blacksmith and soon found work with a wood turner, by what means he kept his family. Later he went inland to Lapeer County, where little by little he became the owner of 120 acres of land and a joinery workshop with a lathe and hydropower. He died many years ago but a son has lived in San Francisco, California, for a long time.

XII.
Beaver Creek.

In Chicago, one met some countrymen that had settled there, and a couple who had come back from Fox River gave a discouraging report on conditions there. This was the reason that three men were sent to find a favorable place for the proposed colony. They took the way south from Chicago, roughly the path where the Illinois Central Railway now passes — a low-lying swampy area, which experienced people did not expect to see built up for a lifetime. This was in the months of August and September when this flat land was dry and overgrown with coarse grass up to a man's armpits. Some of the survivors have uttered suspicions that land speculators had affected their agents, by letting themselves be persuaded into taking this unfortunate direction instead of going northwest, where within twenty to thirty English miles they could have found the most beautiful government land under the sun. Nevertheless, fate wanted it differently. They arrived at the unfortunate Beaver Creek, in Iroquois County, where they expected to find all the conditions for a paradise on earth. They came back with an excellent portrayal of the flat and fertile land where the grass went over their heads in places. The group then bought oxen and wagons and went off to the Promised Land. They cut timber and built for all they were worth, to be finished before the winter. They drove seventy miles to the nearest sawmill after boards, and gave themselves no time to study the topography of the land, otherwise they would have discovered signs that the land they thought to plow the next spring had been under water right up to the month of June the previous spring. They were hardy and bright folk. They had their dwellings in good condition before the rains of fall began; but soon they had to wade through icy water up over their knees when they wanted to go anywhere. When spring arrived, the flat land was under water as far as the eye could see. Many of them had succumbed to malaria and when the heat of summer arrived and the water evaporated, swamp fever claimed its daily sacrifices, and then it was: "save yourself, whomsoever can!" Here is where Ole Rynning's bones were laid to rest. He was a strong and powerful man that no hardship shunned. He lived with a man where one was used to eating porridge and sour milk. The author's brother saw him walk with a pair of his tattered boots through icy water and snow. Finally, he was affected by a pernicious diarrhea that did not ease up, and caused his death.

The few survivors left everything and went over to the Fox River settlement in La Salle County, where some of them still live — among who is a sister of the author. My brother was the only one who still did not want to move; he was there for three years and eventually was able to exchange his place for a herd of cattle that he in 1840 went north with and settled in Racine County, Wisconsin.

Such was the outcome of the settlement at Beaver Creek; something close to the outcome of the colony of *Leifsboder* — 1000 years earlier.

XIII.
In La Salle County.

Above we have seen that Cleng Peerson early on found his way to Chicago and from there west to Illinois' great prairies. Soon he was followed by some of the *Sloopers* in New York, as well as others who had arrived later by themselves. Among those who first settled in La Salle County, Illinois, can be mentioned Gudmund Haukaas, an excellent farmer from Stavanger Parish who arrived from the Norwegian colony at Rochester, N. Y. The very first group of Knud Slogvig's party in 1836 settled in La Salle, and it was difficult to explain why Rynning's party the following year did not go there. The story is that they let themselves be frightened off from there by some countrymen they met in Chicago; they had told them that the Norwegian settlers out there were dying from endemic fever, and that the place was exceedingly unhealthy and the conditions in this settlement as a whole were deplorable. Cleng Peerson had misled them into settling there, and he had always been a Jonah. Such was that story that the party from Bergen was told in Chicago. Now we know that at that time, endemic fever raged through the whole of Fox River valley from Muskego in Wisconsin to the Mississippi River in Illinois, as well as the other river basins out west, but this the settlers did not understand. The Norwegian settlers in La Salle spread rapidly during the steadfast immigration and soon spread to surrounding districts. Norway, Leland, Lisbon, Morris, Ottawa etc. became excellent early centers for this first Norwegian colony in the west. These districts are among the finest and most fruitful of all the Norwegian settlements in the Mississippi valley. The winter is not nearly as harsh as in the far northwest, and the endemic fever of the early years stopped as soon as the land was under cultivation. The country was almost everywhere ready for the plow, and all who would work soon prospered.

XIV.
Ansten Natstad's [Nattestad's] trip to America.

Above it has on occasions been shown that knowledge of America and the people who were moving there, were from Stavanger County, and then especially from Skjold Parish. A further testimony about this is given by Ansten Nattestad in a short story about his trip to America. From this story is the following condensed excerpt: He and his brother Ole Nattestad, from Rollaug's parish in Numedal, in 1835, during a business trip in western Norway, arrived one evening on a farm in Tysvær Parish, Stavanger County. At the farm, there had just arrived a letter from a relative who lived close to Rochester in the state of New York in America. This letter was from a woman to her niece whom she advised to come over and wherein she gave a detailed report about their economic position, on land and on the prospects for Norwegian immigrants. This aroused the two brothers' first attention to America.

One year later, Mr. Nattestad made his acquaintance with the Norwegian government official, Nubrud, an enlightened farmer in Sigdal. This old man was a friend of democracy with great thoughts about America's future both in economical as well as political terms, and his opinions were well adapted to revive and strengthen the prevailing thought about emigration. The two brothers decided then in the spring of 1837 to cast off and go to America. They heard that a ship was to sail from Stavanger with emigrants, and therefore took the road over the mountains in Numedal; but when they arrived, it was still nearly two months until the ship was to depart. They therefore took the chance with a sloop to Göteborg where they were given passage with a big American ship loaded with Swedish iron. For the voyage, they each paid 50 *speciedaler*, and after thirty-two days, they landed at Fall River, Rhode Island. From here, they went through New York, Albany and Buffalo to Detroit, Michigan, where they met with Ole Rynning and his party from Bergen. Together with this group, they now traveled through Chicago to Beaver Creek. They had traveled as sparingly as possible but still the cost of the journey was $100 each. They both soon concluded that America offered many advantages for farmers and laborers and they decided therefore to stay in the New World; but business affairs made it necessary that one of them needed to travel back to Norway. Ansten therefore left the next spring and made his way over through New Orleans, Liverpool and Tønsberg to Kristiania, where he was to take care of the release of Ole Rynning's book about America. About his sojourn in his home village Mr. Nattestad writes: "Though I did not plan to spread stories about America but simply tell of my experiences in the New World to those I spoke with, a rumor of my return went like wildfire through the land. Throughout the winter people came long ways to hear about America and letters came from everywhere with questions about the New World. There were even men who had come twenty-four Norwegian miles [240 km.] away, solely to speak with me. And in the spring of 1838 there were so many people ready to travel, just in Rollaug's parish, that Captain Ankersen's ship in Drammen, which could only take 100 passengers, did not have room, so that a number had to make their way to Göteborg in Sweden."

On this ship, Ansten came back to America. It took nine weeks for the journey over to New York and the passengers paid about $60 each for the passage. On arrival in Chicago, they heard that Ole Nattestad, Ansten's brother, had traveled from Illinois to Wisconsin and had settled in Rock County. To there the majority of the party went and settled in different parts of the said county as well as partly in bordering Stephenson County, Illinois. This was in the summer of 1839. But Ole Nattestad had arrived in 1838 and is normally assumed to have been the first Norwegian settler in Wisconsin.

The brothers Nattestad are regarded as the first emigrants to America from Norway's *Vestland* [West country] and *Østland* [East country], and that the support came from Stavanger County there can no longer be any doubt of. Numedal, Hallingdal, Siljord [Seljord], Hiterdal [Hitterdal], Sætersdalen and other villages in Vestlandet was therefore heavily represented among the early emigrants to Wisconsin. In 1844, it was especially people from Numedal and Vos [Voss] one met on Dane County's great prairies.

XV.
The Emigrant Groups are formed.

After the first emigration group from Bergen in 1837, the emigration from Bergen Diocese increased, especially from Vos Parish, which for a long time was considered as the place that provided the largest number of emigrants. From 1840, there sailed between one and three ships of emigrants yearly mainly from Vos. From there the epidemic spread to Sogn, Lerdal [Lærdal] and Valders [Valdres] townships, of which all have contributed greatly to the emigration flow in its first stages. Though the well-known men Ole Rynning and Hans Barlien had earlier emigrated from Trondhjem Diocese, the emigration never took off in that part of Norway. It was probably told in the beginning that they both died soon after their arrival. Rynning's book is seen as having been main reason that some families from Namdalen came over here as early as 1844. Since then there is no doubt that later people from different parts of northern Trondhjem Diocese came over here, but never in such a degree as from the districts of Bergen and Vestlandet. In the earlier period the emigration from Norway's eastern parts was very restricted, but later it has become rather significant. It will not help to institute any inquiry into the causes of this significant difference in emigration from the different parts of the country. For the most, perhaps living conditions and nutrition contributed towards this.

From the most reliable data the author could find is the above fundamental features of the beginning of the emigration in our time from Norway to America. We shall later discuss a little closer these first settlers' activity in this country and cast a glance at some of the results that are then lessons for countrymen both here and at home.

Above, it is briefly told how it went with the first Norwegian settlers in Morris County, New Jersey. If there at that place there are found any descendants at all from the first colonists, they have not maintained their Norwegian names and there cannot be said to be any Norwegian settlement there anymore. Not even at Beaver Creek is there found any Norwegian settlement — not even a countryman that can point out Ole Rynning's grave! The first settlers in Illinois however, continue to flourish and prosper, not only in La Salle County, but also in surrounding counties. The people here from the beginning have shown great diligence and thrift, and the worldly prosperity is very significant. One, who from home, brought strong religious tendencies has upheld oneself well, while the interest for politics, official positions and other worldly aptitude have not shown any great life signs, at least as far as it has come to general knowledge.

XVI.
Norwegians in Chicago.

From here we come to a slight period of change to mention some of the first Norwegians who settled in Chicago — the focal point for political, social and religious struggles. Pastor P. Anderson, whom one must assume knew about the first immigration to there from Norway, about as well as anyone presently living, expresses briefly as follows:

"1. Halstein Torrisen from Fjeldberg in Norway, with wife and children arrived in Chicago on the 16th October 1836. His first residence was in Wells Street, where Chicago & Northwestern Depot now stands. He was probably the first Norwegian who settled here in the town. In 1848 (the same year I became pastor in Chicago) he moved to Calumet south of Chicago, where he died a few years ago. 2. The first emigrants from Vos also came in 1836, including Nils Røthe and Svein Lothe (the latter from Hardanger), but on what date they arrived is not known. 3. Baar Johnson with wife and five children arrived in the year of 1837. 4. Andrew Nilsen and Anders Larsen Flage, each with their family, arrived in 1839. 5. Endre Iversen Røthe arrived in 1840, and about the same time Lars Davidsen (who now lives at Liberty Prairie, Dane County, Wis.) arrived, as well as Ole Gilbertsen and Anna Bakkethun (later Mrs. Nechlissen) and others. Andrew Nelson thinks that Johan Larsen from Kobbervig in Norway, who still lives here, visited Chicago as a sailor from Buffalo earlier, but settled here in 1836 at the same time as Halstein Torrisen. Anna Bakkethun still lives in Chicago and arrived here with Andrew Nelson, Anders Larsen Flage and others in 1839."

Without doubt, there were more countrymen who settled in Chicago between the years of 1836 and 1840 and we mention them only as being among the first, because we know of them. It needed courage and inclination to settle in Chicago at that time. One needed to saw and split firewood and engage in all sorts of heavy and cumbersome work to survive. The author visited Andrew Flage in 1844 — met him first in 1843 in New York, where he met two of his daughters who had arrived, — at that time, he had a market garden on the so-called canal land, and made a very successful business in vegetables. Since that time, several of the old settlers in Chicago have amassed large fortunes — some of them over half a million dollars. Among the Norwegians in Chicago who early distinguished himself in public affairs, we must in particular mention P. Anderson as our countrymen's first Lutheran pastor whose long-standing and faithful work for Lutheran preservation among our countrymen, deserves to be remembered with gratitude by the present church people in Chicago. The Episcopals during the Swedish Union made very strong efforts to establish their church among the first Norwegians in Wisconsin and in Chicago. At the latter place, Jenny Lind was able to give money to an Episcopal church, which was built on Michigan Street on the north side. Pastor Unonius moved from Pine Lake, Wis., to Chicago and for a time held service in the church; but the small wooden church that was already at that time built in Superior Street, where Pastor Anderson now began preaching, amassed the majority of the Norwegians, and Pastor Unonius soon thereafter moved to New York. I shall not here any longer follow the development of the church among the Norwegians in Chicago; it has too many dark shadows to pursue truthfully, without giving offense.

It was especially those of our countrymen who in Chicago's early days, had the foresight and forethought to invest their savings into building blocks, which so to say, amassed stealthily into large fortunes during this miracle-town's fairytale growth. One will assert that there are now those who posses more than one million, — though perhaps, somewhat exaggerated. The first Norwegian to come into a government position was Iver Lawson — among the Danes, Geo. P. Hansen and among the Swedes, John Nelson — as of later time, their names have multiplied. I know only three Norwegians in Chicago who have been members of the National Legislative Assembly, while from the rural districts, strangely enough, there has not been one single one. However, the Norwegians in Illinois, outside of Chicago, have never put any political interest to light. It is reported that in Chicago there live 50,000 Scandinavians with their offspring — a population large enough by itself for a rather respectable sized city. From this number there are at least 20,000 Norwegians including their offspring.

XVII.
First Norwegian Settlements in Wisconsin.

For several years after the year of 1840, the majority of Norwegian immigrants went to Wisconsin. Above is discussed Ole Nattestad's arrival at Jefferson Prairie in 1838. In 1839 there arrived three brothers from Luraas [in Tinn, Telemark], and with them a travel party of between thirty and forty people to the fairly well known Muskego. These people, who were mainly from Tin Parish, stepped ashore in Milwaukee, and must be seen as the first Norwegian to come directly to this state. The main party incidentally continued on to Chicago and from there overland to the north and to the west. There has been versed a story that the Luraas party were in Milwaukee, misled by land speculators to come out to Muskego's hard forest regions and establish themselves, but I have not found any reliable confirmation on this — which by itself is an implausible tale when all the land thereabouts still belonged to the government. More probable is it that due to the lack of knowledge of the language it became difficult for them to obtain the necessary guidance; otherwise, they could easily have found a better place to settle on. A half score English miles further east and south, in about the same distance from Milwaukee, at that time, was the best prairieland available, not only there where the Norwegian settlements of Yorkville and North Cape are found, but the largest part of the beautiful prairie in Racine County that was yet undeveloped. Development of certain tracts of land in a new country seemed to depend just as much on chance as on a throw of the dice. These people did not lack sharp-sightedness and initiative; they were tough and industrious folk. Had occasion led them some miles further to the southeast, Norwegians would now probably inhabit the beautiful Racine prairie, the same as Koshkonong prairie is now. The name Muskego — at that time in Milwaukee County — was transferred to the adjacent land in Racine County, especially the Town of Norway, where the actual Norwegian settlement is now found.

XVIII.
Heg in Norway [Town of Norway, Wisconsin].

In the fall of the same year (1839) Søren Bakke and Johannesen came north from Illinois, where they had stayed some weeks seeking land, and establish themselves in the later well-known Heg in Norway [Muskego Settlement, often referred to as 'Heg' — Heg's barn served as a receiving station and it became a temporary home for newcomers. Muskego and Heg became the journey's goal. — Odd Sverre Lovoll]. Johannesen was the actual leader and seemed to have been very afraid of prairieland; he always spouted this sentence: "Wood and water are two essential things." And when he abundantly found these things on the shores of Wind Lake, he decided to settle there.

It is easily understood that it must be difficult for the impoverished settler to establish himself on forested land. The densely grown and difficult oak forest is not easy to clear, and it takes under the best of circumstances, a four to five years before one can clear and plow so much that one can harvest enough to sustain the needs of one's family. Therefore, in these years, the settler's endurance was put on a very hard trial. Moreover, it was such here as well, and when also, as it happened in those days, the unavoidable endemic fever arrived, which could continue to plague folks for three to nine months, it is no wonder that the settlement did not flourish or have the same progress as on prairie land. Bakke and Johannesen arrived at New York along with Elling Eielsen in 1839 and went first to the Norwegian settlement in La Salle County, Illinois, from where that fall they came to Muskego and dug winter quarters on the western side of a burial mound from the time of the Indians, where they lived warm and cozy during the winter. The letters being sent to friends in their home villages from these newcomers — yearly brought more and more immigrants, and the location Heg — so called after the arrival of Even Heg — became the Mecca to where Norwegians, who stepped ashore in Milwaukee, mainly headed for. The brothers Luraas and many others however, became fed up with digging up roots in the thick oak forests, and sold their land to newcomers and moved west to the prairie colonies. Johannesen died in his original abode after a period of four to five years, and Søren Bakke returned to Norway, whilst Heg, Skogstad, Thompson, Danielsen and many others remained persisting with the clearing. For a couple of months during summer, Even Heg's barn could be filled with immigrants in transit, as the place had become the first lay-by, on the way from Milwaukee to Koshkonong and farther west.

XIX.
The first Norwegian church in America.

It was here that Messrs. Heg & Reymert began publishing *Nordlyset*, the first Norwegian newspaper in America — about which more will come later. It was here that the well-known Pastor C. L. Clausen had built the first Norwegian church in America in 1844. He arrived here in the fall of 1843, was an amiable, intelligent and pious pastor, and quickly gathered all the scattered settlers in Muskego and Yorkville into Norwegian Lutheran congregations. However, he was not long in Muskego, and moved to Luther Valley at Rock Prairie and was succeeded in Muskego by Pastor H. A. Stub. From memory, Pastor Clausen was the Norwegian Synod's first president, and as he quickly mastered the English language he became of great service to the subsequent Norwegian pastors, and it is no exaggeration to say that he was their right hand at organizing Norwegian congregations among the scattered settlers. It may well be said, that it later went with him as it does with most trail breakers, who through their heart, sacrifice themselves for their deeds, his services were quickly and completely forgotten by the men who had the most to thank him for.

It was also here that the emigrants going through Milwaukee stopped to seek information, advice and guidance from their earlier arrived countrymen, about conditions in the New World, which were relevant to their future, and what was best for them to now do. Hans Heg, Even's eldest son, who fell as a brigadier general in the battle of Chickamauga, had many an interesting story to tell from the tours he made to Jefferson, Rock and Koshkonong prairies with emigrant families. Now a German is living on old Heg [farm], which also is the case of many of the other farms first cleared by the Norwegians. Most of the old settlers are either dead or have moved elsewhere, but of the younger generation, there are many who live on beautiful well-cultivated farms and together with the Norwegians at Yorkville Prairie, there are still enough to sustain one pastor and two churches.

It was also at this place that the well-known lawyer and politician James D. Reymert, in his time played an outstanding role. He built a steam-saw and took on the contract to build a boardwalk from Muskego Center to Waterford — a distance of twelve to fourteen miles. This brought the farmers' oak forests into play and many a remunerative work for oneself and one's beast of burden. For a time he developed a big company, but it is thought that he suffered a loss in the boardwalk company and moved to Milwaukee, and later to New York, where he became a member of the legal firm of Jenkins & Reymert.

XX.
Yorkville Prairie.

The Norwegian settlement at Yorkville Prairie is separated from Muskego at Muskego Creek, by a small river that flows out from Wind Lake and into Fox River near the city of Rochester. The first Norwegians who settled at this place were Mons Aadland from Samnanger, Bergen Diocese, and Nels Johnson from Hiterdal. They both arrived here in 1840. Aadland belonged to the Beaver Creek group and had come over in 1837 with the first ship from Bergen along with Ole Rynning. After three years of residence in Illinois, he and his family moved here. Of his children there are now only three living, two sons who live on large farms that he owned during his lifetime, and the daughter, widow Preus, living in Norway. Nels Johnson moved some years later to Iowa, where he not so long ago died as one of the affluent farmers. The next year in 1841, Hermond Nelsen and family arrived from Hallingdal and settled here. Elling Eielsen joined them and later married the eldest daughter. Aslak Simonsen, Ole Helleiksen, Germund Johnson and others soon arrived so that their number in 1843, when I arrived here, was large enough to fill Aadland's barn with an attentive audience at Eielsen's prayer meetings. It must have been a couple of years later that Elling Spillum, Tyge Hendriksen and others arrived here; but then all available government land was taken so that one needed to purchase from others, and it began to become expensive for people who had little money. Also in this settlement many emigrant groups began to stay over on the journey from Milwaukee or Racine in order to obtain detailed information from their countrymen and to get transport west to places where there was still government land to be found. I, myself, did a couple of such trips to Koshkonong with emigrant families. At that time, it was difficult to obtain lodgings for them as they all only sought after the bare essentials for themselves. I can recall that I was able to get one family in with Mr. Smitbak from Numedal, who was one of the first who settled on the big prairie. I have later heard that he has become a rich man, which due to the location, one could foresee.

XXI.
Ogden and the Norwegians.

Here are a couple of small features to describe conditions at that time. In the summer of 1844 or 1845, there arrived a young Norwegian from Chicago who had a horse he wanted to sell. One of our neighbors bought it, and a couple of weeks later a certain Mr. Ogden (butcher in Milwaukee) arrived with the sheriff and took the horse under the assertion that the horse was his and that he had the right to take his property wherever he found it. The man who had bought the horse had to sue Ogden, and it was undeniably proved that the horse, which was only three years old, was bought in Indiana the previous year and had wintered in Chicago. Ogden had to pay for the horse plus [legal] costs. It was often rather lawless in those days.

Around this time, there was much sickness among the Norwegian settlers in Muskego and it was rumored in Racine that there was the need and the want of food there. Concerned friends collected therefore several wagonloads of provisions that were taken out to Yorkville where a committee was elected to attend to the distribution. When Ogden and his sheriff was out there and took the horse mentioned above, they noticed the wagons of goods, and Ogden's attorney argued during the proceedings on the horse, that the Norwegians must be a gang of thieves as one had seen them with a quantity of stolen goods. I was one of the witnesses in this matter and our attorney called me to explain the connection. As soon as it was said that the mentioned goods were provisions sent out from Racine to sick and needy emigrants, Ogden's attorney realized he had overstepped himself and withdrew the allegations, and the judge who leaned strongly on Ogden's side would not hear any further explanation. I did however add that the plaintiff in this matter was a member of the committee that knew of the food distribution. I later heard from a jury member that this episode removed all doubt with the jury.

There was at this time a widespread *Know Nothing* element among the well to do Americans, and this time of need among the Norwegian immigrants in Muskego's forested areas opened the eyes of the politicians in Racine County. At this time, every town was to maintain their own poor, and now that Yorkville included Muskego, or the present-day Norway, and three other townships, in the next legislature one needed to set aside the Town of Norway separately for fear of the tax burden to the poverty stricken Norwegians. Poor Norway was now to take care of itself! One has to excuse this with the fact that one did not know the Norwegians. When we now see the well cultivated, magnificently built farms, *Norskerne* in Norway, and neighboring towns, we see the prosperity, comfort and aptitude, which appear with them overall, it is excusable if we feel a little pride over our nationality. Those men, who at that time felt threatened by the Norwegian's poverty, have themselves nearly all come closer to the poorhouse than the Norwegians in Racine County have.

XXII.
Travel from Bergen to New York in 1843.

In the spring of 1843, two ships were to sail from Bergen with emigrants to America. Both ships were to be equipped by the shipping company *Gade*. One ship was a bark, which took on eighty passengers, the other a brig, which only took on fifty-two passengers. With the exception of myself and a young man by the name of Nels Torstensen, for whom I paid the passage, along with a young bookbinding apprentice, Øvre from Bergen, all the passengers on board the brig were from Vos Parish, and as far as is remembered it was the same on the bark. However, there was one exception, Cleng Peerson, who came back with this ship from his last voyage to Norway. The departure time on the contract was scheduled for the 1st of May, but the ships were not ready until the middle of the month, and during this time the emigrants had to stay in Bergen and eke out their provisions. Most of them had received letters from friends in America, wherein there was advice and guidance from which they had decided whithersoever to go. None of them was quite without means — some of them were even wealthy folk with $1,000 or more of ready money for the family. The voyage began under the most pleasant of weathers, and with a sweeping easterly, the course was set towards the west, over the North Sea via the Faroe Islands, and within two weeks, we were about halfway to America. We soon began discussing our voyage and said it would be the fastest yet heard of, for with the same progress we would see America in two weeks. However, in the ensuing six to seven weeks we had to constantly struggle with a westerly wind, and sometimes hurricane-like storms, so that what was gained one day was lost the next. The little brig however sailed well and we had skilled officers and crew on the ship.

XXIII.
Illness among the Passengers.

I, who for the last two to three years had roamed the seas and seen the oceans' whimsical moods felt no anxiety on that side; but what during the ongoing westerly storms struck myself and others with a well-founded fear, was a pernicious disease that had broken out among the passengers. The talk among them was that there had been typhoid fever in the area where some of them had come from. The first mate was an acquaintance of mine with whom I had previously made a voyage to England, and I mentioned to him what I had heard. When this was made known to the captain, he became seriously anxious. The shipping company had not given us a doctor but had given the captain a box of medicines so that in an emergency he could take on the role of a physician. At this time, he did what he could, but as it seemed, to no avail, as the disease steadily took grip; two children in one family died and were buried at sea. The eldest was a girl of between ten and twelve years of age; she suffered badly from diarrhea, and an old servant woman of the family gave her a dose of *Hoffmansdraaber* [one part ether and three parts alcohol], which was followed by terrible pain and she died very rapidly. The cadavers were sewn inside canvas with a stone by the feet, and on a plank, they were slid out into the waves during the singing of a verse from a psalm. These children belonged to a respectable and wealthy family and the compassion for them was general. If I am not wrong, there are still two or three children from these parents living in this country. This is not a unique case; I know there were many emigrant families who had to go through similar trials.

On the 4th of July, America's Independence Day, we were still on the open sea, but of late we had started to creep forward in a more lenient weather. There was too much anxiety and dejection for anyone to feel inclined to celebrate our future homeland, its Independence Day. The young man whose passage I had paid for was now very ill, and for a time I feared that he would succumb. But his iron resolve was victorious and he recovered incredibly fast. When we finally had a New York pilot on board, we were still nearly two hundred miles from land. He was a young and daring rascal who did not spare the sails; suddenly there was hauling and bracing and the crew was very lively, and I must admit that it was with great relief to see the rapid progress the ship was now making.

XXIV.
Arrival in New York.

Finally, the east coast of Long Island showed itself to the emigrants' yearning staring eyes as a long, low cloudbank on the western horizon. It was early in the morning and the coast became clearer as we came closer. Later on, Sandy Hook also came into view further south, near the entrance to New York. The emigrants' hopes once more rose and everyone thanked God for having reached land before the disease got the upper hand. We came to anchor in the afternoon at the quarantine station just out from the marine hospital on Staten Island. The conditions on board had been made known, and when the doctor from the hospital arrived, he gave the captain a very serious rebuke as if he was the cause of the disease. The shipping company could have had the benefit of a reprimand as there was no doctor on the ship, but the captain had surely done the best he could. It was a great joy for all of us when we found the bark *Juno,* which had left Bergen the same time as us, in the harbor; it had only arrived the previous day despite it not being an unusually quick sailing ship. Everybody on board was healthy. Of our passengers, there were seven or eight that had to be taken to the hospital, and as none of the doctors understood Norwegian, they commandeered me to be interpreter and I remained three days at the hospital. The doctors did their rounds a couple of times every night and I then needed to be up and go along with them. In the same ward there were some sick German emigrants, and I also became interpreter for them. The families who had ill members in the hospital had to lay over in New York to await the outcome.

XXV.
Departure to the West.

The day before departing New York, I went back to the hospital with a man who had a sister that was ill, though recovering well. He decided to bring her along, even though the doctor assured him that she would die if he discharged her now; I also tried to persuade him to wait, though in vain. I heard later that she had died on the way across the canal. The doctors called the disease *Ship Fever* [typhus] and told me that to some degree it was contagious, so that if I wished to avoid the disease it was best if I left the group. I had promised to go with them up the Hudson River to the city of Troy, where their luggage would be weighed and the overweight paid for, before they went aboard the canal boat. Every adult should have 100 pounds free freight and the remaining freight would need to be paid. Whilst we were doing the weighing, on the wharf there was a group of American gentlemen and ladies who looked at these strangers with much curiosity, and when they saw the Norwegian flat-bread exposed in the emigrants' chests, one of the came over and asked if he could have a taste — but of course, that he must do! The Irish railway was just then finished from Albany to Buffalo. I had decided to go by railway from Troy to Buffalo, and the time had now come to separate from the group. The young bookbinding apprentice Øvre, from Bergen, was just beginning to become ill and I tried to persuade him into joining me, as otherwise he would suffer great pain on the canal boat; but this he did not want to do. Later I heard he had died in Buffalo.

XXVI.
Captain Gasman's [Gasmann's] Group.

At the same time as we, another Norwegian emigrant ship also arrived in New York from Drøbak skippered by Captain [Johan] Gasmann. A brother of the captain, former *Storthingsmand* [parliamentarian] Hans Gasmann and family were also among the emigrants in this group. I saw some of these folk in shipbroker Balken's office where at that time nearly all Norwegian shipping was cleared through customs. The majority of Mr. Gasmann's traveling group went westward from Milwaukee to the settlements at Pine Lake and Rock River, where already some countrymen had settled in these forested parts. Here the Norwegian parliamentarian cleared and built his farm in quiescence without taking any leading part in public affairs, and here he ended his days some years ago. One of his sons attended the military school at West Point and is now, as far as is known, an officer in the United States army. Another has been employed as an agent among the Indians.

XXVII.
Broker Balken and the Emigrants.

Broker Balken was born in Bergen and lived in New York for several years. Therefore, the emigrant's contracts for their transport to the westerly states usually ended up at his office, even though Balken did not seem to have any interest in any of the competing shipping lines. This shipping business with the emigrants to the west was at that time a very large and remunerative business, and the competition between the different lines was very fierce. Representatives of these lines came therefore steadily to Balken's office, and it was usually the captains who acted for the emigrants, since they themselves did not understand how to take care of the essentials. There was a common rumor among the emigrants, which presumably came from earlier immigrant friends, that there was a great deal of deception with these contracts. But that the Norwegian captains were part thereof, I do not think. They were completely honest men who did not embark on taking venture money, but did the best they could for their emigrants. However, as the emigrants knew little, especially about these means of conveyance, they turned often to Mr. Balken for advice. Because of his many years of residence in New York, he should best know the situation and the trustworthiness of the shipping line. Cleng Peerson predicted that the company that we had signed a contract with would deceive our group; and the results showed that he was correct. But from where he had his suspicions, I have never found out.

When the group arrived at Buffalo after the voyage, they should have had a steamship from there to Milwaukee and Chicago, but instead of this they were put on board a sailing ship, and because of calms and head winds, the group was on the journey for over a month. Because of the lengthy journey that the passengers had not counted on, they suffered much because of the lack of provisions. By steamship the journey would at the most taken four days; but in Buffalo there was none who could speak for them, and the written contract which clearly showed that they had paid for a steamer over the lakes, was not put into effect. I had been in Wisconsin for six weeks before the young man for whom I had paid the passage for arrived. He was on the sailing ship until Chicago and left there along with some emigrants who had come via Le Havre — and among them was first officer Wigeland who understood English and was their leader.

XXVIII.
The Runner Menace.

For the emigrant groups that had no interpreter it was at that time very difficult to reach one's destination without being deceived, or delayed on the journey. Being a volunteer interpreter without pay was actually a thankless task; had they been shrewd, most of the emigrants would have been discerning enough to have paid a token for the work. Therefore, later there was a rule that there had to be an interpreter along who was usually paid by the shipping company or the transport company to avoid complications; later the Norwegian shipmasters would often follow along with their emigrants, right through to Chicago. The so-called runner service [menace] (or rather disservice) began already at that time to torment the emigrants and there arrived scarcely a letter back from the America-farers, without therein being warnings against the emigrant-runners, who from the day they stepped ashore till they reached their destination, followed and encircled them as if by a swarm of bees. This scandalous behavior became much worse later and the most sinister was that the runners, almost without exception, were the emigrant's own countrymen who had learned English, and arrived amongst them as if they were some angels of deliverance to guide and protect them against American swindle. Those who had not been warned about them easily attached much credence to them, whilst on the other side, the warnings made the emigrants so suspicious that they did not dare believe the occasional honest person who offered their assistance. Even the later translator, who was of a better class and worked for wages, was often exposed to fierce suspicion. It often happens that traveling expenses are higher than previously expected, and for people who did not understand the discussion, it was quite natural to see swindles everywhere. But this suspicion was excusable because of the scoundrel tricks that now and then came to light. When the runners' act of tyranny in New York, had brought this country for the emigrants into a place of ill repute, and when higher disembarkation money was strongly demanded, the Norwegian emigration began to take the voyage via Québec in Canada, where in the beginning it went better, but it happened here as it happens everywhere. "Wheresoever the body is, thither will the eagles be gathered together." [Luke 17:37]. The runners were not slow in finding their way to Québec and little was better till the emigrants were being transported by steamer or railroad; as then the legislation procedure protected them, and a stricter control were placed on the transport companies that transported the emigrants as well as their agents and interpreters.

I have mentioned this, our voyage, somewhat detailed — partly because the story thereon is relying on personal experience, and partly because the voyage as long as it was with a sailing ship, was essentially a repetition of one as with another, so that much of it may serve as an example for them all.

There was nearly an absolute rule among the first Norwegian immigrants to search for a block of land out in the countryside whereupon they could build and live. It was a rare exception, when any Norwegian farmer would intentionally settle in town. Only when his travel money could no longer stretch would he take work in town, and when it began to go well he would remain where he was. The first emigrants came exclusively from the rural districts of Norway and their first thought was to find a piece of land to cultivate in order to extract therefrom the necessities of life. With sailors and artisans it was different; their livelihood led them naturally to the city. The only exceptions I can recall were the people from Vos in Chicago. Already among the first of them, some settled in town, aye, I knew also of those who returned from Koshkonong back to Chicago to live there, and luck was with those who did not imbibe too much spirits.

XXIX.
The first Norwegians in the Townships of Wisconsin.

Among the first Norwegians I know to tell about in the Town of Racine, was a man from western Norway by the name of Farbjørn Gunleiksen with family. He had a small boardinghouse where the Norwegians from Muskego and Yorkville always visited when they arrived in town, and it shall be said to his praise, that there was never found intoxicating drink in his house. The old ones are now dead but two daughters still live there, and a son lives in Chicago. Racine had for a time a not so small Norwegian population, but as bad working circumstances occurred many moved out onto the land. Now Racine has grown to a thriving factory town of 20,000 inhabitants, and it is told that nearly one third of are Danish.

Milwaukee also had earlier a not so small Norwegian population, mainly sailors and artisans. Among the eldest I can remember was Captain Saveland. He died many years ago, but his descendants constitute a numerous family, several who are out west. A man by the name of Nordbo who used to take in boarders had settled there early, and to him the farmers from Muskego and Yorkville set out for, as well as from Pine Lake and Rock River when they arrived in Milwaukee. When I in 1843 arrived in Milwaukee, I could not find any Norwegians present, but of Swedes, the well-known Mr. Lange in Chicago had at that time a hotel on the west side. James D. Reymert and if I am not mistaken, John Thorson as well, were at that time young sales clerks. John Thorson is now one of the city's leading merchants. The family Kildal, were also apparently among one of the first to settle there. Reinertsen was one of the city's old settlers. His boardinghouse on Clinton Street, which still stands in the same old place under the name Scandinavian House, was generally the meeting place for the city's Norwegian sailors, as well as the place where the Norwegian farmers always found a friendly reception and shelter for themselves and their draught animals when they arrived in town with their wares. A man from Bergen who called himself Frøiseth tried as a merchant but did not last long. With him, I met for the first time the renowned Dr. [Johan Christian Brotkorb] Dass (Dundas), who later settled in Koshkonong. The first Norwegians, who settled in Milwaukee, consisted mainly of sailors and shipwrights. Now the Norwegian population counts several thousand from all social classes, with three Norwegian churches and several associations for mutual support etc. I believe there is a criterion among our countrymen in the cities that they do not like to pay rent, and so try as quickly as possible to live in their own house; this gives them a good foothold and a solid foundation whereupon to build an independent and happy future — something the descendants would do well in remembering. Both during the war as well as the immediate succeeding years, shipping on the great lakes was a very rewarding business, and there were not so few Norwegians in Milwaukee, who at that time collected great fortunes. Many of them skippered their own ships as well as holding shares in others, which as long as the time was good brought in a respectable income. But then the economic depression of 1873 came with changes to economic conditions, of which followed such a sharp decline in freight and prices that those who happened to have invested in the shipping industry suffered great losses; on the other hand, those who had invested their fortunes in land property, were untouched.

XXX.
Reminiscence of the New Settler Life.

Thc first Norwegian settlements on the prairies of Jefferson, Rock and Koshkonong have already been mentioned in passing. And as there is no intention to provide further accounts on settlements, which require quite different sources to draw from than the ones I possess, I will let myself be content with a few personal reminiscences from that time I visited these beautiful and fertile districts. To Jefferson and Rock Prairie I did not arrive until the spring of 1849, and then only in transit. It was said that Jefferson was one of the most beautiful landscapes one had seen, and that seemed to be true. When I traveled through there with Pastor Clausen, nearly all usable government land had been taken, and everywhere we saw well-built farms as if there was an all knowing diligence and prosperity among the farmers.

We stayed over until the next day with Kristoffer Nyhus, one of the first from Numedal who settled there. Pastor Clausen was known thereabouts through his missionary trips to the new Norwegian settlements; and where he was known, he was also welcome; everywhere he came he was very respected and loved among the Norwegian settlers. On this trip we visited Beloit and Janesville, places that were still in their infancy, and arrived finally at Luther Valley at Rock Prairie, where Pastor Clausen at that time owned a flourishing farm. The prairie here is a more grand and hilly landscape than Racine and Jefferson, and I for a long time had heard that the area around Rock River had the name for being very rich and fertile; the land had therefore been taken earlier by American pioneers. However there were at that time enough Norwegians to form a large congregation, and they had themselves a roomy stone building as a church. As belonging to the first settlers, I heard mention Lars Skavland, Gulleik Laugen, and Mr. Gravdal — among others whose names I now do not recall —; they had settled there in 1839, at the same time as those in Jefferson.

XXXI.
In Dane County.

North of Rock County is Dane County with a continuation of the same beautiful prairieland, and it was natural that these eager land seekers from the rocky land on the other side of the ocean felt inspired by these beautiful areas. The first Norwegian immigrants arrived therefore at the same time to Rock and Dane County, that is, 1839 and 1840. They were mostly from Numedal, Vos and Stavanger. Here as elsewhere, their diligence and thrift followed them and produced the same good results — they attained quick cozy homes and an anxiety-free livelihood. The so-called Koshkonong settlement was soon seen as the largest and wealthiest Norwegian settlement in Wisconsin. When I for the first time (1844) arrived there with a load of emigrant luggage, it was said everywhere that all the best land was occupied and that there was no housing to be found for newcomers. At that time, it was understood that one needed to have a forest grove next to one's prairieland. But it was nevertheless true that immigrants crammed themselves in too close to each other in the new settlements. A man from Numedal, whose name I have now forgotten, was so good as to take in the family I was driving for. He lived not so far from the so-called Christiana and was probably one of the first Norwegian settlers. He told about a man from Skien, who had rowed by boat from Beloit in Rock County, when he arrived there in 1839, to seek land. A man by the name of Bjoland from Stavanger had also arrived there in 1839 and had been one of the first to take land on the prairie. A young man from Saue in Vos, was said to be one of the first settlers near Cambridge and later had the name for being the wealthiest farmer among the Norwegians in Koshkonong. Below, by Prof. J. Olsen, may perhaps be of historical interest in honor of Prof. Rasmus B. Anderson's mother's death some years ago. It is partly an excerpt, partly a free translation from an English article in the Madison Democrat:

"As Abel Cathrine Amundsen was the first white woman to settle in the Town of Albion (Dane County), some information of her life will be of interest, especially when her son, Prof. Rasmus B. Anderson, the present United States' minister in Denmark, is so well known. She was born in Sandeid in the southwestern part of Norway. Her father, Bernhardus Arnoldus von Krogh, was a lieutenant in the Norwegian army. Her mother was also from the famous von Krogh clan, which stretches across a whole line of military officers back to a Major Bernhardus von Krogh in Lübeck, who in 1644 arrived in Bremen with soldiers in order to help Denmark against Sweden. He remained in the Danish service, and his only son, George Frederik von Krogh became a colonel for a Norwegian regiment in 1710. His descendants were many and most of them entered the army as officers. In 1830, she married Bjørn Anderson, a farmer's son born near Stavanger in 1801. It is nearly impossible for Americans to imagine with what consternation and indignation this marriage between the officer's daughter and farmer's son was received. That her husband was a Quaker and therefore did not belong to the state church also increased the antipathy against the young pair. They decided then to sail to the land on the other side of the ocean, whose *star* just now began to show itself over the horizon. Therefore, they left Norway in the spring of 1836 with the first group of Norwegian emigrants who came to this land. When they reached New York, Bjørn Anderson and wife, along with a few other families, traveled to Rochester, N. Y. where they lived for two years. Bjørn worked then as a cooper. At the end of this time, they moved to the Norwegian settlement in La Salle County, Illinois, where they also lived for two years. In 1840, Bjørn Anderson went on foot, along with two friends, on an expedition to Wisconsin to find a suitable place for a new home. He chose a stretch of land near Lake Koshkonong and returned to La Salle County. The following spring, with wife and four young children, and the same two companions, they left for their new homes in Wisconsin. They were the first couple who settled in the present Town of Albion, and the hardships and sufferings they then had to endure, seem now like fiction to the younger generation. However, throughout all this hard time they never lost their courage. Both had a rare will power; he was energetic, restless and active, she was gentle, quiet and durable. In the first two or three years, six cents was all the ready money they possessed. With the few products they could spare, he traveled seventy miles over the wild uninhabited region to Milwaukee to buy life's necessities. When he was away, she stayed at home in the log hut with their children, and now and then had Indians as guests. Their struggles in the end paid off and in ten years the first 40 acres had turned into 230 acres, of fertile land. Nevertheless, just as the pioneer life's struggles were over, a new enemy arrived. In the summer of 1850, cholera raged through the settlement and Bjørn Anderson and one son died thereof. Nine children survived him of which eight are still alive. His eldest son, Andrew A., is a wealthy farmer in Goodhue County, Minn.; Abel B., is a pastor in Muskegon, Michigan; Brown Anderson is a merchant in Spring Grove, Minn.; Prof. Rasmus B. Anderson is, as already mentioned, a minister in Denmark. Their four daughters are all married; three live in Minnesota and the fourth in Iowa. In 1854, the widow married Ingebrigt Amundsen. He died in 1861, leaving behind one son."

XXXII.
Tollefson's Experiences.

A farmer, by the name of G. Tollefson, arrived in America in 1843 and now lives in Dane County. He writes an article in an English newspaper about his experience on arriving in America of which the following is here, written: Arriving in New York, a man by the name of Bakke gave a free pass for the Tollefson family and traveling companions to Milwaukee, where they arrived in good form. This town was then on the outskirts of civilization and there were only a few Norwegians in Wisconsin. Tollefson and his family went with Lars Dommerud to Muskego, where among other countrymen they met Even Heg, Reymert and Bakke. Some time thereafter, he went further west and worked for a Sherwood who lived near Clinton, in Rock County. Tollefson says, "I split 600 rails so as to be able to borrow Sherwood's oxen and wagon so that I could bring my parents to Rock County. As I was not accustomed to drive oxen and as I wished to see my parents as soon as possible, I drove the team too quickly. It was not long before the team was tired and they laid themselves down and I did not manage to move them from that place. As of this dilemma I gave them some corncobs, and after a time they stood up and went along after me. This repeated itself several times until it became so that when they wanted maize they would just lay straight down and would not move until they received it. I then arrived at the idea to hang some corncobs on my back and walk in front of the animals. In this manner,

I coaxed them forward and finally I came to my parents. On the homeward journey, we drove more slowly. I have often thought that Sherwood had extraordinary confidence in me, a stranger as well as a newcomer, in that he loaned me the ox team for such a long journey without knowing if I could drive them or not.

"As I wished to own my own land as soon as possible I traveled to Primrose in 1849. Here I met Niels Einarson. There was plenty of land but to find the lot number of what I chose was the question. After much investigation we found a large oak tree a short distance east of where Norman Randal lives. On this tree, it was plain to see the following letters and numbers: N. W. ¼, S. 23, T. 5, N. R. 6 E. There was neither pen nor paper to be found without walking many miles, and something had to be done immediately. I borrowed an axe from Einarson and cut down a small aspen, and after having made it flat on both sides so that it was quite thin, I took my pocketknife and cut in the letters and numbers exactly as they were in the oak tree. With this aspenboard under my arm I went to the land office and put the board and the money on the counter to the clerks' great amusement. They understood the description and I had the land."

XXXIII.
The first battle with the Pastor.

The first settlers in Dane County used to make themselves merry through an occurrence between their first pastor — [J. W. C.] Dietrichson, and a farmer by the name of [Halvor Christian Pedersen] Funkelien. This Funkelien seemed to have been a joker and a jester. He took his pleasure in shocking the pastor with whom he was always in conflict. The pastor's weak point was that he quickly became angry and lost his self-control. In the end, it came so that he forbade Funkelien to come to church. One Sunday he therefore demanded his assistants to throw Funkelien out, as he despite his ban had come to church. The pastor's assistants however remained calm. This enraged the pastor and he stepped down from the pulpit to throw Funkelien out himself. He resisted and there was great commotion in the church. Funkelien sued the pastor and the aforesaid Bjørn Anderson, who was a kind of lawyer, acted as Funkelien's attorney, and the pastor had to suffer by paying a fine. Another newcomer, whom I knew personally, could also tell that he had once sent his wife over to the parsonage on an errand, which had outraged the pastor. He grabbed her so hard by the arm to chase her away that there were bruises caused by his fingers on the woman's arm. From this incident, he was sued once more and had to pay a fine of fifty dollars. One sees from this that controversy between a pastor and the Norwegians in America began early, and it is cited here as probably the first utterance of this kind, among them.

XXXIV.
A Settlers Cabin in Columbia County.

It was in the summer of 1845 when the author erected his pioneer hut in the present Columbia County, and was perhaps the closest opportunity for the glorious land areas of — Spring Prairie, Bonnet Prairie, Lodi and surrounds to come into Norwegian possession, as the American immigration flow had begun to spread towards the north with rapid strides. This is how it happened: When I in 1843 arrived at Yorkville Prairie, Racine County, the best land was occupied and the eighty acres of prairie land I bought was considered to be too low-lying and I was not happy with it. I and another young man, Niels Torstensen, for whom I had paid the voyage for, decided therefore to travel westward to seek land. With a pair of burly oxen and a wagon equipped with a small camp oven, provisions, bedding and other necessary accessories for camp life, we drove off in the month of August in 1845, and set off towards the west, guided by a map of Wisconsin and a pocket compass. We drove directly to Koshkonong Prairie where we had been a couple of times earlier and it was actually from there that the land search was to begin. I had in fact come on the idea that this same stretch of prairie continued further towards the north. We followed the beaten track to Madison where nothing was appealing to the prairie farmer. Madison which had nothing exceptional, except for its natural beauty, and the large Territorial building that looked very stately among the small wooden houses — would however now look very forlorn besides the magnificent Capitol building that the state owns.

We drove a mile from town but became alarmed by the steep hills where the state university now is, and turned towards the east where we located the old road to Fort Winnebago. A countryman by the name of Amund [Endresen] Rosseland who arrived here in 1837 and whom I had known in Norway, I had heard to have moved out here earlier, and I would now visit him. He was to have settled near Dells at Wisconsin River some miles from Fort Winnebago. The land for several miles around the fort was low, swampy and dismal. After a most arduous and boring wandering over sand dunes with brush and swamps, we finally one afternoon reached the place. A half mile from the house we met a Norwegian who was raking hay, and he was so noncommunicative that we could hardly get more out of him than that Amund had gone away and was not expected home for a few days. This, along with the land's character, we made the decision to turn about; but as both ourselves and the oxen were tired, we made camp for the day a little further down where there was water to be found. We were at home in the wagon, and so were the oxen on the rich grassland. We baked our biscuits and fried our bacon, boiled our coffee and ate with an appetite that a prince would have envied us. We returned the same way for about twenty miles to a place an able American by the name of Young, at that time was building his hut. He told us that if we turned off a few miles eastward we would find what we sought, that is to say, good prairieland beside forested land. We followed his advice and soon came to a landscape alternating with both forest and prairie. Here we met a couple of Americans who also were building their houses. One of them was an old pioneer by the name of Gilbert, who wanted to sell us his claim. But when we found out that we had the option of just as good land as his, and also possessed the same right to make a claim, we drove a couple of miles further south and our biggest difficulty was to make a choice, as there was an abundance of satisfying places to choose from. We finally made a choice and began to build our log hut, and soon we could with poetry sing:

"I Dalens Skjød en Hytte laa
Ved Bredden af en Kilde,
Dens Væg var Ler, dens Tag var Straa,
Dens Hegn var Roser vilde."

"In the valley's bosom a hut stood
By the shore of a spring,
Its walls were clay, its roof was straw,
Its fence was roses wild."

It was now the month of September and our first care was to cut hay and build a barn for our oxen for the winter. Thus was the beginning of all the rich and flourishing Norwegian settlements on Spring Prairie, Bonnet Prairie, Lodi, and the other beautiful surrounding prairie tracts. There arrived no other Norwegian settlers there that fall. We were busy getting ready for the winter until the first of November. We heard that a Norwegian by the name of Kleppen had arrived and taken land a little south of where we had settled — but we never saw him. He was a sort of shy hermit who never mixed with other people. The next spring he had sold his claim. When I later in the fall went to Milwaukee to fill out the pre-emption papers on the land, I mentioned the place to people I knew in Koshkonong, and as the immigration from Norway at that time was very extensive, it was foreseeable that the newcomers the following summer would congregate in the Norwegian settlements in Dane

County. I also wrote letters to friends and acquaintances in La Salle County, Illinois, with the consequence that a couple of them moved out there the next spring. The next summer was a busy time in the new settlement. From the visit to Milwaukee, I brought some of the most necessary equipment, such as a plow, harrow and such. Early in spring Peder Frøland, a personal friend of mine arrived. He had arrived out there in La Salle County in 1837, and brought with him a pair of oxen with a wagon and other equipment. The two of us joined forces with the work. When it neared the month of June, the Norwegian emigrants began coming in large numbers to Koshkonong. One party of them had hired Ole Trovatten, an old well-known man in Koshkonong, to come with them to help choose land. I had earlier been acquainted with this man, and when he found that even I could choose land, he soon tired of tramping through forest and over prairie with no other compensation than *thanks for the help*, and he went happily home and left me with the toil. All the land that was thought to be worth taking throughout the whole district was soon in the hands of the settlers. Per Frøland and I now had a team of four pair of oxen and plowed about 100 acres of prairieland that year for the newcomers.

XXXV.
An Indian Visit.

Here I had my first and last experience with Indians. One warm summer's day when I was out in a swamp to cut hay, I saw a herd of deer come fugaciously over a hill on the prairie, and just behind them were some wild hunters following them on horseback. However, the deer seemed at this time to have too large a lead for them to come into shooting range. Soon afterwards, out on the prairie in the same direction, there appeared a long line of people, who were on horseback as well as on foot. It was a group of Winnebago Indians, who had left their reservation and made a raid on the southern counties in the state. Here they had been guilty of some acts of tyranny and the authorities had commanded them to turn back to their homes. It was this group that now on their way north to their reservation were coming by. A couple of their young men came over to me and made signs that they were thirsty. I had a small Norwegian coffee pot with drinking water sitting in the grass and I pointed and made signs for them to drink. Luckily, there was an excellent source [of water] there by the edge of the swamp half a mile from us. I showed them where, by signs as well as I could. Thereupon they left contented thereto, made camp and stayed for three days. The colored [native] Americans treated their women just as harshly as the white Americans treat theirs well, and assist them. The men rode proudly at the head of the group, with their rifles over their knees, whilst the women followed on foot — loaded with provisions, camping equipment etc. When I went home in the evening, my curiosity led me through the Indian's camp to see how they took care of things. There was in this group, a half-blood who spoke a little English. He let me understand that I was not to come into the camp. I did not let this be said twice, as I was everything but feeling good about these wild neighbors' presence. A couple of their women however came to our hut the following day and wanted to swap venison for bread and potatoes. The Indians spent the three days they stayed, with hunting in the forest and on the prairie, and behaved in fact peacefully.

XXXVI.
An Unpleasant Journey.

Here however is an episode from the second year I lived at the place: One day late in fall, I was to make a trip to Madison, which was sixteen miles away and was a hard day's travel there and back with an ox-team. I had been given many small errands by the neighbors and I stayed longer in town than I had expected. On the homeward journey, which went over a huge prairie without any roads, I was caught unawares by a violent thunderstorm. The night was as black as coal and I had to trust the oxen to find the way home. This however went badly, though I did not realize this until they stopped in the middle of some long grass that was higher than their backs. I now had nothing else to do than to come up on the prairie, and unhitch the oxen and wait for daylight. The rain fell in buckets and I lay myself under the wagon, but here it soon became so cold that I could not sleep. The oxen had lain down beside the wagon with the yoke still on. I then grasped with desperation the expedient solution of laying myself flat between the oxen. This helped as I soon was warm and I slept the sleep of the innocent until daylight. I have mentioned these small traits to show our descendants how it often went during the pioneers' first days.

All the good land had now been occupied, and there were many newcomers with family who preferred to buy claims from those who had already built houses and were willing to sell. I sold my claim, including the oxen and other stock that I had bought, and moved back to Racine County.

During the time here mentioned, Norwegian settlements were established at Pine Lake, Rock River, Wiota, Mineral Point and other places. But as I can only tell of personal experiences here, I cannot tell of anything special about them except that the well-known Norwegian government official Hans

Gasmann, was one of the first who (1843) settled at the Rock River settlement and lived there with his family till his death.

XXXVII.
Immigration to Texas and the Death of Cleng Peerson.

The well-known editor [Johan Reinert] Reiersen from Kristiansand, who was on a journey through the western states during an early period of the Norwegian immigration, also came to Texas, which had just then come into the American Union as a state and offered the immigrants very advantageous terms. His portrayal of the land and conditions in Texas led to some emigration groups that went directly from Norway through New Orleans and then to Texas. The following letter from O. Canuteson in Waco, Texas, provides some detailed information about the first Norwegian settlements, and Cleng Peerson's stay, and demise there:

"Cleng Peerson's journey among us in the thirteen or fourteen years that he lived here, I know as well as anyone, as he spent most of the time with myself and father. He was an old man of eighty-three years when he died, and so could not function with the same force as a younger man, but his countrymen's interests and welfare was his life's work until his dying day. I was there and helped, and I self closed his eyes in death's slumber. He told us about all the settlements, and the happenings that he had experienced, and it all could have been on paper. However, in those days I had no idea that something like this would be asked about at some later time, and besides, the struggle for food was to us and nearly all the newcomers so important that there was no thought of any comprehensive recount about these happenings. Father and I arrived from Norway in 1850 and during our stay with our relatives in Illinois old Cleng arrived there. We knew him from before as he had been at our house in Norway during one of his visits. He had now just arrived back from his first trip to Texas. He advised us to go down there as we could buy beautiful land for 50 cents per acre, and so we went. He came with us, as he believed that the climate would better suit him in his old days. He was born on the farm Hesthammer, in Tysvær Parish, Stavanger County. Reiersen must be seen as the man who founded the first Norwegian settlement in Texas. His younger brother still lives in the Bosque settlement. All his other brothers here in the state are deceased as far as I know, however I do believe he has a brother living in Chicago. I have not been in the two settlements in eastern Texas as old Cleng did not want us to stop till we came west of the Trinity River, for he claimed that both the land and health status in eastern Texas compared to western Texas were poor, and in this he was exceedingly correct, which later experience has completely proved. On his first trip, he had actually been as far west as to Johnsons Station, about thirty to forty miles west of Dallas, on the outskirts of the well-known town of Cross Timber, and just a few miles from the now thriving railway town of Fort Worth. We have therefore Cleng to thank for that we arrived at the best district that the state has. As far as the settlement in Bosque County is concerned, I was the first Norwegian who went there, but by no means with the thought of founding a settlement, just to find vacant land for myself and father and a neighbor. Land at that time could be had from the state for nothing; it was just to have the land surveyed and pay ten to twenty dollars for a half-section of the best un-surveyed land that could be found within the state's borders. Soon more countrymen arrived from east Texas and Norway, and it thus became the most important Norwegian settlement in the state. I lived there for fifteen years and mostly worked with land cultivation and a few cattle. I lived in Dallas County for three years before I went out to Bosque, and have now lived here in Waco County for fifteen years. I must not forget to state that the first Norwegian who established himself in Texas as a real settler is beyond all doubt, Johan Nordbo from Østerdalen or Gudbrandsdalen in Norway. He was at that time a very old man, and had probably arrived early in America as he had been in the settlement at Lake Ontario and knew Cleng Peerson from that time. He had also been in Iowa and Missouri, but then finally went to Texas because of the liberal land grants to settlers. We arrived at his house six miles south of Dallas in December of 1850, and he had then lived there, as far as I remember, between twelve and fifteen years. He arrived so early that he received one section of land from the state, and a half section for each of his children who numbered many, and even for a daughter who then lived in Illinois. She intended to come here, but died. Her children came with us and received the land as an inheritance from their mother."

Towards the 1850s, the Norwegians also began to move into Iowa and Minnesota; but as this, which is mentioned earlier, is outside my personal experience, I will let narratives about the immigration thither be in the hands of others.

XXXVIII.
Ole Rynning's Writings.

The man, who after the first emigrants from Stavanger County has applied the greatest influence on Norwegian emigration, is without any doubt, the student Ole Rynning from Snaasen Parish in Trondhjem Diocese. What he in 1838, wrote home from America, was circulated by the thousands throughout all Norwegian rural communities. The proof of how he took care of this call, are written below in an abridged extract from his writings:

The first two questions Rynning answers are in regards to how the country became known. The third is: "How this country as a whole is constituted and what is the reason that so many people journey thither and expect to find a living there?" To this, he answers that the United States has a vast landscape, the major part is flat and arable, but that its extent is so great that there also is a big difference in regards to the weather's kindness and to the richness of the soil. In the easternmost and northernmost states, the climate and the soil is no better than in southern Norway; in the western states by contrast, the soil is usually so fertile that it bears any kind of grain without fertilizer; and in the southern states, there is even cultivated such as sugar, rice, tobacco and several other things that needs a warm climate. Rynning's fourth question is: "Is it not feared that the country will soon be overrun with too many people? — Is it true that the government there will forbid more people to come?" As an answer, he points out that the United States in extent is twenty times the size of Norway, that the larger part of the land has not even begun to be cultivated, and that it is so fertile that it can accommodate more than one hundred times the amount of people found in the whole of Norway. It is not to be feared, he says, that the country would be filled in the first fifty years. The rumor that the government in the United States will not allow more to immigrate there, he says, is false. The American government wishes only that diligent, industrious and moral people will immigrate to the country, and therefore it has not let any injunction emanate in this respect.

The fifth question is: "In which part of the country have the Norwegians settled in? Which is the most convenient and cheapest way for them?" In his answer to this Rynning says that Norwegians are found spread out in many places in the United States. In New York, Rochester, Detroit, Chicago, Philadelphia and New Orleans one shall meet some Norwegians. "However, I know," he adds, "just four to five places that several Norwegians have settled at the same time. These places are: 1) Morri Town [Morristown], Orleans County, New York State, where the first immigrant group of Norwegians settled in 1825. There are now only two or three families left; the others have gone further inland, where they have settled. 2) La Salle County, Illinois State, at Fox River, about one and a half Norwegian miles [9.32 American miles] northeast from the town of Ottawa, and eleven or twelve miles west of Chicago. Here live sixteen to twenty Norwegian families. This colony was founded in 1834. 3) White County, Indiana State, about ten Norwegian miles south of Lake Michigan at Tippecanoe River. Just two Norwegians from

Drammen still live here, who together possess about 1,100 acres of land. 4) Shelby County, Missouri State, where a number of Norwegians from Stavanger settled during the spring of 1837. I do not know how many families there are. 5) Iroquois County, Illinois State, by the rivers Beaver and Iroquois. Here many settled who came over last summer. There are now eleven or twelve families there." Question No. 6 is: "How is the quality of the land where the Norwegians have settled? What does good farmland cost there? What are the costs of cattle and provisions? How high is the day pay?" Rynning describes in his answer the prairie's splendors and fertility. "The price of government land," says he, "has until now been 1¼ dollars per acre, whether the soil has been of the best sort, or of an inferior excellence. The price will be established and the land divided into three classes depending on the quality, whereafter also the price will adjust itself. Accordingly, I have heard that the land in third class will only demand ½ dollar per acre." Here Rynning gives clear indication on how the land was described and selected. The following excerpt of the answer in regards to the prices on cattle and provisions at that time will be of interest: [It is unclear here if Langeland is using (American) dollars as he did above with the cost of the land, or Norwegian Speciedaler. I have assumed that it is Speciedaler as he also mentions the Norwegian Skilling, but it is not definite — Translator] "Here in Beaver Creek, the cost of a tolerably good horse is between 50 to 100 *Daler*; a pair of good work oxen is between 50 to 80 *Daler*; a four wheeled wagon, 60 to 80 *Daler*; a milking cow with calf, 16 to 20 *Daler*; one sheep 2 to 3 *Daler*; an average pig, 6 to 10 *Daler*; pork 3 to 5 *Skilling* per *Mark* [1 mark is a half pound in weight — 1 Skilling is 1/120 of one Speciedaler]; butter 6 to 12 *Skilling* per *Mark*; one barrel [ca. 139 liters] finest wheat flour 8 to 10 *Daler*; one barrel corn flour (flour of maize) 2½ to 3 *Daler*; one barrel potatoes 1 *Daler*; one pound coffee 20 *Skilling*; one barrel salt 5 *Daler*. In Wisconsin Territory, the prices are two to three times higher. Ten miles south of us in Missouri, the prices on most things are cheaper. Daily wage is also very different in the different places and stands rather close in comparison to other things. Hereabouts a capable worker during the winter can earn from a ½ to 1 *Daler* per day, and in the summer, nearly double. Annual salary is from 150 to 200 *Daler*. A servant girl has 1 to 2 *Daler* per week with no outside work except to milk the cows. In Wisconsin Territory, the daily wage is 3 to 5 *Daler*; in New Orleans and Texas it is also very high, but in Missouri it is once again lower. Here at Beaver Creek we could get people to *break* the prairie for us for 2 *Daler* per acre, when we supplied just food for them."

For the seventh question: "What kind of religion is there in America? Is there any type of order or government in the country, or can everyone do as one pleases?" he answers, that here everyone can have their own belief and worship God in the manner one deems correct; and one dare not persecute anyone because one has a different belief. For solace to the not so brave, he assures them that there are laws, government and authority, just as it is in Norway, but everything here is designed to enforce humanity's natural freedom and equality. About the slave trade he says: "The northern states' work at each Congress to have the slave trade abolished in the southern states. But as they always oppose and give the excuse that it is their right to self-organize their internal affairs, there will in all likelihood soon be either a divorce between the northern and southern states or even bloody internal conflict." As this letter was written twenty-two years before the war began, it must be seen as being noteworthy.

Question No. 8 is: "How is schooling and the poor provided for?" In response to this, he tells of the free school system and the Americans' care for their children's teaching and education. Among the Norwegians at Fox River, he says, there are found free schools where the children learn English; but it seems the Norwegian language will die out with the parents. The poor relief he praises as superb. The ninth question that he answers is: "Which language is spoken in America? Is it difficult to learn?" He says that because of immigration there are found many different languages, but the English language is prevailing everywhere. One can, he adds, by daily association with Americans, soon learn so much that one can help oneself markedly. Question 10 is: "Is it dangerous in regards to disease in America? Has one anything to fear from wild animals or of the Indians?" Rynning does not conceal the truth, but says that the unfamiliar climate normally will bring about one or another infirmity among the settlers during the first year, such as diarrhea and malaria. However, they are not very dangerous. Of dangerous beasts of prey there are found none at the places where the Norwegians have settled. Of snakes, there are many, but only a few that are poisonous. The Indians had already been transported far to the west, and nowhere in Illinois was one exposed to attack from them. The eleventh question is: "For what sort of people is it advisable to travel to America, and for whom is it not advisable? What advice against unreasonable expectations." He gives the advice that the Norwegian farmer, artisan and merchants should come. Blacksmiths, tailors, turners, carpenters, wagon makers and such artisans, could easily obtain remunerative work; but for drunkards and those who cannot work or who do not have money to perform speculations, there is no place. "Those who cannot or will not work," says he, "must never expect that wealth and high living is waiting for them here. No, in America, one will achieve nothing without work; but truth will have it that one through work here, can expect to realize better conditions at some time. Many of the pioneers have relied on the miserable huts, which are the pioneers' first homes; but the good folk should however, bear in mind that by moving onto uncultivated land one will not find houses ready for them. Before one has one's land in such a state that it can support its owner, it is not clever to put one's fortune into costly housing."

"What dangers can one especially meet on the ocean? Is it true that those who are brought to America will be sold as slaves?" These are the last questions he answers. About the dangers on the ocean, he says, they are not as terrible as many imagine. When one has a seaworthy ship, an able captain and competent and watchful sailors, he is of the opinion that even then, one must in any case, put one's trust in the Lord. About the slavery rumor, he says: "A foolish rumor believed by many in Norway, which is, that they who wanted to immigrate to America were taken to Turkey and sold as slaves. This rumor is absolutely without foundation. On the other hand, it is true that many who cannot afford to pay for themselves to cross the sea, that the only way for them to come over is that they sell themselves or their service, for a certain number of years, to a man in this country. Many could thereby have come into wicked hands, and have not had it any better than slaves have. No Norwegian, as far as I know, has come into such circumstances, nor is it to fear, when one travels with Norwegian ships and one's own countrymen."

XXXIX.
Nordlyset, the first Norwegian newspaper in America.

Already in the years of 1844 and 1845, it had come into discussion between the more enlightened farmers, that we here, in the land of newspapers, should also have a Norwegian newspaper. And it was two years later, actually in the year of 1847, that Messrs. Heg and Reymert, began publishing *Nordlyset*, the first Norwegian newspaper in America, in their homes in Norway, Racine County. Even Heg was a prosperous man, having just arrived from Norway, and was probably the one who made the outlay for the press and the print shop. James D. Reymert, who was the editor, was an educated young man with great talents, and he had been brought up partly in Scotland and partly in Norway, as he on his mother's side was descended from Scotland. The memorable Free Soil Movement against slavery's advance was at that time very active in Wisconsin. Reymert had taken up this party's ideology and *Nordlyset* was to be the party's organ. It went well in the beginning with receiving subscriptions to the paper, so that the number during the year grew to 200 or thereabouts, but it was hard times for the immigrants, and when it came time to pay, the matter did not seem so idealistic and many of them forgot to send in their subscription. The Democratic Party also had a strong connection between the Norwegian immigrants, and *Nordlyset's* Free Soil policy was opposed by many. As the paper had been in production for nearly two years at a considerable loss, the print shop was discontinued. *Nordlyset* was a four-page paper with four columns on each page. It was released in a rural district and could not get support through advertising. One of Even Heg's sons took charge mostly of the type setting and printing, and as the little paper was only published once a week, the costs were probably not so significant, but with a steady loss of money it could however, not be kept going. The venture had obviously been too early. *Nordlyset* was however advantageous to Reymert in that it brought him onto the political platform. He was in fact his party's elector at the presidential election of 1848, was a member at the constitution convention in 1847, and as well, was voted as a member of the legislature for several years in a row, and played, everything considered, a not so insignificant political role in Wisconsin.

XL.
Demokraten.

It was at the end of 1849, when I committed the folly of buying the print shop from Heg and Reymert, and with O. J. Hatlestad as co-owner, we moved it to Racine and began in 1850 to re-release *Nordlyset*. The Democratic newspapers in Wisconsin had been merciless in their criticism of *Nordlyset*. They said that down there in Muskego' swamps, was an *ignis fatuus* [Latin - foolish fire – will-o'-the-wisp] who wandered around and mislead the Norwegian voters into impassable Free Soil quagmires. This was a satire over the paper's name and had in fact no meaning, but at that time, we did not know of party politics' accepted practice, and were horrified over the paper's name being made fun of. Had we had any political experience, we would have known that such things belong to the order of the day in political papers. As it was, this led to us changing the name of the paper from *Nordlyset* to *Demokraten*. However, we did not use this last name in its party significance, as it should continue to be a Free Soil Democrat, democracy's organ. In the beginning, everything went well above expectations. The subscription list increased to 300; but we soon had the same experience as our predecessors, that the paper could not be published without money. Kindly disposed and enlightened countrymen wrote and encouraged us and spoke of their satisfaction with the paper's work; but money was not to be come by. With a skilled business manager, it is possible we could have survived;

but as we ourselves took care of the work of editing and printing, and neither of us were financiers, the collections were left to well-disposed agents around the settlements. It soon dawned on me that we had bought an [white] elephant that only consumed and never gave anything in return. In other words: as a political paper, it had come too early.

XLI.
Maanedstidende.

I had at the same time entered into an agreement with pastors Clausen, Preus and Stub about printing their ecclesiastical organ, *Maanedstidende*, and as Hatlestad also wished to publish a church newspaper, we agreed to share the print shop. There was actually a prospect that religious newspapers would find better support as the first immigrants mainly consisted of people from country districts, who, for the most part, were not used to read anything other than their religious books, and many of them considered it even a sin to read political newspapers. It was in the 1850s that the memorable battle was going on in congress concerning the law about runaway slaves and slavery propagation in the territories of Kansas and Nebraska. Our small Norwegian newspaper took a lively interest in these proceedings. A series of speeches by men such as Seward, Giddings, Durkee, Hale, Chase and others, whose names are written with immortal writings in the annals of American history, were translated, and comparable editorials were reported. It was the local autonomy and the people's freedom, in battle against slavery's predominance that this was to defend. It is likely I treated this matter too detailed and perhaps one sided, since this was a matter that was consistent with my own personal inclination. Enough said, *Demokraten* did not receive the necessary support and was therefore, after being kept going for one and a half years, closed down.

XLII.
An Old Subscriber List.

Below we show a list of subscribers to *Nordlyset* and *Demokraten*. This list will be of interest to these men's many descendants around here in the west. It is a list of enlightened and liberal progressive men whose memory deserves to be preserved as long as their descendants live in America's West. Many have now joined their fathers, but there are also many who are still alive, and recall our first attempt to establish a Norwegian newspaper in America, and it will also perhaps delight them that they helped to promote a good cause, that is to say, the Norwegian literature's preservation in this country.

Wisconsin.

Norway and Muskego, Racine County.

Anders Kløve.
G. Larsen.
Johannes E. Skoftestad.
Mathias Heimo.
Helge Torsen.
Ole Haagensen.
Niels Nærum.
Jens O. Hatlestad.
Peder Jacobsen.
Bjørn Hatlestad.
Ole Tollefsjorden.
Halvor Lonar.
Niels Brownson.
Ole Mikkelsen.
Thron Thordsen.
Thorkild Hansen.
Thorsten Sjøgaarden.
Knud B. Pedersen.
Syvert Ingebretsen.
Thorsten Hougaasen.
Gunder Goutesen.
Gitle Danielson.
Svennung Johannesen.
Christian Hallofsen.
Christian Christiansen.
Thormod Thorstensen.
Rev. H. A. Stub.
Niels Hansen.
Tyke Hendriksen.
Gudmund Samuelsen.
Halvor Guttormsen.

Rochester, Racine County.

Dr. Blood.
Herbrand Anstensen.
R. E. Ela.
Syvert Johnson.

Beloit, Rock County.

Rev. C. L. Clausen.
T. Tollefsen.
Tollef Numland.
Paul H. Gallager.
H. Ommested.
Hans Christophersen.
Hans Smedrud.
Knud Skjerve.
Hans H. Hansemoen.
Svend Larsen.
Peter Halvorsen.
Peder H. Gaarden.
Gisle Halland.
Gullik O. Gravdal.
C. Halvorsen.
David Anderson.
T. G. Fladeland.
Halvor H. Folkestad.

Cambridge, Dane County.

Windberg & Jørgensen.
Ole Lawrence.

Knud Eriksen.
Ingebret Homstad.

Christiana, Dane County.

Lars Johannesen.
Niri Herbjørnsen.
Iver H. Leimle.
J. Hoff.
Brynhild H. Lønne.
Johannes L. Hole.
John Olson.
Ole Christiansen.
Peder L. Svartskul.
C. Corneliusen.
Niels A. Berg.
Stad Sivertsen.
Anfind Storksen.
Andrew Ellingsen.
O. T. Torgesen.
Lars P. Haugelia.
Ole K. Frovattn [Trovatten].
Dr. Madsen.
Rev. Dietrichson.

Clinton, Rock County.

Ole Knudsen.
Elling Eielsen.
Ansten Knudsen.
Knud Nielsen.
Gullik Knudsen.
H. Poulsen.
Christ Newhouse.
Jens Gulbrandsen.
Peder Thomsen.
Thorsten Nielsen.
O. A. Haadtvet.
Erik Gulbrandsen.

Columbus, Columbia County.

Lars Johansen.
Anders Dælan.
Mons Johnsen.
Peder Langeland.

Deerfield, Dane County.

Ole K. Bakketun.
Ole Olsen Tveten.
Ole Syvertsen.
Aslak Olsen Lie.

Delafield, Waukesha County.

Hans Gasmann.
Hans Rasmusen.
Ellef Bjørnsen.
Chr. Olsen.

Dodgeville, La Fayette County.

John Lie.
Niels Arneson.
Syvert Tallerssen.

Door Creek, Dane County.

Niels Saem.
Christian O. Holo.

Osmund Lunde.

Fulton, Rock County.

Johan Niels Luuraas.

Cedar Grove, Sheboygan County.

Endre Michelsen.
Ole Michelsen.
Knud Aaberg.

Madison, Dane County.

Erik Andersen.
Lars Johnson.
William Andersen.

Manitowoc, Manitowoc County.

C. Andersen.
Ole Andreasen.
Jacob Madsen.
L. Nordboe.
Hans M. Hansen.

Milwaukee, Milwaukee County.

C. E. Jenkins.
Lars Bæver.
P. L. Morin.
Jens Lund.
Abraham Sørensen.
Tønnes Sæveland.
S. Gabrielsen.
C. Sørensen.
M. N. Olsen.
R. Reinertsen.

Mineral Point, Iowa County.

Peder Stenerson.
Ole Thorsen.

Neenah, Winnebago County.

John Nielsen.
Anders J. Dalen.
Aslak Brynildsen.
Søren Wilson.
Ole P. Klokkerengen.
Svend T. Husetoft.

Oconomowoe, Waukesha County.

H. B. Paus.
David Førre.
Thron Thronsen.
Amund Aamodt.
Ole Iverson.
Johs. Lie.
Gunder Naas.
Ole Olsen.
Jørgen Olsen.

Palmyra, Jefferson County.

Sjur Flettre.
S. S. Berkorg.
Rasmus Jacobsen.
Tollef Brynildsen.
Lars Johnsen.
Iver W. Grintland.

Pine Bluff, Dane County.

Thor J. Spaanem.
Halvor Halvorsen.

Sun Prairie, Dane County.

Sjur Johnson.

Spring Valley, Rock County.

Halvor Monson.
G. Guttormsen.
John E. Solem.

Tolands Prairie, Washington County.

Niels Lønningen.
Jørgen Lüberg.
Hans Christophersen.
Halvor Halvorsen.
Christian Moen.
Martin F. Sørensen.

Utica, Dane County.

Bottel Lunde.
K. S. Okere.
Niels Drougsvold.
John O. Herredal.

Port Washington, Washington County.

Amund Olsen.
Salve Tallaksen.

Racine, Racine County.

Andrew Johannesen.
H. Rasmussen.
O. Hedejord.
Knud Lunden.
H. Hansen.
John Larsen.

Yorkville, Racine County.

Mons K. Aadland.
Aslak S. Aa.
Elias Stangeland.
Arentz Wigeland.
Johannes Bjøs [? Njøs].
Ole J. Landsværk.
Peter M. Andsjøn.
Knud A. Aarethun.
John C. Spellum.
Gunder Lunden.
Hans Landsværk.
Steen Sanderson.

Wiota, La Fayette County.

Knud Knudsen.
Niels Nielsen.
Arne Anderson.
Ole Andersen.
Niels L. Finne.
Erik Ingebretsen.
Peter Davidsen.
Helge Olsen.

Illinois.

Amazon, Boone County.

Thor Trahjem.
Kittil K. Moland.
Knud Tveten.
Niels Johannesen.
Kittil O. Blomhaugen.

Belvedere, Boone County.

Hans Anderson.

St. Charles, Kane County.

John Anderson.

Chicago.

Knud Larsen.
Niels Sjursen.
Regina Wigeland.
Lars Dygestien.
Torger Olsen.
Iver Lawson.
Rev. Paul Anderson.
Anders Pederson.
Magnus Nordboe.
Ole Nordhuus.
Jens Gulbrandsen.
Haagen Paulson.
N. P. Løberg.
Lars A. Bryn.
S. G. Bøe.
John Ammundsen.
S. Arentz.
Jacob Hodnefjeld.
Bernt Abrahamson.
E. Stephenson.
Bjørn Nielsen.
Endre Nielsen.
Anders N. Brække.
Niels Johnson.
John Johnson.

Dorr, McHenry County.

Andreas A. Schjeie.
Erik Knudsen.
Mikkel J. Bryn.

Lisbon, Kendall County.

Erik Skjeldal.
Thorkild Henrysen.
Lars Skjeldal.
John Hill.

K. A. Bouge.

Freedom, La Salle County.

Hellik C. Furlie.
Tjerran Osmundsen.
Kittil Kittilson.
Ole Andersen.
Geo. Pedersen.
Helge Olsen.
Made Madesen.
Knud Thomson.

Mission Grove, La Salle County.

Ole Olsen.
Ole Pearson.
Osmund Tuttlie.
Hermand Osmunsen.
Halvor Pedersen.
Christian Olsen.
Ole Knudsen.
Knud Williamson.
Gunlik Johnson.
Peder Ormsen.
Niels N. Nielsen.
Ole Anderson, Jr.
Anders Knudsen.

Norway, La Salle County.

Gudmund Hougaas.
Niels Nielsen.
Halvor Nielsen.
Nels Andersen.
Niels Thomsen.
Rev. Ole Andrewson.

Ottawa, La Salle County.

Henry L. Hellmann.
Mr. Thomson.

Rock Run, Stephenson County.

Ole Olsen Sunne.
Lars O. Andersen.
Ole Andersen.

Wilmoth, Boone County.

Ole Pehrsen.
Peder Torkelsen.
Ole Torkelsen.

Iowa.

Keokuk, Lee County. Jacob Olsen.

Indiana.

Monticello, White County. Peter B. Smith.

Missouri.

St. Louis. Hans Sandberg.
New Washington, Franklin County. L. A. Hansen.

New York.
Kendall's Corner, Orleans County. Ole Osland.
New York City.
F. Knauft. A. Løvenskjold.
John Holfeldt. Chr. Hansen.

Rhode Island.
Providence. N. B. Schubarth.

The following is a list of American and German newspapers that took over from *Nordlyset* and *Demokraten*: New York Weekly Sun, New York; Christian Advocate and Journal, New York; Western Citizen, Chicago, Ill.; Daily Wisconsin, Milwaukee, Wis.; The National Era, Washington, D. C.; The New York Weekly Tribune, New York; Ohio State Tribune, Columbus, O.; Racine Advocate, Racine, Wis.; Wisconsin Argus, Madison, Wis., Wisconsin Free Democrat, Milwaukee, Wis.; Wisconsin Express, Madison, Wis.; Southport Telegraph, Southport, Wis.; Buffalo Telegraph, Buffalo, N. Y.; *Volksfreund*, Milwaukee, Wis.; Wisconsin Banner, Milwaukee, Wis.; Western Star, Elkhorn, Wisconsin.

XLIII.
Other Norwegian-American Newspapers.

After we had shared the print shop, Hatlestad began publishing his *Kirketidende* and struggled for a time in Racine and moved thereafter to Leland in Illinois, where the publication continued until the paper went into the hands of Ole Andrewsen. He moved it to Norway, La Salle County, where it was finally closed down after many years of laborious battle for its preservation.

On Pastor Clausen's suggestion, I decided to move my print shop to Janesville to continue the printing of *Maanedstidende* there. Our agreement was that the pastors themselves would proofread, and Clausen thought that this could be easier done in Janesville than in Racine. Proofreading had in fact caused us much annoyance whilst we were in Racine. As far as I now remember, it was in the summer of 1852 that I moved to Janesville. This move turned out to be a mistake; so instead of receiving more support, the print shop's costs doubled. To be able to typeset *Maanedstidende* I needed several different types. A countryman in Madison, Ole Torgerson, had for some months published a Norwegian newspaper in the interest of Whig's Party, but had been so wise as to close it before it ruined him. I therefore went down there and bought his types and brought them to Janesville. Besides a young boy who wanted to learn the art of printing, and who later became an excellent pastor among his countrymen, I had a Norwegian printer by the name of Conradi, a brother to the well-known professor of the same name. This Conradi was a kind and good-natured man, but sacrificed much of his time to the service of Bacchus. At that time, there was a great shortage of Norwegian printers, and this shortage often gave us many problems.

XLIV.
Emigranten.

Through the course of the first year that [the] *Maanedstidende* was published I wished to sell the print shop, and as the pastors needed to have their organ printed they joined together to create a corporation. This soon came into effect and I sold the print shop to them. It was then moved to Inmansville in Rock County, where Pastor Clausen lived at that time. The pastors had the best opportunity to collect support for printing as they constantly associated with the people in the settlements. The new corporation decided therefore also that in addition to their ecclesiastical organ to publish a political paper, *Emigranten*. Pastor Clausen was to be the editor for *Emigranten*, and the print shop was to be under the management of the well-known emigrant agent John Holfeldt. I stayed with them in Inmansville a couple of months to get the print shop going, and moved thereafter back to my farm in Racine County. The beginning in Inmansville started in the month of January 1853, and the print shop was run for a short time under Holfeldt's management. Pastor Clausen soon became tired of the work, and Holfeldt was very unpopular among the Norwegian emigrants because of his work as an emigrant agent. Later the print shop came into the hands of Consul K. Fleischer, and it seemed to survive reasonably, until after a few years it was moved to, where it later went into the hands of C. F. Solberg as a sole trader. *Emigranten*'s later history is so near to us that it needs no mentioning here. It was eventually merged with *Fædrelandet* in La Crosse and exists now under the name *Fædrelandet og Emigranten* and is published in La Crosse and Minneapolis.

If I do not remember incorrectly, it was in 1850 that a Norwegian newspaper called *Frihedsbanneret* began publication in Chicago. It was published for a few months, but had to cease operation as the finances had come into disorder. Friends of the newspaper sent a man to Racine to have me go down there and take care of the matter; but as I had just gone out to my farm, I luckily escaped falling into a new temptation.

XLV.
Den Norske Amerikaner.

In 1856, the well-known Elias Stangeland began publishing *Den Norske Amerikaner* in Madison, Wisconsin. He had as a man of business acquired some money, but had come into difficulty in obtaining an editor for his paper. As I was personally acquainted with him, he persuaded me to come out there and help him with the editing. Stangeland was present at the convention at the time when James Buchanan from the Democratic Party in Baltimore was nominated as president. The politicians had promised him gold and green pastures if his *Norske Amerikaner* would support their candidate. John C. Fremont was the Republican's candidate and all my sympathies belonged home in this party. I could therefore not edit Stangeland's newspaper as he decided to support the democratic candidate. I left him therefore in all friendliness, and when the politicians kept their promises in their usual manner, Stangeland's *Norske Amerikaner* soon *went the way of all flesh, and joined their fathers*.

It is the advertising business to a great degree, which supports our present gigantic Norwegian newspapers here in this land. This is why we see them mainly in the big cities of Chicago and Minneapolis. Major cities depend on business, business again, on a large population throughout the rural districts. These conditions were missing during our first attempt with Norwegian newspapers. Also fully qualified printers and experienced business managers were missing. The picture I have painted about the birth of Norwegian newspapers in America is therefore not rosy, nevertheless true. The newspaper business has now grown big and powerful and there is now no danger of a timely conflict against our mighty Norwegian newspapers.

It was the above-mentioned conditions in Chicago, which in the beginning gave *Skandinaven* the best foothold and made it so that the funeral orations that had been earlier promised it, never came to be held. With the publication of the *Skandinaven* a new era in our newspaper literature began, and it has steadily gone forward to what it is now.

XLVI.
The Norwegian's Future in America.

That the Norwegian immigration population has been unusually lucky in regards to the districts it has settled, shall be seen more clearly by the subsequent account: An American wrote a few years ago an article where he mentioned some interesting estimates regarding the Mississippi valley and the number of residence who might find home there in the future. That this part of America will become densely populated no-one can doubt, as the land nearly everywhere [here] is very fertile, and of coal there in Illinois, there is just by itself, three to four times the amount as there is in the whole of Great Britain. England has today 500 persons per square mile; Belgium has about the same amount and some of the Chinese provinces have 700. The great wheat-belt on this continent can be considered to stretch from Ohio in the east to Nebraska in the west and from Kentucky in the south to Peace River in British America [Canada]. Calculating this district as 1,500 miles from east to west and 2,000 miles from south to north, we have an area of 3,500 square miles of good fertile land. Something similar is not found anywhere else on this earth. If we now assume that 1,000,000 of these 3,000,000 square miles, are only one third as densely populated as the above examples, or there are about 200 persons per square mile, then we have a population of two hundred million. When one thinks about the United States' present population being merely sixty million, one can get a somewhat clear idea of the Mississippi valley's great future. That this part of America will in the course of time, surpass the east and the Pacific Ocean coast, not only in population but also in wealth and influence, cannot be in doubt. Should now this picture of the future be realized, it is a great possibility that Chicago will be for North America, that which London is now for Europe, the center for trade and business investments, a world-class city, teeming with many millions of inhabitants, a pulsating business center. Let that be as it may. Time often brings unexpected changes with it, which overturns the best of calculations. Nevertheless, it is certain that the first pioneers were notably fortunate in regards to their choice of time and place for colonization. They and their nearest descendants have shown this noteworthy by the progressive and enterprising spirit with which they have already laid for the day in both economy, industry and business, as well as in the scientific and religious areas, so that thousands of those in prosperity, enlightenment and culture can now be stood in rank and file with the earth's best men and women.

The average from the different reports about our population in America is 500,000 (a half million). That is assuming that every ten immigrants have increased by seven since they arrived here. There is no reliable data to go by, but this number is hardly too high. Many of these have arrived in recent years and cannot be included as contributing to the growth we here mention. As far as their wealth is concerned, the farmers and artisan class can be assumed to own from $5,000 to $30,000 per family, whilst merchants and manufacturers each own more than double as much. In regards to education and intelligence, we find their young progeny well represented as pastors, doctors, lawyers, editors, engineers, telegraphists and other important positions, which require careful preparation and a long vocational study. Equally are the many representatives of schoolteachers and professors in higher education. Whilst in the American congress, we have two representatives and another in the country's diplomatic corps, who all do their key positions honor. When one considers the importance of the terrain in the Mississippi valley, which has given our people's descendants a playground through many impending times, then it will surely be admitted that it has gone well with our first immigrants, and those who are still alive can with satisfaction reflect back on the results of the daring steps they made when they cut the apron strings from old Norway and traveled to America.

In ecclesiastical matters, it is nevertheless above all, that progress has been astonishing. In round numbers, the Lutheran pastors among the Norwegians are estimated at something over 400 with a congregation of 125,000. The whole of Norway does not have more than 600 pastors with a population of nearly 2,000,000. From these statements, we should therefore, here in America, be much better endowed with pastors in comparison to the congregation size, than in Norway, and yet there are still complaints over a shortage of pastors, though there are more and more seminaries being built. This must be sufficient proof of our people's great interest and willingness for ecclesiastical affairs. The numbers that we here have indicated, are not given to be accurate, but they come close enough to the truth as evidence of the considerable progress our people have in ecclesiastical development.

Part Two.

I.
An Emigrant's Memoirs about Life in Norway and America.

When I at an invitation from a few faithful friends began the following depiction, I languished by chance without work in Chicago. Before I was actually finished the part that is concerning life in Norway, I was once more back in work, and this journal was laid aside. Since then, I have not had the time or the inclination to pursue them. It is therefore only on the publisher's earnest invitation, that I now in brief, have continued to bring continuity in the rendering. This then also explains the reason that much of the memoirs about life in America appear scattered in several places earlier in this book.

The part that concerns America has become very short and incomplete because of my health of late. I have actually not been able to put pen to paper myself but have had to use a research assistant.

It is an undistorted and trustworthy portrayal of everyday life in Norway and America, partly as I have myself experienced it and partly as how I have perceived the past sixty years, which I intend here to describe. I have received many invitations from my friends to do this, as one thought that such reminiscences from life would not just be read with interest, but that also through long and agile life's experiences, there could be several useful teachings to be had. While at the same time, there could be a small advantage to the history of the Norwegian emigrant. When I now comply with these requests, it does not happen because there in my experiences lie something more distinctive or unusual than in so many of my other emigrating countrymen, but partly to fill some vacant hours, of which I until now have had very few, and partly to make a little contribution to the Norwegian emigration history.

The life of a youth in the fjords of western Norway may appear for many to be pleasant and romantic enough. In a lovely green cove, in the fertile little valley, by the friendly fjord, by the even friendlier tranquil lake, by the foaming waterfall, on the precipitous birch mountainsides, on the rock-strewn slope by the sheer cliff and on the sky high mountain peaks — everywhere in this rocky land's glorious nature, where the plant life fragrance is so sweet, and where the bird song is so enchanting, the awakened spirit could not be other than delighted and happy, and the gay youth could not do anything other than be seized by admiration for the beauty and poetry in this environment, and have adulation for nature's Lord. Nevertheless, it was here as it was everywhere in the world. Only the enlightened can open the book of nature and understand its language; for many of the country's children it was a closed book. At the side of his mother's spinning wheel, the valley's son learned to recite his Lord's Prayer. In the squalid ambulatory school, he probably learned the five parts [The Ten Commandments – The Apostles' Creed – The Lord's Prayer – Holy Baptism - and The Sacrament of the Eucharist] of his small catechism by heart so that a few years later he could come before the pastor and be accepted into the bosom of the church — and with only this, he had also to remain content. He was barely ten years old before all his time and all his energy had to be put to physical toil and drudgery — into toil for his daily bread, where every day returned the same uncompromising and inescapable demands. The arable patches of earth in the narrow valleys were small, the population relatively large, and this poor land could produce no more. During the course of the last 400 years, the country had augmented itself a prolific Danish-German government and a business class that held the power in their hands. The laws had given this imported class a monopoly on everything except on freehold land, and this later became so subdivided because of over-population and so burdened by taxes from a wasteful government, and to keep the ruling class in commanding and in enlightened heights, destitution and ignorance became the Norwegian common man's normal lot. The old Norwegian heroic spirit that throughout centuries was squeezed and subdued under these circumstances, have with unbelievable perseverance still preserved some faint remnants of its days of yore greatness. In the beginning of our century, it endured especially in an unparalleled battle for the daily bread and with an innate loathing to go on poor relief, or go begging.

This is a hard portrayal, and only those who as I, had to go through the struggle from the age of ten, and seen thousands of others do the same, will concede that I am speaking the truth without exaggeration. How incomprehensible is it then, if the eyes of a poor farmer's half-grown boy were closed for beautiful Hardanger's remarkable scenery, which a Wergeland's gusto has harmonized, and a Tidemand's brush has painted? How incomprehensible is it, if his young mind was dulled and dispirited during his adolescence, whilst he every day in his pauper's tattered clothing, trudged barefoot to attain something for his subsistence? Aye, how incomprehensible is it if he came to live and die without knowing his fate's austerity, without other longings and aspirations than to satisfy one's belly's acute demands as do any other beast on the earth? I grew up in a place where I had occasion to see the young sons of the pastor, the chief magistrate, the company chief and the storekeeper being taught by a tutor (the graduate, as we called him). And it was without doubt, the sight of these well-dressed, carefree and cheerful youths, who had nothing else to do than play and gather knowledge, which first made it so, that the painful question, like sharp steel, forged its way into my young heart. "What have I done? And what have they done, so that there should be such a great difference between us?" And when they then ridiculed me because of my ragged clothing and laughed and pointed their fingers at me and called: "look at him!" as I, being bent and crooked under a heavy burden, walked with my nose pointing to the ground, — I then wept and swore and was angry.

Later, I have often looked back on this period as reflection's actual first gleam of light into the dark repressed soul, and even in this moment, I truly believe that providence in its wisdom turned towards the good, the evil thoughts of these sons of gentlemen. Therefore, even though I with indignation in my heart blamed God for this injustice, he saved me from despair and gave me courage and strength to a certain extent to overcome, and patience to carry a difficult and merciless fate. When I was twelve years old, I could only barely read the Catechism and the gospel of Christianity which were the only books (except for the ABC) I had access to. Apart from this, I also could recite the Lord's Prayer and some table prayers [grace], the Ten Commandments and the three articles of faith. And when I read the fourth commandment, I often bowed my head because the storekeeper's son who certainly was not a kind or obedient boy to his parents, should have it so good, whilst I, who so far had never thought of saying no to what my father or mother bade me, should have it so thoroughly hard. My father had in the fatherland's service, been hit by a ball [probably musket ball] in the one knee, and this had become completely stiff. This disability, I can well remember was of great inconvenience to him; he could not arise with a burden on his back and I was then needed to be close at hand to help him up. I was the youngest of ten siblings, and it was cramped for us. Father had a small parcel of cultivated land to use for life, but did not own it. As time went by and my siblings grew up, they had to undertake something on their own, and already by the time I was thirteen years old my father died at an age of fifty-three [62]. Despite his thrift and hard work, my mother was once again left in very restricted living conditions, which through reluctance and affliction she was *granted* by the farm-parcel's owner. In his last year of life, when father noticed my great interest in reading and writing, he used a large part of Sundays to give me lessons. Thus, he often wrote numbers and easy arithmetic with chalk on the bottom of a wooden milk container, and I had now come so far with my reading that I was able to read many interesting stories from the Old Testament, which for me at that time were so extraordinary interesting.

I cannot say with certainty how far my memory goes back. The first event that has imprinted itself into my memory with an indelible mark is when I was weaned off breast milk, and at that time, I was about three years old. The next episode that I clearly remember from that time is when my sister one Sunday had dared to cut my long hair, which mother adored so much. It had just now come into fashion to let one's hair be cut, and sister did not like me to be different from other young boys; but mother would not give her consent. When I that Sunday evening came home minus my long hair my mother wept. This was the first time I had seen her tears, and the impression of this moment I have not been able to wipe from my memory. At the age of four or five, I now and then transgressed mother's strict rules (at least I thought they were unnecessarily strict), but as long as I knew myself guilty, I accepted the punishment with lack of complaint. At this time, I had a strong inclination to try all sorts of small handiworks and was perhaps not without certain mechanical aptitude. One day, mother had lost one of her knitting needles, and as she knew I always was on the lookout for such handy things, I was thereby accused of having taken it, and when I definitely denied having done the crime, I received a right severe punishment. I would probably have forgotten this along with much more from that period of time, if I had been guilty. However, to have been this severely punished when innocent, made a deep impression on me. This impression increased, as my mother soon afterwards found her knitting needle in the ashes by the fireplace, where she probably had lost it, and thereby was so gripped by remorse over the wrong she had inflicted on me, that huge tears rolled down her cheeks. But enough on this.

II.
Preparing for Confirmation.

After my father's death, I was still to stay with mother in father's old house for one year to go before the pastor and made ready by him for confirmation, and then go out into the world to take care of myself as so many others of my defenseless social class. My academic knowledge was still rather second-rate; the only thing I can say about this is that I could read more or less proper from a book and had begun arithmetic in whole numbers. I would now also like to learn to write, but it was difficult getting tuition. An uncle of mine had in his youth come to Bergen, where his rare talents had attracted the attention of a couple of schoolmasters, and they had the fulfillment of giving him a good deal of private lessons. He had thus grasped the bold decision to go the way of the student, which he later had to abandon when the promised support did not happen and he had nothing to contribute. Some influential patrons of the ruling class used their influence to secure employment for him in a vacant teacher and vaccinator position in our parish. He was a keen tutor, and worked with great skill in his vocation. However, his district was not in the parish where I lived and therefore I did not have the benefit of his teaching. Whereas our ambulatory-school was a cripple in both body and soul, full of wailing religious fanaticism, which reinforced the populace in its general prejudices. For instance, it was a sin for people of the working class to want to learn to read and do arithmetic, or to read other books than the Bible and the Gospel of Christianity, and that such was only allowed to people who belonged to the ruling class — the important people as he called them — etc. With these perceptions prevalent among the people, the schoolwork was naturally so much more enjoyable for this lazy person, who fell asleep every second hour of the day. He also thereby won infinitely much in the pastor's esteem, who was one of the loyal men in the social status that did not tolerate new ideas in the heads of sheep, which, — as the ruling social status at that time expressed itself — would just make them *nosewise* (plant wisdom in their noses?). Our ambulatory school was therefore not the place where I could learn to write and learn arithmetic. I found a mass of old papers and letters that had belonged to my father, who in regards to intelligence and skills had been an exception in his class — something that seemed to have gone back through many generations. If there in the family was found anyone knowledgeable in the art of writing at that time when our forefathers, some twenty-four to twenty-five centuries ago, came to the west from the northern Russian forests, traveled down the Norwegian coast and settled along the fjords, I cannot say; if so, it must have been Runic characters that they had used.

The old Gothic writing my father had used was the only model I had for my guidance; there was also not an alphabet to be found nor had I learned to write the individual letters. I naturally could not read his hand, and had for the time being to be content with copying it as best I could. This is how I used much of my Sundays, so that my mother began to rebuke me: "You know that in the spring you shall go before the pastor, and that he probably won't ask if you can write. As far as that is concerned, it may be difficult for you to pass should he hear that you squander your time with writing. You must now stick to the book of questions and learn it well by heart, or otherwise you will not even be enrolled." She was however mistaken in regards to the writing, as it was the young curate, who was to supervise the confirmand, and he was a much more liberal and popular minded man than the old intoxicated parish pastor. Now then, with the book of questions, it was extremely difficult; the content was too difficult for my limited intellectual development, and it was so difficult to learn by parroting and to memorize what I did not understand, that I fell into despair over the task before me. Therefore, I believed that I would certainly be before the pastor for at least three years before I could be confirmed. It was at this time that my abovementioned uncle came from the neighboring parish to visit us; my mother told him about my peculiarities and expressed much anxiety for me; I just wanted to read stories from the Old Testament and sit the whole of Sunday and copy my father's old letters. The roar of laughter from my uncle when he heard this I shall never forget, so ashamed and anxious was I. However, he came up to me, laid his hand on my head and said, "Don't be anxious, my boy; you are a shoot from the old tree. Do not read too much from the Old Testament, the language is after all so tiresome that it will absolutely spoil your want to read. I will loan you some books, and also you will receive examples from me and learn the new system of writing." Had I possessed a kingdom, I would have given it to him in gratitude. He now had holidays from his school, and in his devotion to further public education, he had decided that for a couple of weeks he would experiment with a writing school in our neighborhood. Moreover, despite the common people's prejudices, he succeeded through careful arguments and persuasions, to get seven or eight young boys to take part in the writing school, which he without payment would hold for them. He was a naturally highly gifted, though somewhat eccentric man. He had a lively interest or rather a remarkable enthusiasm for the common youth's education. Although he had a numerous flock of children to support and lived in absolute poverty, he was so thoroughly pleased and happy, and without payment, to be able to spread information and awaken the people to reflection, and awaken them from the fatal sweet sleep of ignorance, from which centuries of a foreign and unregimented yoke had suppressed it. It went well with the writing school. Aye, they were happy, although unfortunately far too short a day. He had peculiar rare qualities to make his teachings enjoyable and instructive. I can especially remember one afternoon when he had received a letter from a young man in the neighboring parish who had benefited from his teaching and had now become an ambulatory-school teacher. He was not good in diction and therefore excused himself in the letter, but added finally, that "*jeg haaber at drage mig* [I hope to leave]." This was too much for our good old teacher; he broke out in his characteristic roar of laughter, lay down on his stomach on a long bench and began to drag himself forward, saying: "*Jeg haaber at drage mig* [I hope to drag myself]! *Jeg haaber at drage mig* [I hope to drag myself]!" and then he laughed again. Such was how he wanted to impress upon us the correct notions about the meaning of words and its correct use.

When his holidays had expired, he went back to his district. Before he left us, he suggested that those of the young boys who wanted to continue with writing exercises, to send him compositions by mail, and then he would correct them and send them back when he had the opportunity. He said, to learn to write letters and words is only the means, but the real purpose of writing is to communicate one's thoughts, and to do this in a clear and straightforward manner, which is much more difficult, and demands much more practice and intellectual development than the mere mechanical skill of writing letters and words. As far as I know, only a few of the young boys took advantage of this friendly offer, perhaps because of mistaken angst that he should laugh at their mistakes. I, for my part, did not let myself be restrained by any such scruples, and therefore wrote many exercises of the simpler everyday topics, which I also received back promptly with the teacher's corrections. To see these corrections become less and more trivial as time progressed and exercises being continued, was not just a little flattering for my vanity. From this, I no doubt could thereof, correctly draw a rational encouragement, to continue with the work.

When spring arrived, I would as was earlier mentioned, go before the pastor to be enrolled with the confirmands. I surely believe that many a criminal in his cell anticipates the day when he will be hanged, with far less fear and angst than I anticipated the day that I for the first time was to be heard by the pastor. I also wondered whether he would be very hard and merciless. Aye, maybe even make himself mirthful on my behalf, and point his finger at me like the young sons of gentlemen had so often done because I was so poorly clothed and was so dumb and clumsy and timid when I came near those who belonged to a higher class. Finally the dreaded day came. Most of the confirmands were accompanied by their fathers and brought presents along for the pastor's kitchen. I who had a father no more, came alone and unfortunately, nor did I have a gift — a very embarrassing situation that almost deprived me of the little rationale I still had left. I became aware of a curious maneuver among several of the accompanying fathers during the waiting time before the enrollment began; I noticed that it depended on getting in first, but I did not know why. One of our neighbors whose daughter was also to be enrolled, and who had promised my mother to bring me along to the pastor, whispered to me that these men wanted to come in first so that their sons would be first on the list and thereby stand first in the row for the catechization. This I had not thought of. Being by nature a little timid creature, I wished mainly to be among the last, and thereby be as inconspicuous as possible. As the neighbor's daughter was not very competent with reading, she did not bother about being among the first either, and she felt that also for my part, it was much better to be moved up than down on the confirmation day. Besides, there were several candidates, who obviously were to be first; among these were the merchant's son, the son of the pastor's assistant along with a son of the parsonage's manager etc. When most of the glory seekers had been in, it became our turn along with some others. Fortunately, it probably so happened, that several of those who just before us had been to the catechization, had only passed this test with mediocre results. When our neighbor's daughter, who was heard before me, also read with a great deal of uncertainty and distress, and because of my rote reading practice, the contrast was rather splendid. The praise I thus gained, gave me back much of my composure and sustained my nerves to such a degree that I almost entirely ceased to tremble, and so could now give a sensible answer as to what I had memorized, as if it was my own mother who asked the questions. When I said that I only had learned by heart as far as the first list of *Pontoppidans*

Forklaring [Pontoppidan's Explanation], the pastor seemed to think that this was very little, compared to my fast rote reading. I had to make a sincere confession to him that the parts I understood I could remember after I had read them a couple of times; but those I did not understand I forgot again even if I read them many times. "We shall get through that," said the pastor kindly, and added that I needed to take this in hand earnestly, and when I again came for appraisal, he would explain. During the enrollment, he mentioned the gifts each confirmand had brought, and here my situation became embarrassing, as I had not brought him anything. Why had I not? — I admitted that I did not know; perhaps my mother had forgotten. She had only mentioned to me that during summer I had to go away to work, at a time I was not needed at home, to earn one *speciedaler*, which was to be given to the pastor when I was confirmed. I promised sincerely to ask mother for a gift, and I hoped she would procure something. Thereby I was excused from this on this occasion. However, it was not that she had forgotten the gift; she knew all about the custom as she had already sent nine of her children to confirmation. The fact was this, that in the time before the pastors were paid a regular wage to read with the confirmands, it would have been rather respectful and seen as a loving appreciation of the diligence he used during the youths' Christian teachings. While now it had turned into a bad custom. Being used by the wealthy to get their neglected children confirmed, without the necessary preparation. Whereas the children of the poor, even if they read better, were given the burden and the time wasting of going two or three years before the pastor, because they had not been able to bring him the necessary gifts. — In short, this scandalous behavior was now nothing more than a present to the pastor to set their children free from needing to learn anything. My mother and an elder brother, who was at home and ran the farm with her, meant therefore that I would learn the book well and when the pastor received his *daler* that would be enough. At the next oral examination, I had the bliss to give the correct answer on a couple of answers that the others had come to grief on; but unfortunately, this good man had the sudden impulse to ask me in the hearing of the whole assembly, if I had on this day brought the gift I had promised him. This humiliation was so upsetting that I wished I could sink through the earth where I was at that time standing. On the brink of tears, I admitted that I had not received anything this time; but I had done what I promised, I had asked mother for something for the pastor. He now held a short sermon as punishment for me, saying that we should not use our poverty to excuse ourselves, several of my siblings were among the wealthiest in the parish, and therefore he could not tolerate any exception just for my sake; it was to set a bad example and encourage others to follow.

I had at first felt humiliated and put to shame; now the hot blood ran to my head and I became angry, but I kept quiet. Nevertheless, in my thoughts I aired my vexation to him. That they can find accord with their dignity to beg can perhaps be correct. However, I cannot beg, be it from my siblings or others. Can I through honest work, earn so much more than I need for food and clothes, I would with the greatest of pleasure give a gift, if not through love, then at least to avoid shame and vexation.

The confirmands' first joint meeting had therefore been disastrous for me; I was ashamed and depressed, whilst the others were excited and happy, and yet in my catechization I had been as good as any of the others. However, my catechization had mainly been about gifts, and there I had sadly come up short. Yet the first joint oral examination had a lucky effect on me, my disinclination to rote reading had disappeared. I had seen how it stood with the others and we now all had the same set homework that had to be learned for the next meeting; this was enough encouragement. Two days had not elapsed before I had every word of my homework at my fingertips, and I could not understand how this had happened; it had come as if by itself.

III.
Work and Reading.

The land area of our farm at home was very limited. On the other hand, we had an extensive but distant outlying field, to where (about ¾ of a Norwegian mile) we often had to walk as soon as the snow was gone in the spring. This was partly to repair fences, hay drying racks, hay barns and so forth, and partly to go farther up to the summer dairy, to prepare firewood and other things for the time when the dairymaids were to move up there with the cattle. On the way to and from the outlying fields, I always read my Pontoppidan's Explanation homework. This was so that I did not waste the slightest amount of time, and it was surprising how easy it was for me. Whilst reading, I did not know it before the road lay behind, even though I was carrying a large supply of food on my back, and during the walk, I did not know it before the lesson was read. There was only one unpleasantness with this type of somnambulating; you see, one always walked barefoot here during the summer, and during reading I continually kicked my toes, against the sharp stones that were everywhere on the path in this rocky mountain district, so that the blood ran. It was worst when old wounds were torn open again; *but every day one must accept the bad with the good*. Bias had thus far not changed places with the enlightenment of common sense — superstition had thus far not given the sinful present-day engineering skill, permission to clear the road to these isolated areas. However, I do not think that one needed more than a little muscle power and simple everyday hands to make many of these foot tracks passable by wagon or sleigh. The greatest portion of hay, for several neighboring farms, was gathered up in these mountains, which consist of steep hillsides and narrow valleys. The steep hillsides do have a small amount of forest, though mainly rocks, and of course, the grass is rather lush. Nevertheless, collection of the hay is very difficult due to the amount of rocks. The grass that is cut on the slopes needs to be carried on one's back, down to the valley to the small hillsides, where the hay drying racks are, and when there is rainy weather, which in these parts is very common, one has the wonderful job of carrying the wet grass, whilst the cold water runs down one's back. As the way up there is long and takes up too much time, one stays there in the hay barns, several nights in succession, while a half-grown boy or girl go home after more provisions, which mainly consists of porridge, flatbread and large winter herring. The dairymaid however, brings milk every morning from the opposite direction, where the summer dairy is. She then worked all day until about sundown, when she returns to the summer dairy, — and often has still a long way to go to find the herd, milk the cows and clean up the dairy. Though all the farmers in these parts spend their life in complete slavery in regards to work, food and clothes, I do however think that the dairymaids here are worst off.

One of our neighbors' wives had the name for being very stingy, and if Eilert Sundt [1817-1875, Norwegian sociologist born in Farsund, Norway] had seen her house cleaning, he would have certainly declared her an unusually dirty sow. Early one morning, when she was to go out to the fields, she could not find a vessel to ladle the mid-day porridge into, and when she happened to see a pair of old stiff leather trousers that belonged to her husband, she had the bright idea to ladle the porridge into one of the legs, which she had tied off at the bottom, then threw it over her shoulder and went off to the outer field, where the men had been for several days. As one was to have one's mid-day meal of this, in itself not so appetizing oat-meal porridge, which was in this ingenious container, the hired hand revolted and refused to eat, which one probably could not blame him for. He declared frankly that when he could not get edible food he just could not work, and prepared therefore to take it easy on his empty stomach. It had been a warm sunny day, and now a thundercloud began to come in fast from the west with all the signs of a farmer's so sinister torrential rain, which in this unstable climate is so common. As it happened, there was a mass of dry hay spread over the ground, which one was about to gather up in the afternoon and put in the hay barn. The woman naturally rushed off as if the devil was behind her to save as much as possible of the dry hay before the rain came, and what brought her rage to a point, was that the relentless hired hand sat quietly and watched. In vain she begged and scolded and wept and threatened; he held firm that "he, who does not get food, can therefore not work." Finally, the big raindrops began to fall, and the day's battle was thereby decided. Only a small amount of the hay had been gathered and in her despair, the woman sank quite defeated to the ground exclaiming: "Our own strength is worth nothing; we are soon defeated!"

As one sees, life in these parts was no game; he who wanted to succeed could not walk on roses. The mode of living was scanty and work was extremely hard and tedious; nevertheless, the summer here was unlike so many other places, not to be compared with the hard winter. To make this understandable, I only need to mention that all the hay that in the summer was gathered in these outfields had in the winter to be carried home on the back. Furthermore, when one knows that the road's length was from ¾ to 1 Norwegian mile, and that it went through deep mountain gorges, over rock-strewn slopes, up and down over steep mountain sides and hills covered with ice and snow, which therefore often made walking along these tracks mortally dangerous, even for those who had nothing to carry. One could easily understand what life was for those who nearly every day, in all sorts of weather, had to make this difficult trip. It has often puzzled me when I have looked back at this life how it happened that I did not become a cripple under this discipline, which had already started at the age of twelve. While I probably now should not underestimate the worth of such a school of experience for a young person, who from an early age was to begin to make a career for himself, I must nevertheless confirm, that there really was great danger to both life and health associated with this winter work. I have later often thought about the lucky circumstance that it was for me when my mother gave up the farm after I had been confirmed and had filled my fourteenth year. With that, I was at least able to leave this place, and notwithstanding the fact that luck did not always thereafter show me a loving hand, I believe nevertheless that it would have been much worse off if I had stayed long at my place of birth. Notwithstanding the fact that this region that I have mentioned, possibly belongs to one of the more difficult and disadvantageously placed regions in the fjord-districts in Bergen Diocese. It is nevertheless not the worst, and I am not very wrong when I say that a farmer's life thereabouts can just about be determined as the average extent of conditions in Bergen Diocese. Many more beautiful, better and handy farms are found there, but on the other side, I do also know that there are found just as many smaller, poorer and worse off farms than those I here have sought to portray.

After this excursion to our outfields, we will return for a moment back to the confirmation. I made this digression to give the reader a picture of the life that I was subjected to during the time of my confirmation.

It made a very disheartening impression on me that before all the confirmands I was to stand disgraced as the one who would not bring the pastor a gift. In my own mind, I came thus to be on a lower level in a more despicable position and was both a poorer and a more atrocious boy than what all the others were. I had not known before that all the confirmands had brought gifts for the pastor's kitchen, but as I now was the only one who was disgraced with an official rebuke, it became clear to me that I was the only one who had not performed this inducement. I therefore made the strongest performance in front of my mother, and with my tears' eloquence, I tried to make her comprehend how unhappy I felt and how hurtful it was for my little sense of honor to have been officially humiliated for such a small thing, which I however meant did not need to cost so much. My arguments, how good I may have thought they were, seemed however not to exert any significant effect, and I once more had to attend without bringing the much desired gift with me. Thus it remained until the approach of summer when my mother one day began to speak to me something like this: "My son, it saddens me greatly to see you so completely neglect your *Explanation of the Catechism*, while you so persistently spend your Sundays and your other spare time on these worldly books that your uncle has lent you. I feel almost certain that you will not be confirmed this year, and I have therefore decidedly made up my mind not to give you any present for the pastor, as I will absolutely, not have it seen as if I am buying your status, when I know that you can learn your religious books whenever you want to. It would therefore also be a wrong both for the pastor and against you if I as such bought you your standing. Were you however a very bright confirmand, the matter would have a much better appearance." — "But I have learned the set homework every single time, mother, and the others are not better; you could after all test me once in a while to get assurance in the matter," I answered. This she did not have time for, and on the other hand, thought it was self-evident that I could not learn my lessons without looking in the book. The next Sunday the pastor had decided to examine the confirmands before the congregation in the church, and then one could hear how we all performed. In this case I felt completely safe with my issue; we had now gone through the book once and had started from the front again; I had not only learnt the book from start to finish, but also totally in my memory were the explanations the pastor at each lesson had given. It seemed to us in all things that did not concern the purse or the kitchen, that the pastor was both a righteous and a kind man. During the catechization, he always asked his questions separately to each one, so that the boisterous loudmouth could not as I had seen, take the words out of the mouth of the more able, but humble and gentle pupil, when this one had already begun to answer. Nevertheless, each one had to be accountable for themselves; and when after repeated attempts and turns at the question, the answer was finally, as far as that is concerned, subsequently open for discussion. In this way, the cleverest did not alone have the chance to answer, but also the others, and when it was answered correctly, the pastor had recently acquired the habit, by a gesture, to draw attention to a place further down the row. In the congregation's hearing he was naturally always thankful for a correct answer when everyone was able to hold their own, hence, when no answer could be had, he considered himself in some degree to be defeated.

That Sunday afternoon my mother was very happy and contented, and the next time we met with the pastor I had a magnificent cheese with me for him. After having waited so long, he probably thought it was insignificant (butter was strictly speaking the correct gift), and presented a sour face, to which I dared to remark that the cheese was sweet. This half-hidden little bit of humor had its effect; cheerfully he took a knife to taste the cheese, and it appeared that I was correct. I had during the course of summer, come to stand on a familiar footing with him. It seemed he had long ago forgotten the affair of the gift and given me many a small proof of support, especially with his detailed explanations during catechization, and I can for that reason as well as his later demonstrations of kindness, remember this man with nothing but thankfulness. During the examination, my vanity had now and then been flattered by answering questions that had been directed at the son of the merchant or the son of the parson's assistant, without being answered. On the day of the confirmation, I was therefore to stand next to these dignitaries. The son of the pastor's assistant was in fact a blockhead, and his father was a very pompous (wanting to climb the social ladder!) man, and it would have been an unforgivable insult to place his son after the widow's underprivileged son. This is how narrow-minded and curtailed was the leaning in those days, even among the leading men of the community. When I paid my *daler* for the confirmation, the pastor had the kindness to ask if I had the desire to become a schoolteacher. Even as a chaplain he did not have this power, but had been ordered by the parish pastor to report to him who of the confirmands he saw as probable candidates to fill these honorable positions. I had not thought about this, but answered that I would however consider it after first hearing advice from my mother and some friends. Certainly, I had the urge to learn all sorts of things, but all my time was being taken up with acquiring clothing and food. Sundays I certainly had free, but I could pay neither for books nor for tuition. Therefore, this time it had to be declined. My thought was to have my mother outfit me so that during winter I could stay with my uncle, if possible, to enjoy the benefit of his tuition. But just after the confirmation, I had the misfortune to receive a very dangerous ax wound in the left leg, whereby the muscle in front of the ankle joint had been so damaged that one thought for sure, I would end up with a stiff foot. This accident kept me at home for the greater part of the winter, but fortunately, the nasty wound healed without leaving any permanent damage. Thus, at this time that I could not assist in carrying hay or chopping firewood, I utilized as well as I could in continuing my reading, writing and arithmetic exercises; but unfortunately only on my own. There was found, after my father, an old German Bible; this, I now took hold of, and without a dictionary, without grammar or oral guidance, I worked tirelessly to learn the German language by comparing verse by verse the German against the Norwegian translation.

In the spring, my mother intended to give up the farm, and I would then be able to go wherever I wanted. As she knew, my natural inclination was towards books so she did not object that I prepared myself to be a teacher. However, she shared her biased opinion and considered an ambulatory teacher's position as one of the lowliest. This was a position that only a few others, apart for crippled and incompetent people, sought. Poorly paid (10 *speciedaler* per annum) and even shoddier quartered. It was a type of infliction that only a farmer was able to accept because he had to; and there were in many a house, misgivings as to whether it was the teacher or the pauper, who stood on the bottom rung. However, she rationalized it thus! This book fuss suited the farmer about as much as the dry land suited the fish; as the fish must give up its spirit because of the lack of water, so must the farmer because of his books, give up his spirit through the of lack of bread. Book learning belongs to the influential; all the easy sources of income belong to him and his family; and when you, my son, will become involved in a unfamiliar position, and adorn yourself with borrowed feathers, it will go with you, as it went with the crow among the peacocks. You will be ostracized by the influential, while brothers from your own class will despise you and refuse to accept you into their circle. If there is a teacher or bailiff's position that can support its man, a notable's son with a feeble brain is sure to get it. A healthy man, such as a cotter, can scrape together enough for the necessities of life and be respected by his peers; but an ambulatory schoolteacher must find himself put into the same class as *John Poverty,* and no healthy girl in the community will share poverty and misery with him. However, as you must now sail on your own sea, and I no longer have work or bread to give you, I will not restrain you. I know that your father's brother's work as a teacher has been noble and beautiful; I know he has sacrificed his own comfort and benefits to his fellow men's advantage, and an active work ability, honesty and frugality has always described his path; but this has not been able to save him from the wrath of attitude. His good intentions have been unappreciated and his work unrewarded. All because his learning and way of thinking has removed him from his own class, while his lineage made it impossible to be accepted in the upper class. I can therefore only give you the advice to learn well what you begin to learn, and perform with diligence and faithfulness that which you undertake to do, and besides, find yourself with patience in the injustice and neglect that our social order seems to impose. Dark as this description was, and true in regard to her limited horizon, I nevertheless thought, or at least hoped, that it was a trifle exaggerated. A youthful dream view places so very beautiful and desirable in that which one has put one's whole heart's desire into. As it goes with a couple of poor lovers who do not see the poverty and misery that face them if they married, so it would also go with me. I had wholeheartedly fallen in love with the Norwegian writing style exercises, and the description of the world [geography], and nothing could deter me from throwing myself into their arms.

Therefore, as soon as I was healthy, I traveled to my uncle's, partly for advice from him, and partly to ask him if he would allow me to work for my board whilst he in his free time would tutor me. It should be here noted, that my older brothers had always vilified me, and often ridiculed me, because of my insane love for books, so that I sometimes was gripped by misgivings that I perhaps played a role just as laughable as Don Quixote when he came to grips with the windmill. If only I had otherwise known at that time, of his heroic exploits.

IV.
A Hard School.

However, it was not a teacher that I wanted to become. The outlook on this road was much too dark and unrewarding. In reality, I had absolutely no certain resolve in this respect. What it was that drove me to academic pursuits, I do not know. I would call it a natural inclination; perhaps it was a subconscious ambitious quest to become, what common sense might dictate that I could not become, or a slight aversion to be what class and birth had decided for me to be. However, I had to and wanted to pursue reading and writing, however hard my mother and brothers rebuked me for it. My uncle had now left teaching and had hold of a small cotter's farm on which he could support a couple of cows and cultivate some potatoes, but managed a carpentry shop as his main income. He was one of these men that in America are called public-spirited men, and filled with a fervent desire to introduce useful reformations among his countrymen. For instance, he had earlier as a teacher, worked on the scholarly path with universal information and intellectual development, to eradicate prejudice. Now, with the introduction of improved tools and work methods, he would remove many detrimental prejudices and old backward customs in cultivation and the agricultural sector in general. To this end, he had fitted out a blacksmith's shop beside his carpentry shop, though he himself was not a blacksmith, in order that he could supply plows, harrows, churns, spades, hoes and a multitude of things that had not yet come into use in this part of the country, and was not even obtainable without ordering from a factory in *Østlandet*. When I during spring visited him, he had his hands full with preparations for the actual enterprise that as yet had not come into operation. He told me that I could get enough hard work and simple lodgings, but he could not offer me any other time for instruction than he needed to apply for his own children's education. Even this for the moment he had to limit very much, but hoped however that this would improve when the workshop was in operation. Naturally, I agreed with every condition, for here at least there was something to learn that did not normally occur with an ordinary farmer; what there was to be learned at an ordinary farmer, I thought I had only learned too well. He still held, as before, a warm interest in education, and though he had been paid with immense ingratitude for his sacrifices in the public school service, he would not dissuade me to follow this path if I should later come to find that I wished to select it. It was you see, that in 1827 I believe, that a new School Act had come from *Storthinget* [Norwegian Parliament], that somewhat improved a teacher's wage, and tried to raise their status in the public eye by demanding a better education and skill from them. Under this Act, the earlier sexton [sometimes also held the position as a school master] position would be withdrawn gradually as the officeholders died. The best suited among the parishes' teachers would then become precentors, and with this extra small source of income, he could increase his miserable wage along with this position's reputedly linked honor, to raise the teaching profession a little in the public's esteem; something that certainly was a most necessary condition; as well as to make its undertakings beneficial by inducing able, gifted young people to choose this profession. This Act now, besides reading, also made writing and arithmetic into fixed teaching courses; but the main thing was that religious training and the teaching task still was and remained as before, in the catechism examination, which assumed intimate acquaintance with the faith doctrine after the five part division.

After having given me this explanation, my father's brother told me how unfortunate it had been for him, when after the death of the old sexton he had sought employment as a precentor and teacher at the home parish permanent school. It was among the farmers then, as now, a general custom to discuss faith doctrines at their social gatherings. The one, who was the most well read in the Bible and could best explain the difficult and partly mysterious places in the scripture, was the wisest man. My father's brother was a friend to man, full of love and compassion for others, and therefore found in Christ a glorious model for his ideas, but always came into embarrassment with the extra-orthodox, when they put forth their heartless theory of belief without deeds and humanity. He was a kind of Henry Ward Beecher, who would rather see the fruits of a loving Christian belief in man's daily usage, and wanted to be consistent and not get hung up with the difficult problems, whereafter he came to condemn the good Christians and upright people, who in the one or the other point could think differently than he — in a word, he was too liberal in his religious conception for the time's dark philosophy of life. Some inconsiderate statements concerning the Holy Scriptures had brought him a couple of fanatics' hostility to light, of which one was an old dismissed schoolteacher. These men pursued him with implacable bitterness, which they naturally called zeal of the *true faith,* or what one now calls *pure doctrine*. His words in their mouths became distorted and misinterpreted and they soon spread terrible rumors about his delusional doctrine and heresy. The numerous youths, who had benefited from his excellent teachings and affectionate association, were his fervent devotees. Most of the parents had him dear, and respected him far differently than was normally done with the wretched ambulatory teachers. However, his enemies went forward with much cunning and in all secrecy, there was a complaint drawn up against him to which they attached a number of signatures, of which several belonged to men who had no idea about what they actually signed. This complaint was delivered to the parish pastor who was an old drunk that lived in idleness and luxuriousness, and in principal wanted to see the public as ignorant and superstitious as possible. A son of the recently deceased sexton was the second one seeking the position as precentor and schoolteacher under the new School Act. He was almost equally well suited to lead the church singing as my father's brother, but in knowledge, culture, teaching skills as well as an ardent interest for the education department, he was only as a child in comparison to him. Naturally, the parish pastor wanted the sexton's son, whose father had belonged to the tail end of the upper class. As the two candidates were to meet with the dean at the same time to be examined, the parish pastor sent a warm recommendation for the sexton's son as well as a complaint against my father's brother for heresy. The complaint had been so completely secretive, that the latter did not know about it till the dean, after the examination was over, read it for him and explained that he, with his knowledge and rare teaching skills, would have been obvious for the position he sought, but because of this testimony against him it was impossible for him to be a teacher. Uncle felt so bitterly disappointed by this slighting as a lazy and incompetent teacher. But most offensive however was that he, by his own class faction, had been duped in such a despicable manner through a secretive complaint, for which falsehood and malice, he could have brought one hundred respectable men's' testimony for each of the incompetent people, who had signed it, if he had known of the complaint. It was neither the first time or the last time bigotry's mistaken zeal had seduced people to give one's own interest a perilous wound. Almost each page of Christianity's history shows examples of this kind on a much larger scale. For nearly nineteen hundred years persecutions for religious beliefs have continued. In our time, one does not burn heretics at the stake or stone them as in bygone times; in our time and in our country, persecutions are done more by words and not acts. Imaginary delusions have for a long time been persecuted by fire and sword so that the religious fanatics' bloodthirsty revenge has brought forth a general disgust among the people, and the gentler seed has changed the public opinion until it has been impossible for the religious insistence to bring anyone to the stake. To stretch teachers of heresy on the pen's torture rack, or put them in the preacher's pillory, is now the highest that can be obtained.

If it has gone thus with the green tree, what would become of the dry, I thought at the end of his narrative; because as a teacher, he was at that time in my eyes, really the green tree over the dry, against what I dared hope to ever be. Had I before had disinclination to the teaching profession, I now had it even more. I was to be with my uncle for three months and had to really work for my board as he was an unusually, hardworking modest man. With all his goodness of the heart, his philosophy could at times bring him to a pure absurdity against both himself and those who worked with him. Early one morning before the sun was up, we left before breakfast, rowed a *Fjerdingvei* [quarter of a Norwegian mile; 2.82 km] over the fjord, then walked probably a *Fjerding* into the forest to cut lumber, which the man who owned the forest would then drive down to the water. We were not finished with this work until late in the afternoon, and did not come home until it was dark, while we all day had worked with all our might. As I was exhausted by hunger, and was often ready to drop to the ground, he laughed in his usual manner of laughter and said, it does us well in both body and soul, as rest is not sweet without one being tired, and food does not taste without one being hungry, nor can one's mind be clear with a stomach overfilled with undigested food. I meant however, that it would have been compassionate if we had been given a little breakfast before we left home. If one worked and sweated hard all day without a mid-day meal, I could not understand how the mind's clarity would be surpassed by one with an overfilled stomach of undigested food, if we had been given a spoon of cold porridge with a little sour milk in the morning before we left. However, I had come to school, and could not show insubordination to my teacher. One other time we had rowed with a large boat on the fjord, to some steep forested mountainsides to cut elm trees for wagon lumber. Suitable trees for what we were seeking were only to be found high up on the mountain to where one could not get to by horse. It was a hot spring day; we worked hard, and the shirt was soaked in sweat; we had nothing to drink, and the thirst was nearly unbearable. True enough, we had food with us this time, but it consisted of salt fish and bread without milk or water. When we were about to eat I suggested that I would therefore run down to a small river that right enough ran a half *Fjerdingvei* below us in the valley to collect drinking water, or otherwise we would be endangering our lives if we now ate the salt fish. My tutor was of another opinion. Man is fortunately so arranged that through habit he can almost learn everything; we should accustom ourselves to patience, learn to overcome difficulties in our youth, then such things would not bother us when we become older; through strong determination, we should strengthen physical weaknesses and keep passions in check. As correct as this philosophy was, I could not however live it in the unreasonable extent he wished to give it. I broke through this time all the barriers and ran down to the creek for water. Without this, I am certain that we would not this day have been able to fulfill the Herculean task that was still left to be done. After our lumber was cut and split into large blocks, it was to be rolled or dragged down the steep mountainside to the water and loaded into the boat, and then to row nearly a Norwegian mile back at night. Had I not already from the age of twelve been hardened in a similar, though less unreasonable school, as to food and drink, I would obviously not have been able to withstand the test.

When the three months had passed, I could for that matter use the broad ax, the saw and the wood plane, so he took me to a rich farmer where he had undertaken to construct a sawmill and gave me the opportunity to work for wages. Now it seemed for me that things were starting to improve, even if just a little. The fare we here received struck me as royal compared to what we were previously accustomed to, and it was also a very interesting family with whom association with was very pleasant. The stay here still stands as a highlight in my memory from this dim and wavering time of my youth. I now often suffered from melancholy and despondency, which made a discouraging impression on my whole being. Inside me, there was a strong ambitious spirit, whose flight was hindered and restrained so completely by external difficult hardships, that I came to be standing in-between these two forces, as a depressed and tottering being. Therefore, I have ever since, continued to remember the friendly contribution and encouragement I found among the young members of that family that I had come into contact with.

When the haying season began, I returned to my home village and worked at my brother-in-law's, who had a good farm. During the work on the sawmill I had received a larger wage than anyone of my age could expect, and my brother-in-law was kind enough to give me the same for the work during summer, so that I in fall had saved a few *daler*, and my mother continued to provide me with the most necessary clothing. My guardian now allowed the sale through public auction the goods, which through the probate court had come to me when my mother gave up the farm; she had you see, since my father's death sat in undivided possession of the estate, as one called it. At this auction the goods were sold at a lofty price and brought in 80 *speciadaler* instead of 54 *speciedaler*, which was the value laid out by the court. This small inheritance I could not receive until I was eighteen years old and it was therefore set aside to accrue interest at the public trustee. During fall, I went once again to my father's brother where he now had his workshop in full swing and was so far making enough so that he could sacrifice a little more time on his children's education, and I also was then given a little tuition. I was now to pay something for my board and also do some work. In this manner, I spent winter. My tutor now told me straight out that it would be fruitless for me to try calligraphy, as I could never master it to a great perfection. He had through drawing and calligraphy won great admiration at the time he frequented the Bergen Sunday school, which was at that time a sort of polytechnic school for the impoverished apprentice boys, and he therefore had to be seen as an authority in this regard. Thus, I occupied myself this winter especially with arithmetic, along with Norwegian and German grammar, in which subjects he held great satisfaction with my progress.

V.
At Bergen Alternative School.

I was now fifteen years old, and in the spring I had to make a specific decision for the future. To help me come to a decision, my father's brother traveled with me to Bergen, and had the kindness to take me to several of his old benefactors among Bergen's excellent pedagogues, among them the celebrated poet Lyder Sagen. I had expressed a great inclination to go to business school to become a clerk and from there work my way through to the commercial world. When old Sagen heard this, he asked how much money I could count on getting when I came of age. Not over eighty *speciedaler* was the answer, — and much more would be needed to be able to pass the business exam under the then, strict regulations. I can never forget how crushing his answer fell upon me: "A merchant without money and a violin without strings resemble each other very much." He wanted to seriously advise me from thinking about the commercial world; a trade, for example a lathe operator for artistic work he thought would be suitable for me. Now that I had heard his opinion, I must sincerely confess that it was completely disheartening if not to say daunting. With Mr. Winding, who at that time was a teacher at the high school, it did not go much better. He was however, willing to give me private tuition by the hour in the necessary subjects (arithmetic, book-keeping, and German business correspondence) for the business exam, but gave me just as gloomy a portrayal of the cashless clerk's artificial position as Mr. Sagen had done. And to have me in complete despair, which he believed, he asked if I could use a cooper's adz and work as a casual hand by filling and making herring barrels, after I had taken the exam, as then it was extremely difficult to get a placement as a book-keeper. It went about the same with a couple of other of my uncle's acquaintances, with whom we had sought advice, and it was now clear to me that the door was closed for me, and that one instinctively, as if one had come to agreement over it on all fronts, had shut me out because of my class. Mr. Winding was however courteous because of his acquaintance with my father's brother, and for 70 *speciadaler* he would prepare me for the examination. I agreed with this, though of course I did not have such money, let alone double as much that was needed, for such a long stay in the city. I would now try my luck, and consoled myself with the thought: In time, a solution will come.

But when I a couple of months later came back to begin my preparations, and already had rented a small room where I had to take care of my own housekeeping, and an old woman who was a housekeeper for the police official who owned the house, would for a small payment assume the responsibility for my washing — the admirable old Mr. W. who had forgotten the whole agreement, seemed not to recognize me again, and asked me naively who my uncle was, if he also was a farmer etc., and declared finally that I must be mistaken and that he was not the man, — even though he knew well it was completely impossible for anyone who had seen this peculiar little hunchbacked man, to mistake him for someone else. Well, here I stood once again, just as embarrassed and bewildered as ever, aye, even to a degree worse, for I could not escape paying the agreed rental for my room, which indeed was only 6 *speciedaler* for six months, but even this, for a young person in my position, was not a small amount to throw away, especially when my entire undertaking in Bergen had met with the most decided disapproval by my mother and my siblings, from whom I also could not expect any help, even though some were fairly well off. They looked upon my whole quest as a youthful folly, a delusion, which late or early, according to their opinion, would unfailingly lead me into trouble. In the midst of my embarrassment, I one day met in the street the merchant's son who had been confirmed along with me. With a few words, I explained to him my position and what a shame it seemed to me to have to abandon my project and return to my home village disappointed and humiliated with my mission unaccomplished. He was very courteous and expressed much concern for me. He asked me to follow him home to his lodgings where he then told me that he had just passed his exam from the business college, and offered, as he had nothing in particular to do, to take over my private instructions for the 70 *speciedaler* and have me ready for the exam. I thanked him courteously for this friendly offer and asked for time to think it over until the following day, when I would once again let him hear from me. The fact was that I had strong suspicion of his ability to give me the necessary preparations; for although he himself had just passed the exam, it did not however follow that he was competent to teach, so that I at a given time could reach the necessary skills in all subjects. During the previous visit to Bergen along with my uncle, we had visited a teacher B., who was a teacher at a so-called special school, that is to say, in one of the city's free schools for the poor, where the so-called alternate method was introduced during the teaching. This was to say, nothing more than that the school was divided into many classes, with one of the best students in each class as the teacher for his class. And where each student during reading exercises, from a printed chart with large writing hanging on the wall, recited every letter in the word and every word in the sentence, along with alternately reading each their own paragraph on the different charts, which of course were designed for the development of the class. This teacher B., who had come from Nordfjord in Bergen Diocese, and strangely enough belonged to the farming class, even though he now had his top coat and shiny boots on, he had presented particularly obligingly when my uncle and I had visited him. From memory, I decided now to counsel him during my feelings of doubt and therefore took the way to the "day nursery," as his school (which originally, as far as I recall, had been one or another charitable establishment) was normally called. Conveniently, I met him just as school finished, and he listened with concerned attentiveness to the story of my disappointment with Mr. W. and about my concerns in regards to my young friend's offer. Before a stroke of good luck had led him into the well paid position, which he now held, he had for a couple of years been a school teacher and precentor in his home village. Step by step, he constantly had luck with him — a favorable wind had always filled his sails, and he had as it seemed by this, become a bit proud and vain, but was nevertheless by nature a happy and kindly fellow. He told me how many young men from the rural area had been sent to his alternate school, partly to learn the new tutoring method, and partly to further educate themselves to be able to obtain school teacher and precentor positions in the rural districts. In the whole he had taken great pains to put the teaching profession in such a favorable light as possible and eventually advised me to attend his school for six months to train me for this profession, and besides had the goodness to offer to give me a couple of hours tuition in German at home in his lodgings. It need not cost me more than what I myself thought best to give him when the time was up. Whether it was divine providence, blind chance or inevitable logic of things that here intervened and changed my direction in life, I shall not here concern myself with investigating. Enough said, I took this man's advice and began under his guidance with all might to prepare myself for a public teacher's profession.

My six-month stay in Bergen this time barley bore the fruit I had expected, the progress I made I had my diligent self-study to thank more for than the help my teacher could give me. In Norwegian grammar and arithmetic, I was one and the same as he. In German he helped me not so little as he was doing this himself and had come a little farther than I; but in his school, it was actually singing and the practical tutoring manner that I made the most progress in, and which I very well could not have mastered in private tuition. He had decided to go on the path of learning and was now preparing to go to university. Becoming a student was his big goal for which he was now aiming, and often filled his mind with the most exaggerated future prominence. Once he had passed *Eksamen Artium* [The General Certificate of Education], there was it seemed, nothing that could hinder him from being a cabinet minister or whatever it was. For the moment, it was Latin that was giving him gray hairs. A young man by the name of Sexe (from my neighboring parish), whom Lyder Sagen, because of a *skjæppe* Hardanger apples [about half a bushel] had obtained entry to the Latin school, came to him in the afternoons to read with him for an hour. This Sexe, who later as a mineralogist had attracted a good deal of public attention — especially since he, because of intrigue, had been dismissed from his position at Kongsberg Silverworks, and therefore by *Storthinget* was granted 800 *speciedaler* annually to continue his studies in geology — was a young man endowed with rare talents, who, at the time when I saw him give private tutoring to teacher B., was soon to go to university to study for the *Artium*. I can remember how he sometimes made fun of Mr. B.'s vanity and folly, but in such a nice way that this one did not notice the bitter irony that was therein. One day, just as I was at the crucial part of tutoring one of the top classes in the school, whilst Mr. B. sat engrossed in his Latin, one of the school's inspectors, *Herr Pastor* Flotman — parish pastor at Nykirken, arrived to hold a visitation [for purposes of inspection and examination] at the school. Surprised at seeing a stranger occupied with the teaching — a stranger in a strange work — he came straight to me, and with a real angry manner asked whom I was and what I was doing here. I, who did not know him or did not know that he was in any special relationship to the school, answered him straight out that I intended to become a teacher in the country and had come here to make myself acquainted with the alternate method. It appeared that this good man, though he had learned very much, still had not learned to put a gag on his own emotions as he was positively enraged and commanded in a stern tone: "Away, young man; we do not teach farmers to be school teachers here!" Then he sought the teacher, who unluckily was sitting behind the desk and crammed Baden's Latin Grammar. I understood now that he must be one of the school's superiors and removed myself as quietly as possible when I began to get a notion that teacher B. had no authority to do what he did with me and several others who had been there and others who were still in the process. How Mr. B. survived this fierce theologian, I do not know; he complained later over this unfortunate affair, and I then heard nothing more about it. B. was for several years at the school and was at least fortunate, in as far as his marriage was advantageous and thereby came into ownership of a beautiful property in town; but I heard later that he had failed the *Examen Artium*. So as not to be surprised by the inspector, we later used greater prudence, but continued nevertheless as before with our work in the school. A schoolteacher from Sogn, also came to practice singing and make himself acquainted with the new teaching method. We took turns to hold watch, but the pastor never came again, as long as I was there.

VI.
Life as a School Teacher.

What I had seen and experienced during my six months stay in Bergen, and the insight I had of the conditions, even among those who could be called the student youth, had more and more reconciled me with the thought of becoming a teacher, and the future that I in this path was to meet. I had, — to use an old proverb, seen with my own eyes — that not everything is gold that glitters. Even in my still so limited world of experience and with my so modest developed concepts about the seriousness of life, it already now began to come to my understanding that it depended less on what our call in life was than on how we fulfilled this call's obligations so as to be pleased and happy here in this world. Hampered, and then again and again being thrown back each time, my zealous quest for knowledge had brought me too near social classes' sharp-drawn boundaries, it went strictly with me as it went with the fox who discovered that the grapes were sour when he noticed that he could not reach them. I began to discover that the social class in many places was like a *whited sepulcher* [St. Mathew 23, 27], which on the outside is wonderful to look at, but on the inside is full of rot and dead bones. Nevertheless, it was several years after this time, that I first wholly learned to use that which the writings say — "Let us not depart our own congregation, as some have done." Under the conditions of the middle class, I learned to see how backward one acted, when one, intimidated by the hard pressure under which the populace groaned, tried to come up into the ruling class to have it better, without thinking that the pressure thereby increased. One saves not the ship by abandoning it; it is treason during the heat of battle to go over to the enemy. To stand in line with one's own, through word and deed, aye, through work, misunderstanding and suffering to try to encourage, comfort, develop and lift them and oneself, higher and higher up to a position of independence, where the great principle of equality holds good as mandatory law for all classes of society, is what the obligation offers, and here the simple teacher can also reap laurels. A people who for 400 years, from one generation to the next, had lived and died in a repressed, downtrodden and relatively anarchical conditions, could not under the 1814 introduced changes in the constitution, rise to any general awareness about one's rights. The few nobles, who at Eidsvold had abolished in the new constitution the seed, from which they at one time had hoped to see the people's tree of liberty germinate, were themselves conservative and wished that the growth of liberty would be slow and even more conservative (some even were against liberty) were their immediate descendants in governing and legislation. At the time I here mention, that is, around 1830, the new constitution had still not in the part of the country where I was at home, produced any visible change in conditions. The people's economic state, enlightenment, ways of thinking, manners and customs were about the same as they had been at the end of the 18th century. The ruling class, as I earlier have shown, consisted of imported German and Danish officials and merchants and their offspring in a descending line, and did not belong to the so-called Norse tribe from where the actual Norwegian people descended. Already, the in our time extolled, (despot) Harald Haarfager deprived the Norwegian farmer in the 9th century one of his supreme rights, the Assessment Court, and with his bloodthirsty sons drove the best and mightiest families to go into exile rather than make themselves salves to the monarchy. The rest of the laws and memories thereof, which ambitious chiefs and protracted civil wars down to the14th century had not been able to destroy and bring into oblivion, was accomplished rather persistently, with the union with Denmark sent, German Junker class and their descendants. With laws, which from end to end were shaped after this classes' wishes and taste, with officials, merchants and power solely in their hands, it was no wonder that their 400 year reigning rule had brought the once so mighty and independent Norse tribe to an unimportant status, which the first half-century after the new constitution, had not been able to dispel. Then when one remembers that the ruling class still, with a few remarkable exceptions, truly stood together in government and legislation from top to bottom in order to preserve their privileges and rights against the democratic tendency, which gradually began to reveal itself, can one make a conception of the meaning that the teacher's work at that time had to have in his own consciousness, if he by the way understood it or was equal to the task. That a sixteen-year old boy, for whose vision only a few fundamental features of this state of affairs began to vaguely show itself, as if in a dim light, was not equal to the task, is unnecessary to add. A good fortune it is perhaps that barely any of that time's teachers had a clear vision on his work's immense significance from this side considered, for otherwise the responsibility and the consciousness of one's own weakness would have frightened away every one of them.

A precentor position had been available in one of the annex parishes in our parish ever since the old sexton's demise, and singing during the divine service was in the mean time directed by one of the pastor's assistants, as none of the parish's three schoolteachers could sing. When I stayed at the alternative school in Bergen, I had written to the chaplain who had read with me for confirmation, and told him that I had now decided to seek for employment as a teacher and precentor and wished preferably to remain in our parish if there was a vacancy. He had informed his parish pastor of this, and had a place ready for me in the said annex parish. When I was furnished with a certificate and a somewhat exaggerated recommendation from teacher B., I went on the journey home, to the parish pastor, to announce myself as a candidate and ask for a letter to the dean, to whom I intended then to address myself to undergo the requisite examination. It proceeded towards the afternoon and the parish pastor had now gone so deep into the bottle that there was no getting any sense from him; but he had recently received an assistant pastor, and this young, friendly little man showed my request all the necessary attention. Equipped with the parish pastor's recommendation and a very advantageous confirmation testimony from my beloved chaplain, I went off to the dean who lived over four Norwegian miles from there. The new assistant pastor did however not know about the affair, with the complaint of heresy, against my father's brother, nor knew, I was a nephew of the accused teacher; otherwise, it may well happen that he would have seen it as his duty to give the dean a hint in this regard. The latter however did not need such a hint, as he subjected me, after what I later learned from others, a quite unjustifiably strict examination in religion. Bible history I had at the tips of my fingers, and as to what incidental reading, writing, arithmetic, grammar, geography, history and singing was concerned, his questions were easy and insignificant except for the singing, which he seemed to be personally interested in. In the arithmetic and grammar test the answers several times seemed to wake his astonishment, without it being clear for me whether this was to my advantage or otherwise. The actual doctrine I had not read through since my confirmation, but yet had it just in my memory, that with a normal catechization I could have passed it with ease, but he decided to make his questions as complicated and as indistinct as possible. My uncle had never taught me in religion, and the good teacher B. had his head so full of declinations and conjugations, that he probably completely forgot that the *Herr* dean might perhaps come to take me down in the dogmatists' mystical depths to see if I was infected by the freethinking of those days. And I will gladly confess that in this field I was less prepared than in the other subjects, though my testimonial from my time of confirmation seemed to show the opposite. The dean's questions were nevertheless very extensive, and several times I showed the answer due respect, whilst I also a couple of times answered wrong. His face became very gloomy, and I now saw clearly that he had a suspicion about my orthodoxy. After a short repose, he said, "You have in the normal subjects given some astonishing answers, but now we are stuck; I do not know what to think about this." I asked if I had permission to explain myself, and thereupon gave a short résumé of the doctrine according to the five parts and declared that this was my teachings as a child. By this indoctrination I had become a member of the Lutheran church, and if herein there was something false, I had learned it from Pastor X., who had prepared me for confirmation, and whose testimony I must be allowed to show. Probably I had here shown too much fervor; even though he never pointed out anything divergent in my knowledge, his characteristic gloom however, remained on his face. I concluded therefore that the explanation had been correct, though my end argument had given affront. I received a rather chilly farewell. I did not ask, and he did not deign to answer either yes or no as to my application, but said dryly, after I had bowed and said farewell, that he would ascribe the parish pastor. I drew from this the inference that *my uncle's nephew*, despite recommendations and good testimonials, had been rejected, and with dark clouds hanging over me, I walked the long journey home.

Two weeks after my homecoming (I still regarded my old mother's house as my home) I received a written request from the parish pastor to report to the annex church in question the following Sunday, to be registered into the office and begin my work as an ambulatory schoolteacher. These ambulatory teachers' wage was actually 10 *speciedaler* per annum with a teaching period of thirty-eight weeks, but those of the parishes' three teachers who were given the position of precentor with which the so-called tithing attached, would in consideration only receive 6 *speciedaler* annually as a school wage. This had already earlier by the parishes' school commission, been decided; but for the so-called precentor tithing there existed no such firm provisions, and it depended simply on new precentor's understanding of how to win the farmer's favor and good will, if the tithing became something or not. So, I was for thirty-eight weeks in the year to go from farm to farm to teach school, and at the year's end accept 6 *speciedaler* in wages along with daily bread in those houses I held school. On Sundays, I was obliged to be at the church and direct the singing as well as make lists of communions, christenings, marriage ceremonies and so forth, and whether I was to receive something for this work, which still was not so little onerous, was of no certainty. Therefore, it was no prosperous office I had come into. However, I had now already begun to see visions, and was determined to seek my fortune in the happy knowledge, which in my opinion should be the fruit of charitable work, and I consoled myself with the fact that in the fourteen weeks, which I in the summer had free, I should work enough for clothes and shoes, — board of course I would get around in the houses I tended. The school went better than expected. I could not carry out the tutoring fully as well as I had learned in Bergen, as I was missing the then necessary equipment, and the different localities to where I came with my school did not allow it either. However, as I seldom in any of the four *roder* [group of farms which keeps up a section of roadwork, by work in kind], of which the district consisted, came to have over twenty, most often only ten to fifteen pupils, it was also not necessary to use the alternate method. In fact, it soon became clear that in itself it was not necessary but just a tool where a teacher had about one hundred children to teach. Class grouping I could utilize with advantage during reading practice, as every class had its own lesson to memorize and every student in the class addressed it in turn. The same could also to a certain extent be done with writing and arithmetic exercises, so that there became more order and system as well as more life, activities and emulation in the school, while one also had the benefit of a partial reciprocal action between the students in each class. During my stay in Bergen, I had already made myself so familiar as far as to tutoring and school discipline, that in this regard I could foresee no difficulty. As for the children, I was so far from having grounds to complain, and because of their diligence, obedience and good manners towards me, they were my greatest comfort under the otherwise so trying and often itinerant schoolwork. The elderly men and women in the district stated often that they had never seen a teacher before, who as such, could commandeer the children's confidence and love, and at the same time be so completely respected and obeyed. The constant interchange between reading, writing, arithmetic, singing practice and catechization made the teaching pleasant and captivating; all tedious frequent cramming avoided; the young brains held in constant activity by portrayal of a continuous line of new concepts and thoughts, which was always addressed and developed in an ascending direction as their comprehension and ability strengthened and grew. The parish pastor was an indifferent man who neglected everything that could be neglected. Thus he had never during the long time he had been in the call, generated any supervision or control of the school system, of which however, he was the legal guardian. Therefore, the public school in his parish had also come into great disrepair, and I soon found out that it was in significantly worse repair than in other parishes. The resident chaplain was a more enterprising man who interested himself in my school. He many times used the opportunity to visit our school when he came to hold divine service in our church. During these occasions, I made him aware of what were my main difficulties, specifically the lack of suitable reading books, multiplication tables, arithmetic books etc., and laid particular stress on how necessary it was for the children in each class to have the same books. I also mentioned that I thought most of the parents would be agreeable to buy the books. However, I could not take it upon myself to introduce the books without the authorization from the proper authorities. This led to addressing the parish pastor, and his assistant chaplain, who had recently arrived, found then a mass of authorized multiplication tables and books distributed by the Department of Education. But since the good, elderly pastor, had placed them in his storehouse and forgotten them — he unfortunately had not, as it was with the bard, re-discovered them at the bottom of his mug, no matter how often he emptied it. The assistant chaplain on this occasion had his attention, through a unique approach, drawn to the public school and became from this moment my sincere friend and defender when I later came into conflict with bigotry. I now received what I had so been missing — charts with spelling and reading practice, Grøgaard's Reader etc. Of religious books, we already had the old ABC, Luther's Small Catechism and Pontoppidan's Explanation, all of which were used during religious teachings and were the basis for catechetical instructions. Of arithmetic books, slates, slate pencils, paper, ink and pens, I stocked at my own expense and sold to those who could afford to buy, and gave to those who could not.

VII.
A Forbidden Fruit.

I had now come onto a good road and found that it already seemed to have begun to brighten. I began to think about giving the brightest among the boys a bit of tutoring in spelling, grammar, as well as geography; but unfortunately, it was a forbidden fruit not found in the school commission's commodities chest. That the boys learned to write and do arithmetic, some of the more conservative parents considered this to be going a bit too far. They could however not explain away the potential therein of the practical use and need for daily life, especially when I could convince them that they through this new method of teaching learned more religion in a given time, than if they spent their whole school time linked to the religious book alone. However, when the small girls also began to want to write and do arithmetic, which I also agreed to, then it was too much. Such a scandal would not be tolerated. If I did not stop with this abomination — if I wanted to continue to introduce this new fallacy, I would be accused before the pastor. I would, they believed, have benefit of being reminded how it had gone with my uncle. I would not even admit that it was a fallacy or heresy to tutor the youth of both genders, to write and do arithmetic, and if one in conclusion wanted to accuse me for this, then one could so do. To be discharged for such a reason I would not be so much against, and daily bread with 6 *speciedaler* per annum in wages, I could surely obtain in another position in life. As the parish pastor was the ex-officio chairman in the school commission, I would in conjunction with the pastor's assistant submit to him the matter for further deliberation. However, before this could be done, a more serious matter came into being. Grøgaard's Reader, which was used in my school, was not teaching correctly — it was heretical. It did not only teach about the five senses and other natural doctrines, but there was also written, that the witch in Endor had not been able to conjure Samuel up from the dead when King Saul wished to counsel with him. She had deceived him by having one whom she had hidden nearby to play Samuel and answer Saul's questions. Aye, true enough, this was bad, but I was however not the book's author, and besides it was the government and the pastor who had supplied this book to be used in the school, and I should use it until the correct person thought it best to replace it with another.

All this agitation led to no result; the young pastor's assistant was definitely on my side, and besides, I had through diligence and hard work at the school, as well as an engaging relationship with both the children and the parents, won a large majority approval and benevolence. At church singing there were found many difficulties, which the pastor as well as I realized would take a long time and much patience to overcome. Many of the elderly in the congregation would not know of the new choral melodies, which headmaster Bohr in Bergen had released, to promote an orderly, rhythmic and consistent singing in the church where the old melodies gradually had become garbled, and were now sung exceedingly dissimilar in the different churches. One could remedy this but encountered many difficulties, which, as there showed unwillingness in the congregations, could not be dismissed in any other way than to teach the youth for a couple of generations, so that prejudices would disappear imperceptibly. In our church there was nearly always present a gigantic man with a stentorian voice. This man was a right old Norwegian Viking, full of pride and vigor. He was also very keen on the changed psalm melodies, and when any of these changes were attempted in the church, he sang in his, as such, "own melody", so that the church walls actually shook. It would not alone be in vain, but it would also be purely ridiculous to challenge him. We had therefore, when all is said and done, — to compromise. At this time, I had constantly in my memory the sentence: "He, who makes friends of his enemies, is greater than he who captures a government." I intended to come into personal contact with those I saw as the major opponents. To move towards a friendly association and come into conversation with them, read with them, sing with them and imperceptibly get them interested in the previous matter. In this manner, I won the way of friendship and conviction little by little, and with so much territory in my district, I sometimes flattered myself that I perhaps would soon be able to operate without opposition, in the public education service.

With singing in the school, and with the confirmed youth, many of whom now had in mind to come to school during winter in order to learn writing and arithmetic, it went much better than in the church. Many people obtained for themselves, the so-called, *Contemporary Psalms* with organist Bohr's numbered chorales, and with the help of these and by assiduous gatherings on winter afternoons in the place where school was held, we had by the end of the first year a choir that with rhythm and precision could sing in unison with the new method. Occasionally, they were given the opportunity to perform in church, but I never dared to go further than to give illustrations, whilst the psalms of the day selected for divine service were always left for the congregation to sing in the old manner. I saw however, that in this manner it would go very slowly with improving the church singing. Aye, even that the experiment would probably fail and my work in that direction would be wasted if the successors to my position were not inspired by the same intellect, and continued the work. Nevertheless, as there did not appear to be any quicker or surer way to reach the goal at the time, I however persisted with patience to do my work as well as I could.

What is remarked above, about opposition against writing and arithmetic practices, against Grøgaard's Reader and against church singing, must not be understood to mean that this opposition was the norm among the people in my district or in the parish. This would be to bestow upon them a shameful injustice. On the contrary, my position as a teacher gradually became much more pleasant than I had at first dared hope for. Only with the exception of a few singularly, very biased dissatisfactions, I was met everywhere with the greatest of kindness and respect. Even though it was not such a small inconvenience associated with having the school gathered in one's living room (to where, one was at nearly every place, shown to during the winter), one vied however to get me to come to their home. So long as the cold of winter did not require a warm room, I usually received one or two candles and a roomy, so-called, formal-parlor, where the school would assemble for several of the farms nearby. I then went to each of the farmers to dine on the agreed upon number of days, whilst the school's assemblage did not change. One realized that the convenience thus, was much better for tutoring. Because in the farmer's living room, all sorts of work was happening, as well as conversations between the farm people, which is a great hindrance to tutoring, and found myself therefore in this arrangement, even though an ambulatory teacher had no right thereto. It was now becoming an honor to have the school assembled at one's home, and one was somewhat jealous of the neighbor who entrusted me with his formal-parlor for the use of the school. In winter however, I came into nearly everyone's house, without, in a sense, that it was their turn, and entering into an agreement for a change. It was usual in this part of the country that not only the womenfolk constantly performed their home crafts in the living room, such as spinning wool, weaving, knitting, sewing, and so forth, but also the men would engage here with one or another handy-craft, especially on the days when one could not perform anything outside. One could make barrel hoops, a second split and cut sticks, a third prepare sleighs or vehicles, a fourth make or repair shoes, a fifth could do carpentry work, etc. It is easy to realize how disturbing this must be for the school's operation and how desirable for this reason alone considered, if one everywhere could have erected these so-called study rooms, even where it was not possible to introduce them, in the rural districts, due to the permanent schooling system. Nevertheless, I for my part already began increasingly to regard the ambulatory school as very recommendable for the teacher who wholeheartedly loved his work and regarded it as something quite differently and higher than just a basic struggle for food. One was thus in fact, in quite a different, friendly and confidential association with parents, children and siblings, in every family in the district. This way one learned to understand each other better; one came into conversation, began to think and develop for each other, one's opinions, hopes and desires. Was the teacher by his knowledge, culture and refined humanely way of thinking, raised above his domain, as according to his call's involvement he should be, he here received a good opportunity to not alone sweep away old ingrained prejudices for a better or equal tutoring system, but also in thousands of different ways to adapt the country dweller's state of mind to useful reforms in the economic, social and political, if not also church issues. He could use the long winter evenings in an exceedingly entertaining and instructive manner in the warm living room surrounded by the entire family circle, speaking of or reading good books on agriculture, cattle breeding, home economics and so forth. He could at other times use accounts of travel by the different foreign people, manners and customs, or historical descriptions from the past and the present, etc., and thereby awaken the thirst for reading, thinking and knowledge among the younger generation, who soon would occupy the older people's place on this life's playground. Should he meet the more mature or more reflective rural man, — newspaper and state economic questions could give a rich material for his evening diversions. The public school never offers the teacher any such occasions for beneficial activity. In the countries where many people have reached such a stage of development, that the teacher's superiority is limited to his professional skills alone, as for instance in the United States, it is different. However, in Norway at that time, we had the opportunity, and I cannot imagine any position so full of interest and having the most wonderful chance with power, to use a lever to help the people's rise from centuries of social order and oppression. It would be impossible in a whole lifetime to forget the joy and the longing with which the young people from the township looked forward to the time when I once more returned to their house with my ambulatory school, or the heartfelt regret with which they again anticipated the time I would leave. The bond, which in a manner, was connected between the young teacher and his contemporaries in the district, was in a different way dedicated and more lasting than the bond made in the dance hall or at the wedding party. It normally happened that housewives and fathers were of the same bond, and one never knew how friendly one was to treat the teacher and make his stay at their home comfortable. How often do thoughts not dwell with relish on the young teacher's happy times, even now when the time of age has colored his locks white, how clear does the picture not stand out of the devoted, loving person, reflected in memory's mirror! Aye, there is magnificence in this, to be able to do with joy, faithfulness and diligence that which one thinks life's duties have lain upon us. In a life, so full of vicissitudes, of joys and sorrows, of fortune and misfortune, there is nothing as such that can evoke joy and comfort as memories from that time.

In pecuniary respect, it was not as bad as it had been depicted in the beginning, thanks to the good will and appreciation, to which one everywhere in the township considered my teaching work. The old sexton tithe, which in the first year did not amount to 5 *speciadaler*, went in the second and third year up to 20 to 25 *speciedaler* per annum, in addition to the very liberal offers, to which one never forgot me, through ecclesiastical dealings. After a lapse of three to four years, I quite unexpectedly received another, rather good source of income. My father's brother had in fact been employed as a vaccinator for the entire widespread and richly populated parish, but now found that his business suffered too much by his long absence in the best part of summer, when this work was to be done. He therefore offered to pass it over to me, or more correctly, to resign in my favor and recommending me as his successor. During the time of learning to use the vaccination lancet correctly, and with the necessary skills, such as learning to judge the vaccination authenticity, I stayed for a month in Bergen with the well-known Dr. Wisbeck. Equipped with his certificate I quietly sent my application to the Church and Education Department. As my father's brother in the last couple of years had neglected this task and quite neglected to make his usual vaccination journeys, it had been strongly suggested for each parish to share this task, so that each precentor was in charge of his own district. I greatly feared that if one was to know that the old vaccinator had resigned, one would enter into an agreement with the government about the contemplated application for sharing, and I expected therefore not to be employed for the entire parish. With luck, the idea of sharing had not reached the government, probably because the county did not wish to have so many uninformed people to take into account, and I accepted quite rightly, the commission as vaccinator for the entire parish. Luck had this time stood by me. As soon as the appointment was known, protests began against my employment for more than my own district, but it was now too late. The government would not overturn its own recruitment. As my predecessor in this connection, as said, had not performed his call, I had in the first two years a rather good harvest in that my calculation, including the seasonal work, went up to around 100 *speciedaler* yearly. Incidentally, I never later reached more than between 40 to 50 *speciedaler* per annum for the vaccination occupation. This was however of a big help. My summer vacations, which I until now had used in working for one or another farmer to help a little with my humble wage, were now completely taken over with vaccination trips. On these travels, I once more had the opportunity to establish many interesting acquaintances, and before many of the parishes' most enlightened and progressive rural men, to put forward my favorite theories about public education and what may be connected with such. I have reason to believe that the seed thus planted was never to be without fruit. At least I remember with great satisfaction, how important farmers came long distances to the places where my meetings were to be held, to speak with me about something that was a great joy for me to hear them mention with so much interest.

VIII.
Journey to England.

In the spring of 1835, after I had come of age and had received my inheritance, and also had saved up most of my earnings, except for what I bought books for, I found myself in the possession of some hundreds of *speciedaler*, of which I could just modestly boast, as none of my own age as far as I knew, could boast of having such an amount of cash. The more my curiosity was fostered by new books, the more widespread and stronger it became. Books could no longer satisfy me; I longed to go out in the world to see and experience some, of that which had come through descriptions to me in too sparse and vague a quality. I had an old teacher take my place in the school, and one of the assistants to take on the church singing, and turned to the parish pastor for permission to be absent for six months. The assistant pastor was to me, always a true friend, and when I explained to him that a good friend in Bergen, who in those days was intending to send a ship to Shields in England, had offered me a free journey to there in company with his son, who was going there to learn the language, he wrought without great difficulty the necessary permission from the old parish pastor, who incidentally was so good-natured that one might nearly persuade him to do anything as long as one would not neglect one's duty. I remember once during a bishop's visitation, when the bishop with firmness insisted that the parish pastor was to visit the ambulatory school, and the pastor in all humility, asked if the chaplain could not do this for him: "No!" answered the bishop exasperated, "You will do it!" — "It shall be done, it shall be done, your most reverend," answered the parish pastor, but however thought that this certainly would never in the remotest way happen, at least not as long as he was alive.

I had already a year ago started to read English, to which the visiting English, who already had begun to visit the fjord districts in Norway, had given me the greatest opportunity. During my stay in Bergen before the departure to England, I was at one of the city's bookstores to buy a couple of English books, at which time I came to say that I just then was about to undertake a voyage to Shields, Newcastle and some other places in the north of England, and therefore wished to make myself a little better acquainted with the language. He did not have the books I asked for, and perhaps it was this that put him in a bad mood, but I much feared that it was this good man's social pride that was unpleasantly affected; as it was, he became very angry and cried out in righteous indignation: "You, to England! What would *you* do in England? A Norwegian farmer to go to England — to learn English! The certitude of your nose however goes too far. Stick to the catechism and the psalmbook, it suits you better." The man was very indignant over what, he in agreement with most of his social companions, saw as a real scandal, to hear such talk from a farmer. I quote a few of the many instances of this kind, which happened to me during the thirty years I spent in Norway. This had not such a small amount of influence on my thought process and later life's destiny, for it showed how the atmosphere was in that part of Norway at that time between the dominant and subordinate classes. Though now everything is so immeasurably changed in this respect, thanks to the younger student body and adherents of New Norwegian's heroic efforts to adjust the gap between the two classes, without which one has finally discovered that it is impossible for Norway to keep up with the times. Pity is that one is a couple of hundred years too late in seeming to have discovered the truth that it depends on the foundation if a building is sturdy and will be lasting, that the multitude's destitution ultimately will devour the minority's riches and, like a magnificent building on a rotten foundation, will fall down in ruin.

The English journey had, as far as I can understand, an important influence on my future career; it was the first, though not the sole cause for a radical turn in my life's purpose for the future. I had as previously said, preferably yearned to go into business, but had nevertheless not dared to look beyond becoming a clerk. However, now I came into direct contact with shipping and foreign trade, and here there opened for me new scenes, positions and situations, of which before I only have had very obscure and imperfect notions. A shipment of grouse and other game from the *Hardangerfjeld* plateau, which I had been given permission to take with me, gave a very encouraging result in that it sold on the English market for more than double of what the price was in Bergen. The clothing wares I bought and brought back for that amount of money, also gave a very pleasing result, and served therefore even more to fortify me in an (as I later found out) exaggerated reason for the advantages of shipping and trade in foreign countries. The outward voyage took place under very favorable circumstances. The sea was relatively calm and with a persistent northeasterly wind, we sailed across the North Sea in three days and nights. It was the first time I found myself on the sea; it was the first time I saw my fatherland's rocky coast quickly disappear and hide behind the North Sea's *humped back*. Everything was wonderful and beautiful and confirmed the truth of the Norwegian poet's words: "The sea is beautiful, when it is calmly turning over a steel-shiny shield to cover the Viking's grave." I naturally had my bunk for'ard with the crew and was thus given a wonderful opportunity to become acquainted with the seaman's way of life and customs, which hitherto had been to me almost totally unknown. The first impression I had of the seaman's general character has by later experiences been wholly confirmed, and Wolf [Simon Olaus Wolff] is correct when he says: "The sea is wonderful, and wonderful sons are eternally nurtured in a primal embrace."

About the stay in England, I can be brief. Nearly all here that met one's eyes was new and different and made incessant claims upon my attention. A game merchant in Newcastle by the name of James Pape, showed me much kindness and went with me to most of the city attractions, amongst which the museum was the most important and had me extraordinarily interested, so that I later often spent a couple of hours here during the day. One had at that time only recently begun with the railroads in England, and I here was given the opportunity for the first time to try the journey with the railroad, from Newcastle to Shields and back. The flat fertile land in the River Tyne's valley district could do nothing but have an extraordinary interest for a person who had never been outside the mountain rich and rocky Bergen Diocese. My trips, partly on foot and partly by the mail coach, out in the rural districts, with stays in the so-called Inns by the wayside, were the most pleasant of the time I spent in England. The language gave me no problems in that I could make myself understood by the people and tell them where I was from, what I wanted and so forth. But, to understand them when they, as it seemed to me, allowed the tongue to go into a gallop, had unfortunately big difficulties and put me often at first into serious embarrassment. It was easy for the English to recognize the words when I pronounced them as they are written, but for me to recognize them from the sound, which often was very different from the spelling, I found it anything but funny, especially when I was caught in stupid mistakes. Nevertheless, after the first week the worst was over. The womenfolk were always easier to understand, as their voices were sharper and clearer for the unaccustomed ear. Mr. Pape's wife, who was responsible for sales during her husband's absence, and who always had so much to speak about, was of great help to me with the pronunciation of words, not only because she always spoke, but also because she purposefully pronounced each word clear and precise. Both she and her husband were very friendly and Christian-minded people; they bade me to come with them to church, where I for the first time heard English divine service. Mr. Pape also one day went with me to one of the city's big public schools, where I had the opportunity to institute some comparisons in regards to the teaching department, which as it happened, I did not find much different from the older schools in Bergen.

The young son of the Bergen shipping company, with which ship I had come over, and had been the main reason for my journey, was to remain at a business office for a year. When our ship after a six weeks elapse in time was ready to sail on the return voyage, came the question to me whether I should go back with the same ship or dare to stay until there was another passage available. The stay was expensive and I considered that under the strictest thrift, my small amount of accumulated capital would probably become rather exhausted, and somehow my six months permission could perhaps expire before I had a new passage back over the North Sea; at that time, there were actually no steam ships between the two countries, as there is now. Just as I one day aboard our ship, which was sail the next morning, stood and discussed this matter with our supercargo, — a proud, self-interested man, whose benevolence I nevertheless had won by running a multitude of errands into the town for him, — there arrived on board another captain from Bergen who sailed for the same shipping company. He said that he had just come up from Shields by railway and expected his ship up at the mouth of the river, as soon as the tide came in. He expected to lay there for several weeks before he was unloaded and once more take on a load of general cargo, which by and large takes a long time. I would therefore have an excellent opportunity to return with him, of which I immediately then came to agreement with. He was a very interesting, friendly and liberal man with whom I later came to be on a familiar relationship, and whom I have to thank for a number of services. The stay in England was thus extended for over three months, and Mr. Pape arranged for a part-time teacher for me, who came and read with me for an hour daily, for a very insignificant compensation.

A trader from Copenhagen by the name of T. Hansen, was living in Newcastle and was the representative for nearly all of the Norwegian and Danish skippers that arrived there. At the time when I was there, there arrived a considerable number of Danish sloops with loads of wheat, as the wheat duties, because of the lack of flour, had been lifted temporarily. This merchant Hansen had a son who also showed me a good deal of kindness during my stay in the town. He was a good-natured, sociable young man, who incidentally seemed to be a loafer, who would do nothing without having fun. Whenever and whereever he met me, he said, "I wish to drink a glass with you," and then he treated, but always only with a couple of small glasses of wine.

I had always found that language studies was that which I could do with ease, and my English began therefore at the end of the three months to become a little respectable, so that Mrs. Pape with great satisfaction could tell me that I now no longer needed to shake my head and say: *nichts verstehe* [understand nothing]. Insofar as the journey, it had therefore not been in vain; nevertheless, the results in other respects were of greater importance to me than language skills, which perhaps would be of little practical use. It had only just now really dawned for me, that the world in a manner lay open for me. Understanding was increased; the busy life in England, with the immense contrast between affluence and poverty had given my life philosophy a different direction; the small Norwegian caste system with its small moral indignations had been pushed into the background at the sight of the colossal factory and land monopolies in England. The business aristocracy began already here, to be as powerful as the nobility was. Accompanied with luck, the talented and industrious plebian could through his trading enterprises, raise himself up to the state of a plutocrat, run for parliament etc. The impressions I had through what I had seen, heard or experienced on my English journey, made me more hopeful, happy and contented in my position, than I had ever before been. I would with faithfulness and diligence, serve my seven years as a teacher, and in the meantime prepare myself for the commercial world, as far as circumstances would allow.

The home voyage with the skipper mentioned above, generated nothing worth mentioning. With a driving westerly, we went in a rapid speed over the North Sea, and in pouring rain, we came at full sail across the Bergenbar after two and a half days' journey. Was it not for the massive duty, which English factory and manufacturing goods were at that time subjected to, the profit would have been enormous on these goods. In those days, there took place, not such a small amount of smuggling along the Norwegian coast. The pilots could certainly tell about many a place where *Havstrilen* [derogatory name of an inhabitant of the coast, especially north and west of Bergen] would fetch loads of costly silk, jewels and the like, from the sides of the ships coming from England, whilst these ships would be behind the scheme. These people are of course complicit in the smuggling and can therefore not make a report without themselves being punished. Rain and stormy weather are of course the most favorable weather for these types of operations, because under these circumstances, only a few people are out and about.

Since there was still a couple of months left of the time that I was able to be away from the school, I spent the time in Bergen, where I always felt better than anywhere else. I had now won more friends here with whom my stay did not cost me, and in return, I now and then read with the children of the house. Some of my informative friends gave me ingress to their private libraries (there was no other public library than the lend-library at that time) and readily lent me the books I wished to read. Reading and private study was actually that which I at that time had intended to use my time for in Bergen; since I was not able to buy many books, and when I went back to my district, there was no one from whom I could borrow. In addition to a continuation of reading practice in German and English, it was especially history and geography as well as a number of travel portrayals, which now occupied most of my time, and I do not recall that any other two months of life have gone faster or been happier than these. On the journey home I reported once more to the pastor; he considered my trip to England from a rational standpoint, pronounced himself very satisfied with my undertaking and added that he wished truly many of the teachers would do something similar. During a visitation of the home parish's permanent school, which the dean held a short time thereafter, I had also arrived to see and hear how it was at our permanent school. As the assistant pastor presented me and told that I had been in England and so forth, it pleased the dean also to speak very approvingly, and he engaged himself with me for a quarter of an hour, without myself noticing any of the dark clouds, which during my religious examination were pulled up over his countenance. At my arrival home, I visited my old mother and several of my siblings. Mother was anything but happy about my adventurous life — which she called my stay in Bergen, my trip to England, aye, even my official trips as the parish's vaccinator. My siblings, who all were older than I was, and were engaged with agriculture in the parish, protested right seriously against the senseless use I made of my money. They complained fervently that I did not utilize this wonderful chance I had, to save together enough money to buy myself cultivated farmland, and prophesized for me, beggary, as an inevitable consequence of my reading madness. One of my brothers had gotten hold of a Norwegian language reader, which belonged to me; from this, he read for me: "I love, I have loved, I shall love" etc. and thereupon cried triumphantly: "The man who can put out money for such meaningless nonsense, must be mad." It mattered little that I took exception that he as such, in a Norwegian language reader, would again find his catechistic matter, but that it however could be helpful for that use. Just as a little plow was able to harrow with or a harrow to plow with, a grammar reader could be a religious book and vice versa. I recalled that from my childhood, in the strictest way, one had punished me for my inclination to reading. That I despite all opposition, had accomplished my purpose as well as possible, but I thought that the result however, was far better than they had predicted for me, and I would essentially give up my belief that also in the future it will go better than what had been predicted. My mother as well as my siblings loved me dearly, and their advice was meant sincerely. They were loyal people in the parish and strictly adhered to the old ancestral customs and the inherited traits, whilst I in my association with books and men of the ruling class, as well as with strangers, had lost much of the old habits; many biases were refined and many a life philosophy was particularly progressively changed. This change manifested itself still clearer in contact with the people in my school district, and it saddens me often to find an increasing incongruity with some of those who previously had for the most, been passive adversaries. In school, I once more worked with renewed vigor and won full appreciation from my superiors as well as a right encouraging appreciation from the majority of the parents in the district. The school commission had arranged a small prize for the best ambulatory school in the parish. There were fifteen districts in addition to the public school, and as my district, in respect of its locality, was less fortunately situated, I had not thought I would have come into consideration for the award. As the assistant pastor was the only one who visited all the schools, we came to an agreement that his recommendation should be decisive, and he did not need to think for a moment before he announced — that in his opinion, there could be no doubt to whom the prize rightly belonged. His reasons were briefly explained and unanimously acceded, and the following Sunday he presented me with the prize in church, before the congregation with a few remarks, that for me, were certainly very flattering. So here I had gained some laurels, of which I had never dreamed — in fact all my thoughts and pursuits of late had been so fully absorbed by my duties and the new changing prospects, that my personal pride, of which I without doubt had my share, was pushed well into the background.

IX.
Attempt to Create a Reading Society.

In a periodical, which name I have now forgotten, I found published a catalogue of books, which the author deemed most appropriate for public libraries. This aroused the thought in me to attempt to create a reading society in our parish. Reading societies and parish societies existed already in some of the parishes, but with us there was yet no such bearing, and I had many a time sincerely felt the lack thereof. Now it became a clear and strong conviction with me that a well chosen, though small parish library, would be of the most effective way for public education's encouragement, and I therefore immediately began with all the zeal and impatience, with which I at this young age, took hold of everything that interested me. There existed in our parish a few more enlightened, open-minded and forward striving men, who had always stood side by side with me in those battles, which the old and the new nearly always conduct against each other. They immediately went head over heels along with my plan; the necessary statutes were prepared, and an invitation to a reading society was issued. Every member was at the commencement to pay 3 *speciedaler* and thereafter an annual subscription of 1 *speciedaler*, which we thought in a few years would give us a respectable little collection of books, provided we received the expected number of members, and hereof naturally, the matter's outcome was dependent. Actually, more signed up than we had dared hope for, and the society soon counted thirty members. For the first purchase, we actually had nearly 100 *speciedaler*. A committee of five members was elected to compile a list of the books that we should buy first. As far as I now recall, it was Henr. Wergeland, who had done the compilation for the parish library's catalogue which I had found, and from this the committee now made its choice, and it was to me delegated, to travel to Bergen and attend to the buying. From some old scraps of letters that are still found in among my papers, I herewith write the names of some of the books that were found in the first collection that was bought: *Sverdrups Magazin,* 4 Volumes [Sverdrup's Magazin on Agriculture]*; Norges offentlige Ret* [Norway's Public Law]*; Priis's Haugekunst* [Priis' Cairn Craft]*; Platous Geograf* [Platou's Geography]*; Primons Lexikon* [Jacob Carl Frederik Primon's Dictionary of foreign words and expressions, with equivalents, used in the Danish language. Published in 1807.]*; Det vigtigste af Naturlæren* [The most important of Nature Lessons]*; Filosofi for ulærde* [Philosophy for beginners]*; Jurks Naturhistorie* [Jurk's Natural History – Zoology – Botany]*; Neumans Haandbog* [Possibly Henry Neuman's Maritime Pocket Dictionary]*; Paludans Raad for syge* [Paludan's Advice for the Sick]; *Husdyrenes Behandling* [Animal Husbandry]; *Abildgaards Heste- og Kvægavl* [Abildgaard's Horse and Cattle Breeding]; *Boyes Regnebog* [Boye's Book of Arithmetic]; *Holst's juridiske Haandbog* [Holst's Legal Handbook]; *Odeens Regnebog* [Odeen's Arithmetic Book]; *Blatz om Havekunsten* [Blatz – on the art of gardening]; *Viborg om Svineavlen* [Viborg – on pig farming]; *Willaume om Mennesket* [Willaume – on man]; *Newton for Ungdommen* [Newton for Youth. Textbook for the higher religion classes. Published 1806.]; *Kunsten at blive rig og lykkelig* [The Art of becoming Rich and Happy]; *Falch om Fiskeri* [Falch on Fishing]; *Hus- og Reiselæge* [Home and Ambulatory Doctor]; *Hirschfeldt om Frugttræer;*[Hirschfeldt – on fruit trees] *Dalgas Lærebog i Agerbruget* [Dalga's Textbook of Agriculture]; *Mallings store og gode Handlinger* [Malling's Great and Good Deeds]; *Naturlæren og Naturhistorien* [Lessons in Nature and Natural History]; *Haandbog for Omgangsskoler* [Handbook for Ambulatory Schools]; *Munthes Fædrelands Historie* [Munthe's History of the Fatherland]; *Platous Verdenshistorie* [Platou's World History]; *Odelsmands Tanker* [Thoughts of a Freeholder – Commonly known as Ola-boka, was a freeholders thoughts about Norway's plight, by John Nergaard. The book is an attack on the official class and a call to the farmer to employ political means to better his lot.]; *Almanakmanden* [The Encyclopedia Man], etc., etc. I have here mentioned this many of our books, so as to show how difficult it was at that time and in this area where I lived, to be able to satisfy the public; for this choice of books, which I was mainly given the blame for, brought me so many troubles that I can never forget it. I had no personal knowledge myself about these books, and it never occurred to me that in such books there could be found anything offensive to religion or the church, morals or ethics. Yet, the reading society, because of its books, was showered with the most serious accusations of unbelief and depravity by those who had worked against the undertaking, so that even some of members became frightened and wanted nothing more to do with the matter. As far as I can remember, it was the last mentioned book, which tried to explain the astronomical calculations in our almanacs and make the basis of astronomy understandable for the everyday person, that first aroused suspicion and resistance. In there, one found written and explained, the principle that that the sun did not revolve around the earth, but that it was the earth's daily movement on its axis that produced the sun's apparent journey around the earth. Also that it was the earth's annual motion in an oval circuit that produced the season changes — not the sun's movement towards the south or north, which one until now, had normally believed. It was thought this book would therefore make the Bible's word a lie, where it states that God, because of

Joshua's prayer, made the sun stand still in the sky for a whole day, to give him time to complete his enemy's defeat in a pitched battle that was happening at that time. It contained then a heretical and soul corrupting doctrine, and those that belonged to the reading society must be unbelieving Huns and Turks, of which one was not to speak of in the community. Now that the superstitious suspicions had awakened, it was not long before there was found one or another item that was wrong in almost every book, and therefore it was indeed wrong to read in secular books. Reading should only be used for reading the Word of God, and therefore it was a dreadful blasphemy to read about horse diseases and the swine husbandry —it was all *Historiebøker* [storybooks] and mendacious fables one had received for one's money. They who read such books must therefore be heathens, as there was not found in them a single word of God.

This time I had actually badly underestimated myself; to come with explanations did not help and the indignation was so great that the pastor did not dare to defend me. I had also not consulted him as to which books we should choose, and could therefore not expect him to make himself unpopular with the community, from whom he received his offering and tithing, at least not with defending the books, which he himself must not have seen as appropriate for reading by the populace. As far as the members were concerned, about half of them began to buckle under the strain and began to ask for their money back as they did not wish to own any part in such books, or be known to be a member of a society that acclaimed beliefs such as these. The other half, which consisted of more enlightened and unprejudiced men of a younger age, closed formation around me, determined not to be bullied by such an unreasonable fanaticism. As for the wavering members, they showed them that they were laughable in their ideas and asked them to explain how it could be a larger sin to read about animal husbandry, tree planting, horticulture etc. than to speak of this, which they often did. As far as the earth's and the sun's movement was concerned, then it was just as easy for the Almighty to let one as the other stand still, if he thought best, and that one probably better not worry oneself over God's providential secrets. Moreover, there was after all considerable disagreement between the theologians themselves concerning this passage, and it must therefore seem best for the laypeople not to get hung up in these difficult places, which simply would cause anxiety and discord; but rather let the church's appointed authorities decide. At least one should give a little time to read these books themselves and see for oneself what really was taught in them, see what they actually were about, and not let oneself be upset by people, who one knew still showed opposition to all knowledge and enlightenment. They, who then, after such a full and impartial examination, continued with their intention to walk out, would receive their contingent back. The final outcome was that only just a few resigned, less because of their superstitions, than because their reading ability and intellect development was so restricted, that they could not read and even less understand most of the books, and therefore found very little interest in them. However, whilst these departed, others with greater reading ability and less fettered thoughts, signed themselves up as members, so that the venture actually did not fall through, but nevertheless became much crippled and restricted in its activities. Even my own work at school was thereby placed in a shadow, which in several places made it chilly and unpleasant for me. And when it was actually among them, that I was to try to win support for the case of enlightenment — the healthy had you see, no need for a cure, but for those who were ailing — I felt much more distress because of my position. The pastors were enlightened men, and one of them I could even call liberal. Between themselves, and with their professional brethren, they often laughed mutually at the common people's narrow-mindedness; but they were careful, clever conservative men, who meant that one should not for the sake of an idea, make enemies among those one could need one day to benefit from. Besides that, it went quick enough with the new reforms, which perhaps could lead one to where one did not want. Our opponents therefore had their zeal much inflated, when they found that the pastor, who hereto had always assisted me in regards to all school matters, now did not give me any further praise. A couple of years later, from the Church and Education Department, there came a regulation in regards to parish libraries, wherein the pastor in every parish was to decide which books should be allowed to be acquired in the reading societies. Herewith, was aroused for the first time my attention for the government's politics —a matter I until now had not thought much about. I saw now that one in higher places did not wish it to go quickly with public education, but that smidgens had to be distributed slowly and dispersed with a wary hand over a long time period so as to avoid revolutionary tendencies; such as the government politics were, such must also the official stand throughout the country be. I for my part had come too far, and so had many of my young friends in the parish. Hence, in the later years, several of the young school teachers, as well as others who intended to become teachers, began to come to me to receive tutoring, and there in a manner appeared a type of spontaneous teacher's college, which promised important results. It was possible that I had come outside my designated field of activity. A few faithful friends in the ruling class made me understand that if I was not careful I could easily receive a contrary wind, which would be more dangerous than the people's bigotry. A letter I had written to a friend in regards to a good many official questions, and wherein I partly pointed out the barriers how the caste system was hindering public education, had through the recipient's negligence come into the wrong hands. When I one day, during a sitting of the *Storthing*, was waiting in the office of the bailiff where I was to receive my vaccination fee, I opened a book that was on the windowsill to look into it. Among one's peers this would not be an offence against etiquette; on the contrary, it is after all something normal that one show the waiting person good manners, by giving them a newspaper or book to while away their time whilst one cannot entertain them with conversation. However, here there were no peers, and the clerk who was present became very indignant over my impertinence and asked in an incensed tone what it was I was doing. It was not a book for farmers (it was a Danish novel whose title I have forgotten). My superior had shown me too much kindness, I had become rude and paid my benefactors with ingratitude, as one had found out that I was a pettifogger and one will sure enough put a stopper to my work among the public. Before I could reply or give an explanation to this man of compliments, whom I did not even know, the bailiff came in and immediately attended to my business without uttering a word, and it was only some time later I found out that my letter had been the object of Mr. Bailiff's attention.

X.
Commercial Enterprises.

All these things in conjunction with the decision I had earlier stated, that had been conceived during my trip to England, determined me now to resign as soon as my contract had expired. In truth, I had already after my homecoming from England, bought a share in a large *Hardangerjægt* [small cargo ship with a half deck and sails] and had contributed to some commercial enterprises, without even so far as to have used some of my own time therewith. Had it not been for the forbidding cold — for want of calling it by any better name, — which I met both from above and from below during my work with the promotion for public enlightenment, it is nevertheless very likely that I would have stayed with the teaching profession, which I by nature almost seemed destined. Now however, there was no doubt left in me as to what I should do. I had you see, still far from gone through the school of life long enough, I had still not by a long shot gone through the trials, the adversity and the suffering, which are challenged to bring forth the wisdom and temperance, without which a fiery youthful nature never rightly knows what best serves him. The mature experiences later showed me that I had tensed the bow too hard. Why not be patient and temporize? Why not cast off something of secondary importance here and there, to still save the main concern? Rome was not built in a day. When one could use centuries to complete a single church building to praise the Lord, why not be content with laying stone upon stone in the glorious building of public education, without being anxious that it was going so slow? There is yet another building that must be constantly built upon from generation to generation, without being able to say that it is finished. However, it lies not in the heart of the young's nature to seek comfort against ingratitude and misunderstanding in one's intentions, and continues with integrity; this belongs to the ripe old age. I nevertheless had many devoted and loyal friends, who sincerely lamented the decisive step I was now to take and assured me that I would come to regret it. I myself had a sense of apprehension hereof when I looked back at the years I had here spent. I had however had it so good, and I had been privileged to work with greater success in my simple call, than my predecessors. The children had always loved, respected and obeyed me; my like aged had all loved me and enjoyed my company, tutoring and advice. The bonds of friendship that had here been linked would now once more be cut, and I was again out among strangers to break a new path. But sentimentality did not have any great hold over me, ingratitude and misunderstanding was nevertheless the coin one most wanted to pay with for the position I held, whilst trade and shipping's changing scenes and storms, promised a far more unrestricted playground for a spirit that had never been satisfied without a restless motion.

At the time here mentioned, the so-called *Hardangerjægter* had come into a great deal of use. Some industrious and enterprising men had in a short time, saved together fortunes from the rich fisheries, which at that time went along the west coast of Norway both in winter and in summer. With a cousin who had some experience in the field, I decided to try my luck as a skipper. I do not here intend to give any detailed report on the three busy and eventful years I spent in this business. The experiences I had cannot have any great general interest, and it is perhaps enough to say that what lady luck in the one year generously gave, she often took back the following year. Sometimes I owned a couple of thousand *dalers,* and then again, nearly nothing, and when the earning of money in the world of trade is always the main thing, there seemed to be a long prospect in reaching the desired goal. The thought of immigrating to America was therefore again strongly manifested within me. I sold therefore what personal effects I had, and when all accounts were settled, I had with all my toil and drudgery, not been able to save as much as one thousand *daler*. Now, whether it is blind chance or inevitable fate that makes it that the one person can barely touch a business without fortune favoring him, and another person with all his diligence and thoughtfulness can never win the favor of lady luck. Herewith, let it be as it may. The outcome was that I in the spring of 1843 left for America.

XI.
Life in America.

About this journey, it is told a little earlier in this small book, and it shall not here be repeated. Also about the pioneer life in Wisconsin it is earlier told, so that it does not here seem necessary to add more. About what little I was able to accomplish between the pioneers in the so-called Yorkville Settlement, I can be brief. Public education was, as one has seen, my obsession. As a former teacher I lived for the interest of the education system, had an active part in the creation of an English school for the district, worked for the creation of a school library, debate societies and singing societies. I wrote an application to the postal service in Washington about establishing a postal route through the settlement. Equipped with numerous signatures and a request from the Legislature of Wisconsin, the application was sent to Washington where it was immediately granted and a postal route established. It is nearly thirty years now, since the North Cape post office was established, and K. Adland, who is still in office, was appointed postmaster. This post office is in the center of the settlement and has exercised an incalculable influence for enlightenment and progress in the community. Had this postal route not been opened just when it was, three months later, it would have been sidetracked elsewhere, and the people in the settlement would have needed to go six to ten miles to the post office. One can scarcely calculate what effect this would have on correspondence and newspaper reading. It was always with satisfaction that I saw the ever-increasing astuteness and development of all that was good and useful among the Norwegians in this place. Moreover, it gladdened me to know that it had fallen to my lot to make the first steps in this direction. In another place in this book it is discussed my part of the publication of the first Norwegian newspaper in America and shall not be repeated here.

In the year of 1860, I was a member of the legislature, and as such, it fell again to my lot to do my neighborhood a service. There was you see, in the Town of Norway, a stretch of swampland of 2,500 acres, which belonged to the so-called Drainingsfond and owned by the state. To give this land to the Town of Norway I sent in a bill, compiled with great care by one of the state's best lawyers. This bill became, after a hard struggle, accepted by both houses and became law. This land was then sold to the surrounding farmers for a low price and the proceeds were used for its draining by means of ditches. Instead of having so far been a source for malaria and other diseases for the surrounding population, it now became a good source of income as a rich hay and pastureland, and the said law must be seen as being of not so little use for the neighborhood.

It had long been discussed by my friends in Chicago, that I should come there and make a new attempt with a Norwegian newspaper; but when I myself had found the experience costly and also seen how unfortunate it had been for others, I could not give them any encouraging answer. Finally, in the summer of 1865, Mr. John Anderson came out to my farm in Racine County, when he on a visit to his wife's parents found himself in Racine. He had arrived in Chicago with his parents at a very young age and had learned the art of printing at the *Chicago Tribune*, and my friends had recommended him to me as well suited to manage the printing business. Nevertheless, there was at that time nothing definite decided, as I still had misgivings about engaging myself with this hazardous venture. Early in spring of the following year, he once more came out there and brought with him a letter of recommendation from Iver Lawson, wherein it stressed the idea of a little monetary support, should this be needed, as well as assurance that he regarded Mr. Anderson competent as a printer and business manager. This conquered my scruples and the result was that the first edition of *Skandinaven* was published on the 1st June 1866. Mr. Marcus Thrane had a couple of months earlier begun his *Norske Amerikaner* in Chicago. Furthermore, we had the two leading Norwegian newspapers in Wisconsin, that is, *Emigranten* in Madison and *Fædrelandet* in La Crosse. Everyone therefore thought that our enterprise was hopeless and would end with defeat of the *Skandinaven*. Hereof one became disappointed as the *Skandinaven* found unexpected support from the people, and when Mr. Thrane delivered his subscription list to the *Skandinaven* for a small incentive, the *Skandinaven* quickly gained a large circulation and its future was secured. My work as editor of the *Skandinaven,* lay us too near for here to need any further mention. As an old abolitionist, I was always an avid champion of the Republican Party's principles as long as I managed the editorials, and how much or how little this had to do with the paper's fortunate progress with the people, I do not know. Probably it was a skilled business performance and a thrifty management of the print shop that saved the paper from the fate that had been predicted.

My defense for the American public school, apart from my political activity, was probably the highlight of my editorial work and led to the unexpected honor that one of Chicago's elementary schools was named after me.

The lengthy discussion about slavery and public schools attracted a widespread attention and credited greatly to the paper's circulation everywhere that Norwegians lived.

In 1880, I was through a suggestion by Editor [Ferdinand A.] Husher, nominated as one of Wisconsin's electors on the Republican ticket. This was a tribute, which presumably should be a reward for a long and faithful service to the party, and I do not deny, that the nomination could as such have its worth; but seen from a worker's standpoint, who shall feed himself through hard work, it is the monetary value he for the most looked at. For the day that the voters spent in Madison during the election, they received $2.50, whilst the stay in the hotel cost them $3.00 — hence, a loss of 50 cents. It is often so that when an office has a monetary value, there are thousands who apply, and it is difficult to obtain. It is the general experience I have had in political affairs, and I suppose that this was the reason for this tribute to be given to me without I having asked thereof. I am not ungrateful for the favor my countrymen had shown me during the convention by their united appearance for me. However, when it later was told in my neighborhood, that I had now been given a government office that would immediately make me a rich man, depended on, as one will see above, a misunderstanding of the matter.

What later happened in Washington and also came into view in such a sad way in their struggle concerning the change, has put me in great hesitation over party politics and given me a loathing for it. I have therefore advised my countrymen for greater independence and versatility in their political activities. President Garfield's assassination, the shocking political ambition chasing in Washington, Blaine's intrigues against Roscoe Conkling, his opinion to Garfield on backbone [standing up to the opposition], from which Conkling's defeat was instigated, the republican's election defeat in New York and Cleveland — all this opened my eyes for party politics' destruction, and the danger, which through the blind fury of the party, endangered the country, and I came to a full and firm conviction that the great republican majorities had brought ruthless politicians to the forefront, and that it had become a necessity to use the brakes to hold them in check. The parties are to keep each other in check, and this they could only do when their voting numbers were somewhat similar. A bit of independence among the voters is therefore good — aye, this is apparently the election's essence. The same also happens when our countrymen seek nominations. When a convention ignores our nationality and so to say, spits in our faces, we should not cry and bawl like a thrashed child, but hit back as adults at the ballot box. It is the only weapon that causes anxiety for the politicians, and they who use it get their wish until the next time; therefore, one shall of course have the majority vote for one's ticket.

Nordmændene i Amerika.
Nogle Optegnelser om De Norskes Udvandring til Amerika.
Af Knud Langeland.

Chicago.
John Anderson & Co., Udgivere,
183, 185 og 187 N. Peoria Street.
1888.

Skandinavens Boghandel.
Skandinavens Bog— og Accidentstrykkeri,
Indbunden i Skandinavens Bogbinderi,
183, 185 og 187 N. Peoria St., Chicago, Ill.

Indledning.

Vistnok ville ikke vore Efterkommere paa den vestlige Jorddel, efter Aarhundreders Forløb, saaledes maatte søge forgjeves efter Oplysninger om deres Fædres første Indvandring til Amerika, som vi nu med Begjerlighed forgjeves søger at løfte Forgangenhedens Slør fra vore Forfædres Indvandring til de skandinaviske Lande. Mod en saadan Tomhed og fuldstændig Mangel paa historiske Vidnesbyrd er Menneskeslægtens fremskredne Tidsalder Borgen. Selv om vi forudsætter som en Mulighed, at Historien, med sin Tilbagegang og sine mørke Tidsaldere, gjentager sig i de kommende som i de forbigangne Aarhundreder, vil dog neppe den skandinaviske Indvandring til Amerika forsvinde af Historien, saalænge der paa Jordens Kreds findes en Levning af vor Nationalitet, for hvem saadanne historiske Minder har nogen Interesse. Det er ikke et saa fjernt Syn paa Sagen, som har bevæget mig til at nedtegne disse Erindringer. Men der er en nærliggende Fremtid, som udentvivl vilde føle Savnet af slige Optegnelser og med rette beklage sig over vor Forsømmelse og Ligegyldighed i denne Henseende, om vi nu allesammen, enten af Mistillid til os selv, eller af andre Grunde, ventede paa, at dygtigere Hænder, eller Mænd med bedre Anledning, skulde paatage sig Gjerningen, indtil alle de tidligere Indvandrere med deres personlige Erindringer og oplevede Erfaringer laa i Graven, hvorfra deres Erindringer ikke mere kunde hentes op. At gjøre sit til at afhjælpe et saadant Savn hos vore nærmest paafølgende Generationer burde derfor fritage Nedskriveren fra Beskyldninger for Indbildskhed og Forfængelighed. Lad derimod ret mange gjøre saadanne Optegnelser, selv om de — ligesom mine — iføres en simpel Hverdagsdragt. Det er ikke Meningen at levere noget fuldendt historisk Arbeide, men derimod det Tømmer og de Stene, som den simple Arbeider bringer den øvede Bygningsmand, for at han deraf kan opføre den historiske Bygning. Vilde nu til Ex. en Mand fra hvert Udvandringsselskab levere saadanne Optegnelser, fik man snart et rigt Forraad, som ved en øvet Haands Bearbeidelse kunde gjøres til noksaa interessante Aarbøger. Mon ikke Tiden snart er kommen til at gjøre en Begyndelse hermed, og mon ikke det snart bliver for sent at kunne naa dette Maal?

Det er Forfatterens Bidrag til dette Maal, som hermed frembæres.

I.
Folkevandringer.

Folkevandringer synes at have foregaaet fra Menneskeslegtens første Tider. Udvandringer blandt Noas tidligste Efterkommere omtales hyppig i Bibelen, ja Gud befalede endog Abraham at udvandre. "Vorder frugtbare, formerer Eder og opfylder Jorden," var et Bud, som stemmede med Naturens Orden, thi det udgik fra Naturens Herre. Da Græsgangene paa Bethels Sletter blev altfor indskrænkede, trættede Hyrdefolket om dem, og Abraham og Lot drog hver sin Vei. Saaledes antages det at have gaaet til mellem Menneskene i de forhistoriske Tider, og senere bærer Verdenshistorien nok af Vidnesbyrd om større og mindre Folkevandringer.

Mægtige Stammer trængte frem fra forskjellige Dele af Asien mod Vesten gjennem Egnene ved det sorte Hav og Donaulandene. Gotherne trykkedes ind paa det store romerskke Riges Grændser, fordi Hunnerne væltede sig ind paa dem fra Østen. Efter de historiske Granskeres Mening skal disse Folkebevægelser være udgaaede fra det gamle Iranien eller de nuværende indiske og persiske Høilande. Til disse Udvandringer regnes ogsaa den germaniske og den norrøne Folkestamme, som i to ligeløbende Linier er draget fra Øst mod Vest, indtil de ned gjennem Tiden naaede lige til Østersøen, hvorfra de har udbredt sig mod Syd og Nord og endelig sat sig fast i de tydske og skandinaviske Lande. Den bekjendte norske Historiker [Jakob Rudolf] Keyser holder for, at vore Fædre er komne til de sidstnævnte Lande en 400 á 500 Aar før vor Tidsregning, og at den norrøne Stamme dels er gaaet over den bothniske Bugt, dels nord om samme, og at de derfra er trængte mod Syd; at der paa den Tid allerede fandtes Nomadefolk, som kaldtes Finner, Lapper, Kelter og Kimbrer; at disse efterhaanden trængtes afveien — Finnerne mod det yderste Norden i Norge, Sverige og Rusland,

Kelterne og Kimbrerne mod Syd og Vest lige til England, Irland og Skotland — og at endelig Norrønerne trængte de gothiske Germaner, som var komne til det sydlige Sverige, Danmark og Slesvig, længere mod Syd og Vest, hvorved atter Anglerne og Saxerne trængtes fra deres Opholdssteder over til Brittanien.

II.
Amerikas Opdagelse.

Flere Aarhundreder senere drev Harald Haarfagers Undertrykkelser mange af vore bedste nordiske Fædre over til Island og Færøerne, hvorfra de paa deres Søreiser tilfældigvis opdagede Amerika. Sagaerne fortæller, at Nordmændene foretog mange Reiser til Landet i Vesten, som de kaldte Vinland, og anlagde en Koloni ved Kysten af Massachusetts, som de kaldte Leifsboder. Da den sorte Død indtraf omkring 1350, glemte man i Norge og Island Veien til den nye Verden, og Formodningen er, at de norske Kolonister i Leifsboder, da de ingen Tilførsel mere fik fra Moderlandet, blandedes med Landets Urindbyggere, Indianerne (de saakaldte Skrællinger). Der er en dunkel Anelse om, at de Gravhøie og andre Oldtidsminder, som paa mange Steder forefindes i de Forenede Stater og som ikke kan skrive sig fra Indianerne, maaske er Spor af de mellem dem værende Nordmænd. Hermed være det nu som det vil. Meget mere sandsynligt er det, at Kristofer Kolumbus paa sin bekjendte Reise til Island har først hørt Fortællingen om det mod Vest liggende Vinland og at dette gav Anledning til hans Opdagelsesreise mod Vesten, som endte med Amerikas Gjenopdagelse i 1492.

III.
Udvandrings - Aarsager.

Aarsagerne til Folkevandringerne kan være forskjellige: dels Nomadelivet og de ufuldkomne Jagtredskaber, hvorfor store Landstrækninger behøvedes for det i Stammerne tilvoxende Folketals Underholdning; dels de barbariske Tider, da den Stærkere uden videre med Magt fordrev den Svagere; dels maaske ogsaa ifølge Stammens frie Valg og Beslutning.

Nordmændenes Vikingetog maa ansees dels som ligefremme Overfald og Plyndringer i Nabolandene, dels som en raa Tidsalders Øvelsestogt og Krigsførelse. Vi læser, at de paa disse Tog ofte besøgte Englands, Irlands og Skotlands Kyster saavelsom Tydskland og Frankrige; at de i det sidstnævnte Land stiftede en Koloni, som endnu kaldes Normandiet og hvorfra Normannernes Erobringshære udgik, som erobrede England osv.

Spaniernes første Udvandring til Amerika efter Kolumbus' Opdagelse bestod af en Skare Eventyrere, som søgte did for at finde Guld og Sølv, og det var først senere at de begyndte at anlægge Kolonier. Under Dronning Elisabeths [I] Regjereng kom Englænderne til Østkysten af Nordamerika og efter nogle forgjeves Forsøg lykkedes det dem at stifte en Koloni i Virginia. Det synes især at have været Handelsinteressen, som besjælede dem, medens paa samme Tid Puritanerne og Hugenoterne reiste til Amerika for at søge Religionsfrihed og undgaa de haarde Religionsforfølgelser, som de maatte udstaa i deres Hjemlande, England og Frankrige. I 1624 anlagde nogle Nordmænd en Koloni i det nuværende New Jersey, og en By, som de kaldte Bergen, bærer endnu dette Navn. I den samme Egn anlagdes ogsaa en svensk Koloni, men Hollænderne, som dengang havde nedsat sig i New York, var saa talrige, at de absorberede alt omkring sig, indtil de selv maatte bukke under for det engelske Element.

Vor Tids nordiske Standsaristokrati gjør Fordring paa at nedstamme fra de gamle til Norge og Sverige indvandrede Høvdingeætter, og at Bønderne nedstammer fra de Livegne eller Trællestanden. Historiens Vidnesbyrd bekræfter ikke denne Forudsætning. Det er derimod hævet over al Tvivl, at den nuværende Embedsstand og de saakaldte øvre Samfundslag oprindelig stammer fra den tydske Adel, som gjennem de tydske Konger i Danmark importeredes for at skaffe dem Levebrød og Magt i Embederne og være den fornødne Støtte for Kongemagten.

IV.
Det første norske Udvandrerselskab.

Det er en Afdeling af den gamle Heltestammes Efterslegt, de norske Bønders Udvandring til Amerika i den nyere Tid, vi her skal omtale. Alle saavel skriftlige som mundtlige Beretninger, Forfatteren har kunnet raadføre sig med, samstemmer i, at Cleng Peerson fra Skjolds Præstegjæld i Stavanger Amt var den, som egentlig gav den første Anledning til de norske Bønders Udvandring til Amerika. Det var i Aaret 1821, at han og en Kammerat ved Navn Knud Eide forlod Fædrelandet for at undersøge Forholdene i Amerika. Religionstvang blev paa den Tid temmelig strengt udøvet i Norge, hvor der viste sig Tegn til Afvigelser. I Stavanger Amt var Hauges Tilhængere talrige, og dernæst havde Kvækerne ikke saa faa Tilhængere. Disse sidste blev især stærkt forfulgte. Forfatteren ved, at Fortællingerne om Kvækerforfølgelserne ikke er nogen tvivlsom Tradition. Paa Præsternes Anklage kom Lensmanden med sine Mænd og tog Kvækernes Børn med Magt og førte dem til Præsten for at døbes og for at konfirmeres, og hvis Forældrene ikke kom til Alters som de andre i Menigheden, blev de mulkterede—ei at tale om, at de maatte betale sin Afgift til Statskirken, uagtet de selv ikke benyttede den. Dette Forhold var den nærmeste Aarsag til, at de to nævnte Mænd udsendtes af Kvækerne for at undersøge Tilstanden i Amerika. Der er flere paalidelige Mænds Udtalelser om, at dette forholder sig saa, og derfor ser vi ogsaa, at der, da Cleng Peerson efter tre Aars Ophold i Amerika kom tilbage i 1824, organiseredes det første norske Udvandringsselskab i Stavanger, som næsten udelukkende bestod af Kvækere fra Stavanger og Skjolds Præstegjæld. Det var de ofte omtalte Sluppefolk, et Selskab paa 52 Personer, som med eget Skib afgik fra Stavanger den 4 Juli 1825. Efterfølgende om dette Selskabs eventyrlige Reise til Amerika gjengives dels efter Ole Rynnings lille Bog om Amerika (trykt i Christiania 1838), dels efter mundtlige Fortællinger fra enkelte af Deltagerne selv.

"I 1821 kom en Person ved Navn Cleng Peerson, fra Stavanger Amt i Norge, over til New York i de Forenede Stater. I 1824 var han en Snartur tilbage til Norge, og ved hans Fortællinger om Amerika vaktes hos flere Lysten at reise didhen. Et Udvandrerselskab paa 52 Personer kjøbte en liden Slup for 1,800 Spd., som de lastede med Jern for at gaa til New York. Skipperen og Styrmanden vare selv delagtige i denne Spekulation. De passerede gjennem Kanalen og løb ind i en liden Udhavn paa Kysten af England, hvor de begyndte at sælge Brændevin, som der er en forbuden Vare. Da de mærkede hvilken Fare de derved havde udsat sig for, maatte de i største Hast igjen søge tilhavs. Formedelst Skipperens Ukyndighed eller Modvind kom de saa langt Syd som til Madeiraøerne. Her fandt de en Tønde Madeiravin svømmende paa Havet, hvilken de halede til sig og begyndte at pumpe og drikke. Da hele Mandskabet var beskjænket, kom Skibet drivende som et Pestskib ind i Havnen, uden Kommando og uden at heise Flag. En Bremer som laa paa Reden raabte til dem, at de øieblikkelig maatte heise Flag, dersom de ikke vilde hilses af Fæstningens Kanoner, som virkelig alt vare rettede mod dem; og nu fik omsider en af Passagererne Flaget fat og fik det heiset. Efter disse og flere Farer naaede de endelig New York. De havde i det hele været 14 Uger fra Stavanger til Amerika. Imidlertid var ingen død paa Reisen og alle Mand vare friske ved Landingen. I New York vakte det almindelig Forundring, at de Norske havde vovet sig over det vide Hav paa et saa lidet Fartøi, hvilket hidtil var uhørt. Ved Uvidenhed eller Misforstaaelse havde man bemandet Skibet med flere Mand, end de amerikanske Love tillode, hvorfor der blev lagt Arrest paa Skipperen med Skib og Ladning. Nu kan jeg ikke med Vished sige, enten Regjeringen af sig selv hævede Arresten, i Betragtning af vore gode Landsmænds Uvidenhed og barnagtige Fremfærd, eller om Kvækerne alt nu havde taget sig af dem; nok er det: Skipperen slap fri og Skib med Ladning gaves Eierne tilbage. De tabte dog meget ved sammes Salg, som ikke indbragte dem mere end 400 Dollars. — Ved Kvækernes Sammenskud fik de Hjælp til at komme længere ind i Landet. To af Følget nedsatte sig i Rochester og en af disse ved Navn Lars Larsen hvis Enke bor endnu der. De øvrige kjøbte sig Land 5 Mile nordvest for Rochester i Morris County. Her maatte de give fem Daler for en Acre; men da de ikke havde Penge at betale med, skulde Betalingen erlægges terminsvis i ti Aar. Enhver kjøbte omtrent 40 Acres. Landet her var tæt bevoxet med Skov og tungt at rydde. De 4—5 første Aar vare derfor meget møisommelige for disse Folk. De led ofte stor Nød og ønskede sig kun tilbage til Norge; men de saa ingen Mulighed til at komme der, uden at opofre den sidste Skjærv af deres Formue, og de vilde ikke komme tilbage som Tiggere. Dog — velgjørende Naboer understøttede dem, og ved egen Flid fik de omsider deres Jord i saadan Stand, at de kunde leve af den, ja leve bedre end i deres gamle Fødeland." Saavidt Rynning.

V.
Rochester-Settlementet.

Efter andre Meddelelser bør endnu tilføies, at Lars Larsen, der bosatte sig i Rochester, ansaaes som Selskabets Leder og var den eneste, som forstod lidt Engelsk. Han er nu for mange Aar siden død, men flere Medlemmer af hans Familie lever vist endnu, nogle i Rochester, andre i Chicago. En Søn studerede ved Frankean-Synodens Læreanstalt og virkede som luthersk Præst blandt sine Landsmænd, men døde i en tidlig Alder. De, som kjøbte Land i Kendall og Morris Countier, flyttede dertil i November Maaned, netop da Vinteren begyndte. Landet deromkring var endnu lidet bebygget, og det var vanskeligt for dem at faa Arbeide og end vanskeligere at finde Husly for Vinteren. Fire og tyve af dem slog sig sammen og byggede et Loghus, der netop var stort nok til at give hver af Beboerne et Fladerum af en Kvadratfods Størrelse. Stuvede sammen i denne trange Hytte havde Nykommerne visselig Brug for en god Del Taalmodighed, og alene en urokkelig Tro paa en bedre Fremtid kunde under disse Omstændigheder opretholde Modet og gjøre deres Stilling nogenlunde taalelig. Tærskemaskinen var endnu ikke kommen i Brug, og ved at tærske for Naboerne med Pleiel fortjente de det Nødvendige til Livsophold. De fik nemlig for dette Arbeide hver ellevte Bushel af Udbyttet. Det følgende Aar begyndte de at rydde det Land, de havde kjøbt; men da dette var bevoxet med tæt Skov, gik det kun langsomt med Rydningen. Dog kunde de den anden Sommer høste Hvede af 2 Acres. Dette gav dem Mod til fortsatte Anstrængelser, men det maa dog siges, at de første 4—5 Aar bragte disse Folk mange

Skuffelser og Sorger. Det gik dem, som det siden er gaaet saamange af deres indvandrede Landsmænd: de ønskede sig tilbage til Norge, og dertil havde de maaske god Grund. Men de kunde ingensteds komme af Mangel paa Midler, og selv de Faa, som kunde bestride Tilbagereisens Udgifter, vidste kun altfor godt, hvad det vilde sige at komme tomhændet hjem, og de forblev i Amerika, uanseet denne uheldige Begyndelse.

VI.
Fra 1825 til 1836.

Dog, ved hjælpsomme Naboers Medvirkning og egen Flid fik de efterhaanden saameget opryddet af det frugtbare Land, at de havde Fødevarer nok til eget Forbrug. Udsigterne blev nu bedre; de begyndte at indse, at Amerika tilbyder den stræbsomme Arbeider mange Fordele, og de opmuntrede, i Breve til deres gamle Hjem, Landsmænd at søge deres Lykke paa denne Side Havet. Følgen heraf var, at der i Aarene fra 1825 til 1836 vedblev at udvandre ikke saa faa, men de reiste i smaa Selskaber med Skibsleilighed, enten over Göteborg i Sverige, Hamburg i Tydskland eller Havre i Frankrige, fra hvilke Steder der ofte gaves Skibsleilighed til de Forenede Stater. Fra Göteborg reiste Emigranterne med amerikanske Skibe, som førte svensk Jern til Amerika; men denne Leilighed var usikker og man blev ofte nødt til at henligge flere Uger for at vente paa Skibsleilighed. Man begyndte derfor at tage til Hamburg, hvor den tydske Udvandring alt længe havde været i regelmæssig Gang med de saakaldte amerikanske Paketskibe. Men ogsaa her mødtes de norske Udvandrere af den Vanskelighed, at hvis man ikke var indskrevet en 2 à 3 Uger iforveien, maatte man ligge over indtil den næste Paket afgik. Dette førte da til, at mange lagde Veien over Havre i Frankrige, hvor Tilgangen af Udvandrere var mindre, medens Paketfarten var omtrent den samme som fra Hamburg. En Ven af Nedskriveren, ved Navn Gjert Hovland, en oplyst og frisindet Bonde fra Hardanger i Bergens Stift, var en af dem, som i 1831 reiste til Amerika over Göteborg, og skrev mange fortrinlige Breve til Norge.*) Da han var vel kjendt i flere Præstegjæld i Bergens Stift, cirkulerede hans Breve vidt og bredt i hundreder af Afskrifter og vakte stor Interesse blandt Folket. For ikke ret mange Aar siden levede han endnu i en høi Alder i Ottawa, Illinois.

**) Forfatteren har seet en Afskrift af et Brev fra Gjert Gregoriussen Hovland, skrevet fra Morris County, N. J., i 1835, hvor han da havde boet 4 Aar. Heraf sees, at han med Familie forlod Norge den 24 Juni 1831; de reiste over Göteborg og afgik derfra den 30 Juli s. A. De ankom til New York den 18 September. Han kjøbte 50 Acres Skovland, som han arbeidede paa i 4 Aar og derpaa solgte med $500 Gevinst. I 1836 kom han til Illinois og boede ikke*

langt fra Ottawa i La Salle County, hvor han døde i en meget høi Alder. I dette Brev skrev han meget rosende om den amerikanske Lovgivning, Lighed og Frihed, i Modsætning til Standsaristokratiets Udsugelser i Norge. Raadede alle, som kunde, til at komme til Amerika, da Skaberen ingensteds havde forbudt Mennesket at bosætte sig, hvor det vilde osv. Hans Breve blev afskrevne i hundredevis og omsendte i de norske Bygder, og havde udentvivl en meget afgjørende Indflydelse paa Udvandringen.
Nordmændene i Amerika. 2.

VII.
Udvandringen i 1836.

Endelig kom en af Sluppefolkene ved Navn Knud Slogvig tilbage til Norge i 1835 efterat have opholdt sig ti Aar i den nye Verden. Han opholdt sig for det meste i sin Hjembygd i Skjolds Præstegjæld, og Efterretningen om hans Hjemkomst løb som en Budstikke fra Mand til Mand med utrolig Hurtighed. Allevegne fra i Bergens Stift og Stavanger Amt reiste Folk lange Veie for at tale med ham. Tre af Nedskriverens Paarørende, som reiste fra Bergen i 1837, var blandt dem, som i Vinteren 1836 besøgte ham, og kom hjem fulde af Amerikafeber. To Brigger i Stavanger, som tilsammen kunde føre 160 Passagerer, udrustedes af det kiellandske Rederi i Foraaret 1836; de reiste under Ledsagelse af nævnte Knud Slogvig til Amerika. De havde en heldig Overreise, besøgte sine Landsmænd i Rochester og fortsatte derpaa Reisen til Chicago. De bosatte sig hovedsagelig i La Salle County, 70 Mil Vest fra Chicago, i det saakaldte Fox River Settlement, som den paa sine eventyrlige Vandringer ustandselige Cleng Peerson da havde udpeget. Efter hvad han fortalte Forfatteren, da han ved sit tredie Besøg til Norge opholdt sig i Bergen Vinteren 1843, var han den første norske Emigrant, som kom vestom de store Indsøer og beføgte Chicago og andre Steder i Illinois, men Aarstallet og de nærmere Omstændigheder desangaaende kan jeg nu ikke mere angive, da de Optegnelser, som dengang gjordes, er gaaet tabt. Om han personlig ledsagede dem eller blot gav dem Anvisning paa Stedet, erindres ikke. Men en interessant Skildring, som han gav mig om sine eventyrlige Opdagelsesreiser udover Illinois' græsrige, blomstrende Prærier, og hvorledes han paa en Fodtur fra Chicago første Gang kom op paa en Høide, hvorfra han kunde overstue de naturskjønne, henrivende Egne, hvor det norske Settlement ved Fox River nu findes, men hvor der dengang ikke fandtes et Hus undtagen med flere Miles Mellemrum i Skovkanten langs Fox River, hvor enkelte Amerikanere var begyndt at flytte ind — den er endnu i friskt Minde. Næsten død af Hunger og Strabadser paa sin lange Vandring gjennem et ubeboet Land, kastede han sig i Græsset, takkede Gud, som havde ladet ham komme og se dette af Naturen saa vidunderlig rigt udstyrede Land, og trøstet og styrket paa Sjælen, glemte han sin Hunger og sine Lidelser. Han tænkte paa Moses, da han fra Nebo Bjerg saa ud over det forjættede Land, som Gud havde lovet hans Folk.

VIII.
Fox River Settlementet.

Veiledet af Cleng Peerson, og opmuntret af hans Beskrivelse over denne Egn, var det, at Indvandrerselskabet fra Stavanger i 1836 kom til Fox River og dannede det andet norske Settlement i Amerika. Hvormeget disse Folk, saavelsom de, der senere kom til disse Egne, har at takke ham for, og som de maaske aldrig har tænkt paa, vil paa en tydeligere Maade fremgaa, naar vi nedenfor kommer til at fortælle om det paafølgende Aars norske Udvandreres Skjæbne i det ulykkelige Beaver Creek Settlement. Vel er det saa, at Koldfeberen næsten overalt i Vesten i mere eller mindre Grad angreb Nykommerne under Landets første Opdyrkning; men paa høitliggende Land, fjernt fra Sumper og Moradser, var denne Hjemsøgelse forholdsvis let overstaaet. Dette var Tilfældet ved Fox River.

Vi har i det Foregaaende seet, at det første Udvandrerskib reiste fra Norge allerede i 1825 — altsaa nu 62 Aar siden; at den næste direkte Udvandring fra Norge først fandt Sted 11 Aar senere, da de 2 kiellandske Brigger i 1836 førte 150 Emigranter fra Stavanger til New York. Det er ogsaa i det Foregaaende kortelig omtalt, hvorledes der i Mellemtiden næsten hvert Aar reiste Folk, enten enteltvis eller i Smaaselskaber, over andre europæiske Havne til Amerika. I det Efterfølgende skal nu omtales det tredie direkte Udvandrerselskab, nemlig det fra Bergen i 1837.

IX.
Det tredie Udvandrerselskab.

Om denne Udvandring kan Forfatteren tale af egen personlig Kundskab, saavel om, hvad der som indledende Skridt gik forud for samme og paa en Maade forberedte Jordbunden for Udvandring blandt de bergenske Bønder, som om de nærmeste Aarsager dertil. Ved et rent Tilfælde fandt Forfatteren i en Vens Bogsamling i Bergen en Tydskers "Reiser i Amerika." I Sextenaarsalderen er Indbildningskraften gjerne meget levende, og da der i denne Bog forekom endel livsfriske Billeder af de fjerne Egne, den Reisende havde besøgt, saavelsom af det Indtryk, han havde modtaget af Land og Folk i den nye Verden, læstes den med en Romans Tillokkelser. Her var udførlig Besked om den tydske Udvandring til Amerika. Med denne Rejsebeskrivelse i Lommen drog jeg en tidlig Sommermorgen bortover Solemsviken og opefter Lyderhorns bratte Sider. Deroppe læste og drømte jeg om den nye, underlige Verden langt borte i Vesten. Taagen havde sænket sig ned over Fjordene, mellem Øerne ved Bergensleden, men deroppe om Bjergets Top var det klart Solskin. Det var første Gang jeg saa dette for Bjergegnene særegne, herlige Syn. Har min prosaiske Natur nogensinde været paavirket af poetisk Inspiration og Løftelse, var det i denne Stund, medens Øiet skuede ud over Taagens solbelyste Flade og i det fjerne Vesten skimtede Nordhavets blanke Skjold, der syntes at hæve sig i lige Høide med Fjeldet. O, hvorfor kommer slige Øieblikke saa sjelden i det almindelige Menneskes Liv! Og langt ude mod Vest, tusinder af Mile derude, ligger det Land, hvorom jeg læser, ligger den store, endnu saa lidet bekjendte Verdensdel, med sine Hemmeligheder og sine Undere. Til dette Lyspunkt i mit Livs tidlige Foraar knytter sig altsaa mine første Erindringer om Amerika, om det Land, som nu i næsten et halvt Aarhundrede har været mit andet Fødeland. Fra denne Tid søgte jeg alle de Bøger og Reisebeskrivelser, jeg kunde faa fat paa angaaende Amerika, og sammen med en Onkel af mig begyndte vi at samle videre Oplysning om den nye Verden, saavel gjennem Bøger som de mundtlige Fortællinger fra Stavangerkanten, som nu begyndte at versere i Bygderne angaaende Cleng Peersons Udvandring og Tilbagekomst, dog uden at vi endnu for Alvor tænkte paa Udvandring. Ved en uegennyttig Vens Hjælp fik jeg i 1834 Anledning til et 6 Maaneders Ophold i England, ved hvilken Anledning jeg samlede en Del Pamfletter og Bøger om Amerika og den engelske Udvandring. Paa denne Maade spredtes der i vor Omkreds en bestemtere og paalideligere Oplysning om Forholdene i Amerika og om Reisen dertil. Dette gjorde, at mange latterlige og urimelige Historier, som nu jevnlig sattes i Omløb blandt Folket, ikke fandt den fornødne Tiltro. Langsomt men stadigt udbredte Tanken sig om Udvandring til Amerika; flere og flere sluttede sig til det lille Tal, som for Alvor begyndte at tale om at sælge sine Jorder og reise. Da var det, at Bergens Bisp skrev sit Hyrdebrev til de bergenske Bønder over Texten: "Bliv i Landet, ernær dig redelig!" Hvadenten han glemte det eller han ikke ansaa det passende for Anledningen, nok er det, han anførte ikke det andet Skriftens Bud: "Vorder frugtbare, formerer Eder og opfylder Jorden." Dette sidste havde Bønderne holdt fast paa: de fleste af dem havde talrige Familier, og da Jorden derhjemme var meget vel opfyldt, medens de nu hørte, at en stor Del af den nye Verden endnu var folketom, besluttede de at blive Bispens Raad ulydige og drage til det nye Kanaan, som flød i Melk og Honning.

X.
Aarsager til Reisen.

Ved Besøget hos Knud Slogvig fik vi en fuld og sikker Bekræftelse paa, hvad vi tidligere havde hørt og læst. Dette var i Vinteren 1836. Samme Aars Høst kom den bergenske Skibskaptein Behrens med Barkskibet "Ægir" hjem fra en Fragttur til Amerika, og da han fik høre, at flere formuende Landsmænd i forskjellige Egne af Amtet havde solgt sine Jorder og søgte Skibsleilighed til Amerika, bestemte han sig til (han var nemlig baade Reder og Fører), at indrette sin gode "Ægir" (Havets Gud) for Passagerfarten, og Kontrakt blev afsluttet om Overreisen det næste Foraar, 1837. Kaptein Behrens havde i New Yorks Havn seet tydske og engelske Emigrantskibe ankomme og vidste god Besked om Skibsrummets Indretning og om de amerikanske Love og Havnevæsen for Emigranternes Vedkommende. To tydske Præster, der skulde hjem for at samle Bidrag til Kirkebygninger, var endog fulgte med ham til Europa, og han var gjennem dem bleven vel underrettet angaaende den tydske Emigration, som nu i mange Aar havde foregaaet efter en stor Maalestok og især var gaaet over Baltimore til Pennsylvania.

Kundskaben om Forholdene i Amerika vilde dog ikke have ledet til denne første Udvandring fra Bergen. For de flestes Vedkommende var det de trange Tider, indskrænkede Næringsveie og store Fattigskatte, som lagde det tunge Lod i Vægtskaalen. Dog ved jeg, at der for enkeltes Vedkommende var andre medvirkende Aarsager. Den gamle, for Folkeoplysningen altopofrende Skolemand N. P. Langeland, der havde valgt den studerende Vei, men af Mangel paa Midler havde maattet standse paa Halvveien og tage fat paa Folkeskolen, var bleven uretfærdig bedømt af en overtroisk og uvidende Almue. Geistligheden fandt, at denne altfor radikale Tænker ikke var nogen passende Mand til at lede Folkeundervisningen i denne meget konservative Landsdel, og hans Lærervirksomhed begyndte at blive et altfor utaknemmeligt Arbeide. Bistaaet af et lidet Antal trofaste og oplyste Venner, men forfulgt af et større Antal uvidende Bigotter, hemmedes hans gavnlige Virksomhed; han lønnedes med Utak for sine ædleste Bestræbelser og de Baand, som bandt ham til Fædrelandet og den Gjerning, han elskede saa høit, løsnedes. For hans Vedkommende var nok dette den ledende Aarsag til Udvandring, og dette Forhold virkede da ogsaa bestemmende paa mange af hans Venner og Paarørende. Men med alt dette maa det dog fastholdes, at uden den bedre økonomiske Udsigt, som aabnede sig for Familien i det rige, tyndtbefolkede Amerika, med det milde Klima og den frugtbare Jordbund, vilde neppe nogen af dette Selskab have reist til Amerika. Som hørende til dette Selskab kan nævnes, foruden den her omtalte Lærer Langeland: Mons Aadland, Nils Frøland, Anders Norvig, Anders Rosseland, Thomas Bauge, Ingebrigt Brudvig, Thorbjørn Veste osv., som alle havde en talrig Familie, samt et Antal løse Personer, hvoriblandt Døvig, Rosseland, Bauge, Frøland, Norvig, Hisdal, Tøsseland o. fl., af hvilke mange endnu lever i Illinois som Velstandsfolk, hvilket ogsaa er Tilfældet med mange af de Ældres efterladte Børn. Ialt bestod Følget af 84 Personer. Saavidt nu erindres betalte de 60 Spd. for Overreisen til New York for hver voxen Person, og det Halve for Børn under 12 Aar.

XI.
Ole Rynning.

Det var først efterat den foreløbige Overenskomst var afsluttet med Kaptein Behrens og efterat Skibsrummet var bleven indrettet for Reisen, at den ved sin lille Bog om Amerika bekjendte Student Ole Rynning fra Snaasen i Trondhjems Stift, kom til Bergen for at slutte sig til Selskabet, om hvis Afreise han først havde faaet Underretning gjennem en Annonce i Bladene, hvorpaa han havde sat sig i Korrespondence med Rederiet i Bergen. Han havde saaledes ikke ringeste Andel i at bringe denne Udvandring til Udførelse. Hvad der egentlig drev ham til Udvandring, kan jeg ikke med Vished sige. Efter nogle Ytringer af Kaptein Behrens lod det til, at Rynning var mere demokratisksindet og sympathiserede mere med Bondestanden end godt syntes for hans mere aristokratisksindede Fader, Provst [Jens] Rynning. En Forlovelse, som Faderen ansaa for en Misalliance, skulde saaledes være den nærmeste Aarsag til hans Reise til Amerika. Saadan var idetmindste Kaptein Behrens' Opfatning, og vist er det, at Rynnings Væsen gav Indtryk af en dyb Melankoli, der meget let kunde have sin Grund i en saadan Omstændighed. At hans Bestemmelse dengang var, efter en Tid at vende tilbage til Norge, idetmindste paa Besøg, deraf gjorde han ingen Hemmelighed. Dette fremgaar ogsaa af et Vers, som forekommer i en Sang, han under Overreisen forfattede og som blev afsungen paa Havet ved en liden Festlighed paa Amerikas Frihedsdag den 4de Juli, hvori det hedder:

Nu ligger Norges Klippeland
Saa dybt i Skjul bag salten Vove,
Men Længslen higer til den Strand
Med gamle, dunkle Egeskove,
Hvor Graners Sus og Jøklers Drøn
Er Harmoni for Norges Søn.

Men om end Skjæbnen bød ham der,
Som fordum Bjørn af Leif, at tjelde,
Han vil dog stedse have kjær
Sit gode gamle Norges Fjelde,
Og længes ømt, med sønlig Hu,
At se sit elskte Hjem endnu.

De var 8 Uger paa Reisen fra Bergen til New York og Passagererne stod sig idetheletaget godt. Kaptein Behrens fortalte adskilligt om Overreisen, da Forfatteren senere traf ham i Bergen. Da disse Bønder, der aldrig før havde seet Havet, saa dette at være roligt, tabte de snart Frygten for dets Raseri. Fiolen kom frem og man begyndte at dandse paa Dækket; dog maatte Kapteinen snart gjøre Indsigelse herimod, da Balsalonen (Dækket) led altfor meget af Damernes og Herrernes Sko, som var stærkt beslagne med Søm. Paa Søen kom et stort amerikansk Paketskib dem saa nær, at man ved en feilagtig Manøvre kom sammen, og da Søgangen var høi og Skibene ikke strax kunde komme klar af hinanden, kom Passagererne med sine Øxer og begyndte at hugge i Tougværk og Ræer; de troede, deres sidste Time var kommen, men de slap dog med Skrækken. Skibene fik ikke nogen stor Skade.

Alle Beretninger stemmer overens om, at Ole Rynning var en sjelden ædel og menneskevenlig Mand, der opofrede meget af sin Tid og sine Evner i sine Medreisendes Tjeneste. Disse viste ham ogsaa derfor, saavelsom paa Grund af hans Sprogkundskab, den mest uindskrænkede Tillid. Han var en af de tre, som af Reisefølget blev udsendte fra Chicago for at udse et passende Sted for dem at nedsætte sig, da de allerfleste af dem agtede at blive Farmere.

Reisen fra New York var den Gang meget besværlig mod hvad den nu er, og kostede for disse talrige Familier langt mere end de havde regnet paa. Da de kom til Detroit, Michigan, havde den ovenfor omtalte N. P. Langeland ikke flere Penge, men derimod en Familie paa 8 Personer. Hans andre Venner i Selskabet havde lovet at hjælpe ham igjennem til Chicago, men nu var de blevne modløse og bange over de mange uforudsete Udtællinger, og vilde ikke gjøre flere Udlæg. Han steg altsaa med sin Familie iland i Detroit. Udsigten var visselig ikke lys, men han var en ihærdig Arbeider og tilmed en dygtig Snedker og Smed, og han fik snart Arbeide hos en Blokkedreier, hvorved han opholdt Familien, og kom siden ind i Landet til Lapeer County, hvor han efterhaanden blev Eier af 120 Acres Land og et Snedkerværksted med Dreiebænk og Vandkraft. Han er død for mange Aar siden, men en Søn har længe boet i San Francisco, California.

XII.
Beaver Creek.

I Chicago traf man enkelte Landsmænd, som havde nedsat sig der, og et Par var komne tilbage fra Fox River og gav en nedslaaende Beretning om Forholdene dersteds. Dette var Anledningen til, at tre Mænd blev udsendte for at søge et for den paatænkte Koloni gunstigt Sted. Disse tog Veien mod Syd fra Chicago, omtrent af den Vei, hvor Illinois Central Jernbanen nu gaar — et lavtliggende, sumpigt Strøg, som erfarne Folk ikke ventede at se bebygget i en Menneskealder. Det var i August og September Maaned, da dette flade Land var tørt og bevoxet med grovt Græs, der gik en Mand op under Armene. Nogle af de Gjenlevende har ytret Mistanke om, at deres Udsendinge blev paavirkede af Landspekulanter, af hvilke de lod sig overtale til at tage denne uheldige Retning, istedetfor at gaa Vest eller Nordvest, hvor de inden 25 à 30 engelske Mile kunde have fundet det deiligste Regjeringsland under Solen. Men Skjæbnen vilde det anderledes: de kom til det ulykkelige Beaver Creek i Iroquois County, hvor de troede at finde alle Betingelser for et Paradis paa Jorden. De kom tilbage med glimrende Skildringer over det flade Land med den rige Jordbund, hvor Græsset tildels gik dem over Hovedet. Selskabet kjøbte nu Oxer og Vogne og drog afsted til det forjættede Land. De tømrede og byggede af alle Kræfter for at blive færdige før Vinteren. De kjørte 70 Mile til nærmeste Saugmølle efter Bord, og gav sig slet ikke Tid til at studere Landets Topografi, ellers vilde de vistnok have opdaget Spor af, at det Land, de tænkte paa at pløie næste Foraar, havde staaet under Vand lige ned i Juni Maaned sidste Foraar. Det var haardføre, flinke Folk. De fik sine Boliger i god Stand, førend Høstregnen begyndte; men de maatte snart vade gjennem Is og Vand op over Knærne, naar de skulde nogetsteds hen. Da Foraaret kom, stod det flade Land under Vand, saalangt Øiet kunde naa. Mange af dem var allerede bukkede under for Koldfeber, og da Sommervarmen kom og Vandet fordunstede, begyndte Sumpfeberen at kræve sine daglige Offere, og da hed det: "redde sig hvo som kan!" Her var det, at Ole Rynnings Ben blev liggende. Han var en hilsestærk og kraftfuld Mand, der ingen Besværligheder skyede. Han boede hos en Mand, hvor man var vant til at spise Grød og Surmelk. Forfatterens Broder saa ham gaa med et Par sine sønderrevne Støvler gjennem Isvand og Sne. Endelig blev han angreben af en ondartet Diarrhoe, som ikke mere lod sig standse og blev hans Dødssygdom.

De faa gjenlevende forlod alt og drog over til Fox River Settlementet i La Salle County, hvor nogle af dem endnu lever — deriblandt en Søster af Forfatteren. Min Broder var den eneste, som endnu ikke vilde flytte; han blev der i tre Aar, og fik endelig bortbyttet sit Sted for en Flok Kreaturer, hvormed han i 1840 drog nord paa og bosatte sig i Racine County, Wisconsin.

Saaledes blev Udfaldet af Kolonien ved Beaver Creek. Noget nær det samme som Udfaldet med Kolonianlægget i Leifsboder 1000 Aar tidligere.

XIII.
I La Salle County.

Vi har ovenfor seet, at Cleng Peerson tidlig fandt Veien til Chicago og derfra vestefter over Illinois' store Prærier. Snart fulgtes han af enkelte af Sluppefolkene i New York og Andre, som var komne enkeltvis senere. Blandt dem, som først bosatte sig i La Salle County, Illinois, kan nævnes Gudmund Haukaas, en fremragende Bonde fra Stavanger Amt, som kom fra den norske Koloni ved Rochester, N. Y. Den allerstørste Del af Knud Slogvigs Følge i 1836 nedsatte sig i La Salle, og det er vanskeligt at forklare, hvorfor Rynnings Følge det næste Aar ikke ogsaa gik did. Beretningen er, at de lod sig afskrække derfra af enkelte Landsmænd, som de traf i Chicago; disse kunde nemlig fortælle, at de norske Nybyggere derude holdt paa at dø af Klimatfeber, at Stedet var overmaade usundt og at Forholdet i dette Settlement idetheletaget var beklageligt. Cleng Peerson havde forledet dem til at nedsætte sig der, og han var og altid havde været en Ulykkesfugl. Saa lød den Beretning, Selskabet fra Bergen fik i Chicago. Nu ved vi, at der paa den Tid herskede Klimatfeber gjennem hele Fox River Dalen fra Muskego i Wisconsin til Mississippi-Floden i Illinois, saavelsom ved de andre Elvedrag i Vesten, men dette forstod Nykommerne sig ikke paa. De norske Nybygder i La Salle udbredte sig hurtigt under den stadig tilstrømmende Indvandring, og strakte sig snart til omliggende Egne. Norway, Leland, Lisbon, Morris, Ottawa osv. blev tidlig fremragende Midtpunkter for denne den første norske Koloni i Vesten. Disse Egne hører til de smukkeste og frugtbareste af alle de norske Settlementer i Mississippidalen. Vinteren er langtfra saa barsk som i det fjerne Nordvesten, og den i de første Aar herskende Klimatfeber ophørte, saasnart Landet kom under Dyrkning. Landet var næsten overalt færdigt for Ploven og alle, som vilde arbeide, kom snart i Velstand.

XIV.
Ansten Natstads [Nattestads] Amerikareise.

Det er ovenfor leilighedsvis bleven paavist, hvorledes Kundskaben om Amerika og om, at Folk holdt paa at flytte derover, udgik fra Stavanger Amt, og da især fra Skjolds Præstegjæld. Et yderligere Vidnesbyrd herom giver

Ansten Nattestad i en kort Beretning om sin Amerikareise. Af denne Beretning gjøres følgende sammentrængte Uddrag: Han og hans Broder Ole Nattestad, af Rollaugs Præstegjæld i Numedal, kom i 1835 paa en Forretningsreise paa Vestlandet en Aften ind paa en Gaard i Tysvær Sogn, Stavanger Amt, hvor man netop havde modtaget Brev fra en Slægtning, som boede i Nærheden af Rochester i Staten New York i Amerika. Dette Brev var fra en Kone til hendes Søsterdatter, hvem hun raadede til at komme derover, og hvori hun gav en udførlig Beretning om deres økonomiske Stilling, om Landet og om Udsigterne for norske Indvandrere. Herved vaktes de to Brødres første Opmærksomhed for Amerika. Et Aar senere gjorde Hr. Nattestad Bekjendtskab med Storthingsmand Nubrud, en oplyst Bonde i Sigdal. Denne gamle Mand var en Frihedsven med store Tanker om Amerikas Fremtid saavel i økonomisk som i politisk Henseende, og hans Meninger var vel skikkede til at gjenoplive og bestyrke den allerede opstaaede Tanke om Udvandring. De to Brødre besluttede altsaa i Vaaren 1837 at kaste løs og reise til Amerika. De hørte, at et Skib skulde afgaa fra Stavanger med Emigranter, og tog derfor Veien over Fjeldene fra Numedal; men da de kom frem, var det endnu næsten to Maaneder før Skibet skulde afgaa. De tog derfor Leilighed med en Jægt til Göteborg, hvor de fik Skibsleilighed med en stor Amerikaner, lastet med svensk Jern. De betalte for Overreisen hver 50 Spd., og efter 32 Dage landede de i Fall River, Rhode Island. Herfra kom de over New York, Albany og Buffalo til Detroit, Michigan, hvor de traf sammen med Ole Rynning og hans Følge fra Bergen. Sammen med dette Selskab reiste de nu over Chicago til Beaver Creek. De havde reist saa sparsomt som muligt, men alligevel kostede Overreisen dem 100 Dollars hver. De kom snart begge til den Slutning, at Amerika tilbød mange Fordele for Jordbrugere og Arbeidere, og de bestemte sig derfor til at forblive i den nye Verden; men Forretningsanliggender gjorde det nødvendigt, at en af dem maatte reise tilbage til Norge. Ansten reiste altsaa næste Foraar og lagde Veien over New Orleans, Liverpool og Tønsberg til Kristiania, hvor han skulde besørge Udgivelsen af Ole Rynnings Bog om Amerika. Om sit Ophold i Hjembygden skriver Hr. Nattestad: "Skjønt jeg ikke lagde an paa at udbrede Efterretninger om Amerika, men fortalte simpelthen mine Erfaringer i den nye Verden til dem, jeg talte med, gik dog Rygtet om min Tilbagekomst som en Ild gjennem Landet. Hele Vinteren kom der Folk lange Veie for at høre om Amerika, og Breve indløb fra alle Kanter med Forespørgsler om den nye Verden. Der kom Mænd endog 24 norske Mile ene og alene for at tale med mig, og om Vaaren 1838 var der saa mange Udvandrere reisefærdige alene i Rollaugs Præstegjæld, at Kaptein Ankersens Skib i Drammen, som kuns kunde tage 100 Passagerer, ikke kunde skaffe Plads for alle, saa en Del maatte lægge Veien over

Göteborg i Sverige."

Med dette Skib kom Ansten tilbage til Amerika. Det var 9 Uger paa Reisen over til New York, og Passagererne betalte omkring 60 Dollars hver i Fragt. Ved Ankomsten til Chicago fik de høre, at Ole Nattestad, Anstens Broder, var reist fra Illinois til Wisconsin og havde nedsat sig i Rock County. Didhen reiste da de allerfleste af dette Selskab og bosatte sig paa forskjellige Steder i nævnte County samt tildels i det tilgrændsende Stephenson Co., Illinois. Dette var i Sommeren 1839, men Ole Nattestad var kommen i 1838, og antages almindelig for at have været den første norske Settler i Wisconsin.

Brødrene Nattestad ansees for de første Udvandrere til Amerika fra Norges Vest- og Østland, og at Stødet dertil kom fra Stavanger Amt kan der ikke længere være nogen Tvivl om. Numedal, Hallingdal, Siljord, Hiterdal, Sætersdalen og andre Bygder paa Vestlandet var derfor stærkt repræsenterede blandt de tidlige Udvandrere til Wisconsin. I 1844 var det især Numedøler og Vossinger man traf paa Dane Countys store Prærier.

XV.
Udvandrernes Antal formeres.

Efter det første Udvandrerselskab fra Bergen i 1837 tiltog Udvandringen fra Bergens Stift, især fra Vos Præstegjæld, som længe ansaaes for at være det Sted, der afgav det største Antal Udvandrere. Fra 1840 afgik der hvert Aar fra 1 til 3 Skibe med Emigranter, næsten udelukkende fra Vos. Derfra udbredte Epidemien sig til Sogn, Lerdal og Valders Bygder, som alle har ydet store Bidrag til Udvandringsstrømmen i dens første Stadier. Skjøndt de bekjendte Mænd Ole Rynning og Hans Barlien tidlig udvandrede fra Trondhjems Stift, slog dog aldrig Udvandringen ret an i denne Del af Norge. Det kom kanske i Førstningen af, at de begge døde saa snart efter deres Ankomst. Rynnings Bog ansees for at have været den ledende Anledning til, at nogle Familier fra Namdalen kom herover saa tidlig som 1844. Siden er der vistnok efterhaanden kommet Folk fra forskjellige Egne af nordre Trondhjems Amt herover, men aldrig i den Grad som fra Bergenskanten og Vestlandet. I den tidligere Periode var ogsaa Udvandringen fra Norges egentlige Østland meget indskrænket, men senere har den dog været ganske betydelig. Det kan ikke nytte at anstille nogen Undersøgelse af Aarsagerne til denne mærkbare Forskjel i Udvandringen fra de forskjellige Landsdele. Mest har maaske Livsvilkaar og Næringsveie bidraget dertil.

Efter de paalideligste Data, Forfatteren har kunnet finde, er det ovenanførte Hovedtrækkene af Begyndelsen til vor Tids Udvandring fra Norge til

Amerika. Vi skulle i det efterfølgende lidt nærmere omtale disse første Indvandreres Virksomhed i dette Land samt kaste et Blik paa nogle af de Resultater, som derved ere indvundne for Landsmænd baade her og i Fædrelandet.

Ovenfor er kortelig fortalt, hvorledes det gik med de første norske Nybyggere i Morris County, N. J. Hvis der paa Stedet overhovedet findes nogen Efterkommere af de første Kolonister, har de ikke vedligeholdt sin norske Betegnelse, og der kan ikke siges at være noget norsk Settlement der mere. Heller ikke ved Beaver Creek findes noget norsk Settlement—ikke engang en Landsmand, som kan udpege Ole Rynnings Grav! Det første Nybygge i Illinois derimod vedbliver at blomstre og trives, ikke alene i La Salle County, men i omliggende Counties. Befolkningen her har fra først af vist stor Flid og Sparsomhed, og den timelige Velstand er meget betydelig. En fra Hjemmet medbragt stærk religiøs Tendents har vedligeholdt sig godt, medens Interessen for Politik, Embedssøgning og anden verdslig Intelligents ikke har vist nogen store Livstegn, idetmindste saavidt det er kommet til almindelig Kundskab.

XVI.
Nordmænd i Chicago.

Herfra komme vi ved en let Overgang til at nævne nogle af de første Nordmænd, som bosatte sig i Chicago—dette Brændpunkt for politiske, sociale og religiøse Kampe. Pastor P. Anderson, der maa antages at kjende til den første Indvandring dertil fra Norge omtrent saa godt som nogen Nulevende, udtaler sig i Korthed saaledes:

"1. Halstein Torrisen fra Fjeldberg i Norge, med Hustru og Børn, kom til Chicago den 16de Oct. 1836. Hans første Bopæl var ved Wells Street, hvor Chicago & Northwestern Depot nu staar. Han var nok den første af bosatte Nordmænd her i Byen. I 1848 (det samme Aar jeg blev Præst i Chicago) flyttede han til Calumet syd for Chicago, hvor han døde for nogle Aar siden. 2. De første Emigranter fra Vos kom ogsaa i 1836, deriblandt Nils Røthe og Svein Lothe (den sidste fra Hardanger), men hvad Dato de kom hertil vides ikke. 3. Baar Johnson med Hustru og 5 Børn kom i Aaret 1837. 4. Andrew Nilsen og Anders Larsen Flage med hver sin Familie kom i 1839. 5. Endre Iversen Røthe kom i 1840 og omtrent paa samme Tid kom Lars Davidsen (som nu bor paa Liberty Prairie, Dane Co., Wis.), Ole Gilbertsen og Anna Bakkethun (senere Mrs. Nechlissen) o. fl. Andrew Nelson mente, at Johan Larsen fra Kobbervig i Norge, som endnu lever her, besøgte Chicago som Sømand fra Buffalo tidligere, men bosatte sig her i 1836 paa samme Tid som Halstein Torrisen. Anna Bakkethun bor endnu i Chicago og kom hertil sammen med Andrew Nelson, Anders Larsen Flage o. fl. i 1839."

Uden Tvivl nedsatte der sig flere Landsmænd i Chicago mellem Aarene '36 og '40 og vi nævne disse kun som værende blandt de første, fordi vi kjender dem. Der hørte Mod og Driftighed til at slaa sig ned i Chicago dengang. Man maatte nære sig med at sage og kløve Brænde og forrette alskens tungt og besværligt Arbeide. Forfatteren besøgte Andrew Flage i 1844—traf ham først i 1843 i New York, hvor han mødte to af sine Døtre, som da kom over—da havde han en Kjøkkenhave paa det saakaldte Kanalland, og gjorde en ganske heldig Forretning i Grøntsager. Siden den Tid har flere af de gamle Settlere i Chicago samlet store Formuer—nogle af dem opover en halv Million Dollars. Blandt Nordmænd i Chicago, som tidlig gjorde sig bemærket i offentlige Anliggender, maa især nævnes P. Anderson som vore Landsmænds første lutherske Præst, hvis mangeaarige trofaste Arbeide for Lutherdommens Bevarelse blandt Landsmænd fortjener at erindres med Taknemlighed af det nulevende norske Kirkefolk i Chicago. Episkopalerne gjorde, under Svenskeren Unonius, ganske alvorlige Anstrængelser for at etablere sin Kirke blandt de første Norske i Wisconsin og i Chicago. Paa sidstnævnte Sted formaaedes Jenny Lind til at give Penge til en Episkopalkirke, som byggedes paa Michigan Street paa Nordsiden, og Pastor Unonius flyttede fra Pine Lake, Wis., til Chicago og holdt for en Tid Gudstjeneste i den; men den lille Trækirke, som allerede da var bygget ved Superior Street, hvor Pastor Anderson nu begyndte at prædike, samlede Størsteparten af de Norske til sig, og Pastor Unonius flyttede snart derefter til New York. Jeg skal ikke her længer følge den kirkelige Udvikling blandt Nordmændene i Chicago; den har altfor mange Skyggesider til at kunne følges med Sandfærdighed uden at give Anstød.

Det var især de af vore Landsmænd, som i Chicagos tidlige Dage havde Fremsyn og Omtanke til at anlægge sine Spareskillinger i Byggetomter, der saa at sige kom sovende til store Formuer under denne Vidunderbys eventyrlige Fremvæxt. Man vil paastaa, at der nu er dem, som eier over en Million, hvilket dog maaske er noget overdrevet. Den første Nordmand, som kom ind i offentlige Stillinger, var Iver Lawson—blandt Danskerne Geo. P. Hansen og blandt Svenskerne John Nelson—i den senere Tid er deres Navn Legio. Jeg kjender kun tre Norske i Chicago, som har været Medlemmer af Statens lovgivende Forsamling, medens der fra Landdistrikterne, mærkeligt nok, ikke har været en eneste. Men de Norske i Illinois, udenfor Chicago, har jo heller aldrig lagt nogen politisk Interesse for Dagen. Det angives, at der bor 50,000 Skandinaver, med deres Afkom, i Chicago—en Befolkning stor nok til en ganske respektabel By for sig selv alene. Af dette Antal er vel mindst 20,000 Norske, iberegnet deres Afkom.

XVII.
Første norske Settlementer i Wisconsin.

Efter Aaret 1840 gik i flere Aar Størsteparten af de norske Indvandrere til Wisconsin. Ovenfor er omtalt Ole Nattestads Ankomst til Jefferson Prairie i 1838. I 1839 kom de tre Luraasbrødre, og med dem et Reisefølge af mellem 30 og 40 Personer, til det noksom bekjendte Muskego. Disse Folk, som hovedsagelig var fra Tins Præstegjæld, steg iland i Milwaukee og maa ansees for de første Norske, som kom direkte til denne Stat. Iøvrigt vedblev Hovedstrømmen at gaa over Chicago og derfra over Land mod Nord og Vest. Der har verseret en Historie om, at Luraasselskabet blev i Milwaukee forledte af Landspekulanter til at komme ud til Muskegos haarde Skovtrakter og nedsætte sig, men jeg har ikke fundet nogen paalidelig Bekræftelse paa denne i sig selv usandsynlige Beretning, da alt Land deromkring endnu tilhørte Regjeringen. Sandsynligere er det, at det formedelst Ubekjendtskab med Sproget faldt dem vanskeligt at faa den fornødne Veiledning, ellers kunde de let have fundet et heldigere Sted at sætte Bo paa. Et halvt Snes engelske Mil længer Øst og Syd, i omtrent lige Afstand fra Milwaukee, laa dengang det bedste Prærieland ledigt, ikke alene der, hvor de norske Settlementer Yorkville og North Cape findes, men den største Del af den deilige Prærie i Racine County var endnu ubebygget. Bebyggelsen af visse Trakter i et nyt Land synes at bero ligesaameget paa Tilfældet som et Tærningkast. Det manglede ikke disse Folk paa Skarpsyn og Foretagsamhed; de var haardføre og driftige Folk. Havde Tilfældet ført dem nogle Mil længer i Sydost, vilde nu sandsynligvis den smukke Racineprærie været beboet af Norske ligesom Koshkonongprærie nu er det. Navnet Muskego—dengang i Milwaukee County—overførtes paa det tilstødende Land i Racine County, specielt paa Town of Norway, hvor det egentlige norske Settlement nu findes.

XVIII.
Heg i Norway.

Om Høsten det samme Aar (1839) kom Søren Bakke og Johannesen nordover fra Illinois, hvor de havde tilbragt nogle Uger med at søge Land, og nedsatte sig paa det senere bekjendte Heg i Norway [Muskego Settlementet, der ofte omtales som 'Heg' — Hegs laden fungerede som en motagende station som blev et midlertdigt hjem for nyankomne. Muskego og Heg blev reisens maal. — Odd Sverre Lovoll]. Johannesen var den egentlige Fører og syntes at være meget bange for Prærielandet; han førte stedse den Sætning i

Munden: "Ved og Vand ere to uundværlige Ting," og da han i rigeligt Maal fandt disse Ting ved Bredden af Windlake, besluttede han at bosætte sig der.

Det er let forstaaeligt, at det maa være tungvindt for den fattige Nybygger at nedsætte sig paa Skovland; den tætvoxende haarde Egeskov er ikke let at rydde, og der medgaar under de bedste Omstændigheder en 4—5 Aar inden man kan faa ryddet og pløiet saameget, at deraf kan høstes det Fornødne til Familiens Ophold. Disse Aar sætter derfor Nybyggerens Udholdenhed paa en meget haard Prøve. Saaledes gik det og her, og naar saa dertil kom den i de Dage uundgaaelige Klimatfeber, som kunde vedblive at plage Folk i 3 til 9 Maaneder, er det ikke at undres over, at Settlementet ikke trivedes eller fik den samme Fremgang som paa Prærielandet. Bakke og Johannesen kom over New York sammen med Elling Eielsen i 1839 og reiste først til det norske Nybygge i La Salle County, Illinois, hvorfra de samme Høst kom til Muskego og grov sig en Vinterbolig i den østlige Side af en Gravhaug fra Indianernes Tid, hvor de levede lunt og hyggeligt om Vinteren. Disse Nykommeres Breve til sine Venner i Hjembygderne bragte aarlig flere og flere Indvandrere, og Stedet Heg—saaledes kaldtes det efter Even Hegs Ankomst—blev det Mekka, hvortil de Norske, som steg iland i Milwaukee, fordetmeste stevnede. Luraasbrødrene og mange Andre blev imidlertid kjed af Rodhugningen i de tykke Egeskove og solgte sit Land til Nykommere og flyttede vestover til Præriekolonierne. Johannesen døde i sin oprindelige Bolig efter en 4—5 Aars Forløb, og Søren Bakke vendte tilbage til Norge, medens Heg, Skogstad, Thompson, Danielsen og mange flere vedblev ihærdig med Rydningen. Even Hegs Ladebygning kunde for et Par Maaneder hver Sommer være fyldt af Emigranter paa Gjennemreise, da Stedet var bleven til den første Holdeplads paa Veien fra Milwaukee til Koshkonong og videre vestover.

XIX.
Den første norske Kirke i Amerika.

Det var her DHrr. Heg & Reymert begyndte at udgive "Nordlyset," den første norske Avis i Amerika—hvorom mere senere. Det var her den velbekjendte Pastor C. L. Clausen fik bygget den første norske Kirke i Amerika Aar 1844. Han kom herover om Høsten 1843, var en elskværdig, begavet og gudfrygtig Præst og samlede snart de spredte Nybyggere i Muskego og Yorkville om sig til norsklutherske Menigheder. Han blev imidlertid ikke ret længe i Muskego, men flyttede til Luthervalley paa Rockprærie og afløstes i Muskego af Pastor H. A. Stub. Saavidt erindres var Pastor Clausen Norskesynodens første President, og da han snart blev det engelske Sprog mægtig, var han de tidligst efterkommende norske Præster til stor Tjeneste, og det er ikke for meget at sige, at han var deres høire Haand ved Arbeidet med at organisere norske Menigheder blandt de spredte Nybyggere. Det maa vel siges, at det senere gik ham, som det gaar de fleste Banebrydere, der af Hjertet opofrer sig for sin Gjerning, hans Tjenester glemtes hurtigt og fuldstændigt af de Mænd, som havde mest at takke ham for.

Det var ogsaa her de over Milwaukee kommende Emigranter standsede for at søge Oplysning, Raad og Veiledning hos sine tidligere ankomne Landsmænd angaaende de Forholde i den nye Verden, som nærmest vedkom deres Fremtid, og hvad der nu for dem var det bedste at gjøre. Hans Heg, Evens ældste Søn, der faldt som Brigadegeneral i Slaget ved Chickamauga, vidste at fortælle mangen interessant Episode fra de Ture, han gjorde til Jefferson-, Rock- og Koshkonongprærie med Emigrantfamilier. Nu bor der en Tydsker paa det gamle Heg, hvilket ogsaa er Tilfældet med mange andre af de af Nordmænd først ryddede Farme. De fleste af de gamle Settlere er enten døde eller flyttet andetsteds hen, men af den yngre Slægt er der endnu mange, som bor paa deilige, veldyrkede Farme, og i Forening med de Norske paa Yorkvilleprærie er de endnu talrige nok til at sutinere en Præst og to Kirker.

Det var ogsaa paa dette Sted den velbekjendte Sagfører og Politiker, James D. Reymert i sin Tid spillede en fremragende Rolle. Han byggede en Dampsag og tog Kontrakt paa at bygge en Plankevei fra Muskego Center til Waterford—en Veilængde af 12 til 14 Mil. Herved kom Farmernes Egeskove i Pris og mange fik et lønnende Arbeide for sig selv og sine Trækdyr. Han udviklede for en Tid en stor Virksomhed, men man troede, at han led Tab hos Plankevei-Kompagniet, og han flyttede til Milwaukee og senere til New York, hvor han blev Medlem af Sagførerfirmaet Jenkins & Reymert.

XX.
Yorkvilleprærie.

Det norske Settlement paa Yorkvilleprærie adskilles egentlig kun fra Muskego ved Muskego Creek, en liden Elv som løber ud af Søen Windlake og falder i Fox River ved Byen Rochester. De første Nordmænd, som bosatte sig paa dette Sted, var Mons Aadland fra Samnanger, Bergens Stift, og Nels Johnson fra Hiterdal. De kom hertil begge i 1840. Aadland hørte til Beaver Creek-Selskabet og var kommen over i 1837 med det første Bergensskib sammen med Ole Rynning. Efter 3 Aars Ophold i Illinois flyttede han og Familie hid. Af hans Børn er der nu kun tre, som lever; de to Sønner bor paa de store Farme, han i sin Levetid eiede, og Datteren, Enkefru Preus, bor i Norge. Nels Johnson flyttede nogle Aar efter til Iowa, hvor han for ikke ret længe siden døde som en af de mest formuende Farmere. Det næste Aar 1841 kom

Hermond Nelsen med Familie fra Hallingdal og bosatte sig her, til dem sluttede Elling Eielsen sig, og blev senere gift med den ældste Datter. Aslak Simonsen, Ole Helleiksen, Germund Johnson o. Fl. kom snart til, saa at deres Tal i 1843, da jeg kom hertil, var stort nok til at fylde Aadlands Lade med opmærksomme Tilhørere ved Eielsens Opbyggelser. Det var vel et Par Aar senere, at Elling Spillum, Tyge Hendriksen og flere kom hertil; men da var alt brugbart Regjeringsland optaget, saaat man maatte kjøbe af andre, og det begyndte at falde dyrt for Folk, som havde lidet Penge. Ogsaa i dette Settlement vedblev mange Emigrantselskaber at standse over paa Gjennemreise fra Milwaukee eller Racine forat skaffe sig nærmere Oplysning hos sine Landsmænd og faa Skyds vestover til Steder, hvor der endnu fandtes Regjeringsland. Selv gjorde jeg et Par saadanne Ture til Koshkonong med Emigrantfamilier. Det var dengang vanskeligt at faa Husrum for dem, da de alle søgte at hjælpe sig med det Allernødvendigste. Jeg kan erindre, at jeg fik en Familie ind hos Hr. Smitbak fra Numedal, som var en af de første, som nedsatte sig paa den store Prærie. Jeg har senere hørt, at han var bleven en rig Mand, hvilket alt i Omgivelserne ogsaa da lod forudse.

XXI.
Ogden og de Norske.

Her et Par Smaatræk forat betegne Forholdene paa den Tid: Der kom om Sommeren '44 eller '45 en ung Nordmand fra Chicago, som havde en Hest han vilde sælge; en af vore Naboer kjøbte den, og et Par Uger derefter kom en vis Mr. Ogden (Slagter i Milwaukee) med Sheriffen og tog Hesten under Paastand, at Hesten var hans og at han havde Ret til at tage sin Eiendom, hvor han fandt den. Manden, som havde kjøbt Hesten, maatte anlægge Sag mod Ogden, og det blev ubestridelig bevist, at Hesten, der kun var 3 Aar gammel, var kjøbt i Indiana det foregaaende Aar og var overvintret i Chicago. Ogden maatte betale for Hesten med Sagsomkostninger. Det gik ofte temmelig lovløst til i de Dage.

Omkring denne Tid var der megen Sygdom blandt de norske Nybyggere i Muskego og det rygtedes i Racine, at der var Nød og Mangel paa Fødemidler hos dem. Velgjørende Menneskevenner samlede derfor flere Vognlæs Proviant, som blev bragt ud til Yorkville, hvor en Komite blev udnævnt til at besørge Omdelingen. Da Ogden og hans Sherif var derude og tog den ovenomtalte Hest, lagde de Mærke til dette Gods, og Ogdens Sagfører paastod under Proceduren om Hesten, at de Norske maatte være en Tyvebande, thi man havde seet hos dem en Mængde stjaalent Gods. Jeg var et af Vidnerne i denne Sag og vor Sagfører opfordrede mig til at forklare Sammenhængen.

Saasnart det var sagt, at det omtalte Gods var Proviant sendt ud fra Racine til syge og trængende Emigranter, saa Ogdens Sagfører at han havde forløbet sig, og frafaldt sin Paastand, og Dommeren, der heldede stærkt til Ogdens Side, vilde ikke høre videre Forklaring. Jeg fik dog tilføiet, at Citanten i Sagen var Medlem af den Komite, som forestod Uddelingen. Jeg hørte siden af en af Jurymændene, at denne Episode fjernede al Tvivl hos Juryen.

Der var paa denne Tid et udbredt Know Nothing-Element blandt de velstaaende Amerikanere, og denne Trængselstid blandt de norske Indvandrere i Muskegos Skovtrakter aabnede Øinene paa Politikerne i Racine County, thi dengang skulde hvert Town forsørge sine egne Fattige, og da nu Yorkville omfattede Muskego eller det nuværende Norway og tre andre Townships, fik man i næste Legislatur Town of Norway afsat for sig selv af Frygt for Skattebyrderne til de fattige Norskes Ophold. Stakkels Norway skulde nu faa skjøtte sig selv! Man faar undskylde dette med, at man ikke kjendte Normændene. Naar vi nu ser de veldyrkede, prægtig bebyggede Farme, Norskerne i Norway og tilgrændsende Towns bebor, ser den Velstand, Hygge og Intelligents, som overalt viser sig hos dem, er det undskyldeligt om vi opvarmes af en Smule Stolthed over vor Nationalitet. De Mænd, som dengang skræmtes over de Norskes Armod, ere næsten alle komne nærmere Fattighuset end Nordmændene i Racine County.

XXII.
Reise fra Bergen til New York i 1843.

Om Vaaren 1843 skulde der reise to Skibe fra Bergen med Emigranter til Amerika. De blev begge udrustede af Rederiet Gade. Det ene var et Barkskib, som indskrev 80 Passagerer, det andet en Brig, som kun tog 52. Med Undtagelse af mig selv og en ung Mand, Nels Torstensen, som jeg betalte Overreisen for, samt en ung Bogbindersvend, Øvre fra Bergen, var alle Passagerer ombord i Briggen fra Vos Præstegjæld, og saavidt nu erindres var det samme Tilfældet ombord i Barkskibet. En Undtagelse herfra var dog Cleng Peerson, som kom tilbage med dette Skib fra sin sidste Reise til Norge. I Fragtkontrakterne var Afgangstiden fastsat til den 1ste Mai, men Skibene blev ikke færdige før til midt ud i Maaneden, og i denne Tid maatte Emigranterne henligge i Bergen og tære paa Nisten. Størsteparten af dem havde modtaget Breve fra Venner i Amerika, hvori der gaves dem Raad og Veiledning og efter hvilke de havde bestemt, hvorhen de agtede sig. Ingen af dem var ganske uden Midler; nogle af dem var endog velstaaende Folk med $1,000 eller mere i rede Penge paa Familien. Reisen begyndte under det behageligste Veir, og med en strygende Østenvind sattes Kursen mod Vest over Nordsøen via Færøerne og om to Uger var vi omtrent halvveis til Amerika. Man begyndte saa smaat at snakke om, at vor Overreise vilde blive den hurtigste man endnu havde hørt om, thi med den samme Fremgang i to Uger til vilde vi se Amerika. Men i de paafølgende 6 til 7 Uger maatte der stadig kjæmpes med Vestenvind, sommetider orkanagtige Storme, saaat hvad der blev vundet den ene Dag tabtes den næste. Den lille Brig holdt dog godt Søen og vi havde dygtige Officerer og Mandskab ombord.

XXIII.
Sygdom blandt Passagererne.

Jeg, som i de to til tre sidste Aar havde flakket om paa Søen og seet Havets Lunefuldhed, følte ingen Bekymring fra den Side; men hvad der under de vedvarende Vestenstorme indgjød baade mig og andre en velgrundet Frygt, var en ondartet Sygdom, som var udbrudt blandt Passagererne. Der fortaltes mellem dem, at der havde været Nervefeber i den Egn, hvorfra en Del af dem var komne. Første Styrmand var en Bekjendt af mig, med hvem jeg tidligere havde gjort en Reise til England, og jeg omtalte for ham, hvad jeg havde hørt. Da Kapteinen fik det at vide, blev han alvorlig bange. Rederiet havde ikke givet os Læge med, men forsynet Kapteinen med en Kasse Mediciner, forat han i Nødstilfælde kunde fungere som Læge. Fra den Tid gjorde han hvad han kunde, men, som det syntes, uden nogen Nytte, thi Sygdommen greb stadig om sig; to Børn i en Familie døde og blev begravne i Søen. Det ældste var en Pige paa 10 til 12 Aar; hun led meget af Diarrhoe, og en gammel Tjenestepige i Familien gav hende en Dosis Hoffmansdraaber, som fulgtes af forfærdelige Smerter og hun døde meget hastig. Ligene indsyedes i Seildug med en Sten ved Fødderne og paa en Planke lod man dem under Afsyngelse af et Salmevers glide ud i Bølgerne. Disse Børn tilhørte en velstaaende og respektabel Familie og Medfølelsen for dem var almindelig. Tager jeg ikke feil, er der to eller tre Børn efter disse Forældre, som endnu lever her i Landet. Det her anførte er ikke noget enestaaende Tilfælde, jeg ved at der var mangen Udvandrerfamilie, som maatte gjennemgaa lignende Prøvelser.

Den 4de Juli, Amerikas Frihedsdag, fandt os endnu i rum Sø, men i den sidste Tid var det dog begyndt at krybe fremad med et mere lempeligt Veir. Der var nu altfor meget Ængstelighed og Forstemthed til at nogen følte sig oplagt til at høitideligholde vort tilkommende Hjemlands Frihedsdag. Den unge Mand, jeg havde betalt for, var nu meget syg og jeg frygtede en Tid for, at han kom til at bukke under, men hans Jernnatur seirede og da kom han sig utroligt hurtig. Da vi endelig fik en New York Lods ombord, var vi endnu næsten et Par Hundrede Mile fra Land, men han var en ung djærv Krabat, der ikke sparede paa Seilene; i et væk blev der halet og braset og Mandskabet fik det meget livligt, og jeg maa tilstaa, at det var en stor Lettelse at se den raske Fremgang, Skibet nu gjorde.

XXIV.
Ankomst til New York.

Endelig viste Østkysten af Long Island sig for Emigranternes længselsfuldt stirrende Blikke som en lang, lavt i den vestlige Horisont liggende Skybanke. Det var tidlig i Morgenstunden og Kysten blev tydeligere alt som vi kom nærmere. Efterhaanden kom ogsaa Sandy Hook tilsyne længer Syd, nær Indseilingen til New York. Emigranternes Haab steg atter og alle takkede Gud fordi vi havde naaet Land, før Sygdommen tog mere Overhaand. Vi kom om Eftermiddagen til Ankers i Kvarantænehavnen lige ud for Marinehospitalet paa Staten Island. Tilstanden ombord var bleven anmeldt og da Hospitalslægen kom ombord, gav han Kapteinen en meget alvorlig Irettesættelse, som om han var Skyld i Sygdommen. Rederiet kunde havt godt af en Tilrettevisning, fordi der ikke fulgte Læge med Skibet, men Kapteinen havde visselig gjort det bedste han kunde. Det var os Alle en stor Glæde, da vi paa Havnen fandt Barkstibet "Juno," som afgik fra Bergen samtidig med os; det var først ankommet den foregaaende Dag, uagtet det skulde være en ualmindelig Hurtigseiler. Alle var friske der ombord. Af vore Passagerer var der en 7—8, som maatte bringes paa Hospitalet, Da ingen af Lægerne forstod Norsk, lagde de Beslag paa mig for at være Tolk, og jeg forblev paa Hospitalet i tre Dage. Lægerne gjorde sin Runde et Par Gange hver Nat, og jeg maatte da op og være med. Der var i samme Ward nogle syge tydske Emigranter og jeg blev da samtidig Tolk for dem. De Familier, som havde Syge paa Hospitalet, maatte ligge over i New York for at afvente Udfaldet.

XXV.
Afreise til Vesten.

Dagen før Afreisen fra New York fulgte jeg tilbage til Hospitalet med en Mand, hvis Søster var syg, men dog i god Bedring, og han besluttede at tage hende med, uagtet Lægen forsikrede ham, at hun kom til at dø, hvis han tog hende ud nu; jeg søgte ogsaa at overtale ham til at vente, men forgjeves. Jeg hørte siden, at hun døde paa Veien over Kanalen. Lægerne kaldte Sygdommen Skibsfeber og fortalte mig, at den til en vis Grad var smitsom, saaat hvis jeg vilde undgaa den, var det bedst jeg forlod Selskabet. Jeg havde lovet at være med dem opover Hudsonfloden til Byen Troy, hvor deres Tøi skulde veies og Overvægten betales, før de kom ombord i Kanalbaaden. Hver Voxen skulde have 100 Pund frit, og Resten betales Fragt for. Da vi holdt paa med at, veie, var der paa Bryggen et Selskab amerikanske Herrer og Damer, som betragtede disse Fremmede med megen Nysgjerrighed, og da de saa det norske Fladbrød blotstillet i Emigranternes Kister, kom en af dem hen og spurgte, om han maatte smage—ja bevares, det maatte han nok. Eriebanen var netop da bleven færdig fra Albany til Buffalo. Jeg havde besluttet at tage med Jernbanen fra Troy til Buffalo, og Tiden var nu kommen til at skilles fra Selskabet. Den unge Bogbindersvend Øvre fra Bergen var nu begyndt at blive syg; jeg søgte at overtale ham til at gjøre mig Følge, da han ellers paa Kanalbaaden vilde komme til at lide meget ondt; men det vilde han ikke. Senere hørte jeg, at han døde, da de kom til Buffalo.

XXVI.
Kaptein Gasman's [Gasmann's] følge.

Paa samme Tid som vi kom ogsaa et andet norsk Emigrantskib til New York fra Drøbak, ført af Kaptein [Johan] Gasmann. En Broder af Kapteinen, forhenværende Storthingsmand Hans Gasmann med Familie var ogsaa blandt Udvandrerne i dette Selskab. Jeg saa nogle af disse Folk paa Skibsmægler Balkens Kontor, hvor dengang næsten alle norske Skibes Indklareringsforretninger besørgedes. Størsteparten af Hr. Gasmanns Reisefølge gik vestover fra Milwaukee til Settlementerne ved Pine Lake og Rock River, hvor allerede nogle Landsmænd havde nedsat sig i disse Skovtrakter. Her byggede og ryddede den norske Storthingsmand sin Farm i Stilhed, uden at tage nogen ledende Del i offentlige Anliggender, og her endte han sine Dage for flere Aar siden. En af hans Sønner gjennemgik Militærskolen i West Point og er nu, saavidt vides, Officer i de Forenede Staters Arme. En anden har været ansat som Agent blandt Indianerne.

XXVII.
Mægler Balken og Emigranterne.

Mægler Balken var Bergenser af Fødsel og havde boet i New York i flere Aar. Paa hans Kontor var det derfor at Indvandrernes Kontrakter om Transporten til de vestlige Stater sædvanlig afsluttedes, skjønt Balken ikke syntes at være direkte interesseret i nogen af de konkurrerende Transportlinier. Denne Fragtforretning med Emigranter til Vesten var paa den Tid en stor og lønnende Forretning, og Konkurrensen mellem de forskjellige Linier var meget levende. Representanter for disse Linier kom derfor stadig til Balkens Kontor, og det var sædvanlig Kapteinerne, som handlede for Indvandrerne, da disse selv ikke forstod at varetage det Fornødne. Det var et almindeligt Rygte blandt Emigranterne, som formodentlig havde det fra tidligere indvandrede Venner, at der under disse Kontrakter foregik en hel Del Snyderi, men at de norske Kapteiner var delagtige deri, tror jeg ikke; de var idetheletaget hæderlige Mænd, som ikke indlod sig paa at tage Stikpenge, men gjorde det bedste de kunde for sine Emigranter; men da de ligesaalidt som Emigranterne kjendte specielt til disse Befordringslinier, rettede de sig gjerne efter Hr. Balkens Raad, som paa Grund af sit mangeaarige Ophold i New York bedst maatte kjende Forholdene og Liniernes Paalidelighed. Cleng Peerson forudsagde, at vort Selskab vilde blive bedraget af det Kompani, det sluttede Kontrakt med, og Udfaldet viste, at han havde Ret, men hvorpaa han støttede sin Mistanke fik jeg aldrig at vide.

Da Selskabet kom til Buffalo skulde de efter Overenskomsten have Dampskib derfra til Milwaukee og Chicago, men istedetfor dette blev de bragte ombord i et Seilskib, som under Vindstille og Modvind blev paa Reisen over en Maaned. Paa Grund af denne langvarige Reise, som Passagererne ikke havde regnet paa, led de meget ondt af Mangel paa Proviant. Med Dampskib vilde Reisen i det høieste have medtaget fire Dage; men i Buffalo var der ingen med dem, som kunde tale deres Sag, og den skriftlige Kontrakt, som tydelig udviste at de havde betalt for Dampskib over Søerne, blev ikke gjordt gjældende. Jeg havde været sex Uger i Wisconsin før den unge Mand, jeg havde betalt for, kom frem. Han var med paa Seilskibet til Chicago og kom derfra sammen med en Del Emigranter, som var komne over Havre, blandt hvem der var en Styrmand Wigeland, som forstod Engelsk og var deres Anfører.

XXVIII.
Runnervæsenet.

For de Emigrantselskaber, som ingen Tolk havde, var det paa den Tid meget vanskeligt at komme frem, uden at blive bedraget og forsinket paa Reisen. At være frivillig Tolk, uden Betaling, var forresten et utaknemmeligt Arbeide; havde de forstaaet sin egen Interesse, vilde vist de fleste af Emigranterne været skjønsomme nok til at betale lidt for Arbeidet. Det blev ogsaa derfor senere til Regel, at der maatte følge Tolk med, som sædvanlig blev betalt af Rederiet eller Transportkompaniet forat undgaa Forviklinger; ofte fulgte senere de norske Skibsførere med sine Emigranter lige til Chicago. Det saakaldte Runnervæsen (rettere Uvæsen) begyndte allerede da at plage

Emigranterne og der kom neppe et Brev tilbage fra Amerikafarerne uden at deri advaredes mod Emigrant-Runnerne, der fra den Dag de steg iland, indtil de naaede deres Bestemmelsessted, omringedes og forfulgtes af dem som af en Bisværm. Dette Uvæsen blev senere meget værre, og det uhyggeligste var, at Runnerne næsten uden Undtagelse var Emigranternes egne Landsmænd, der havde lært Engelsk, og indfandt sig iblandt dem som nogle Frelsens Engle, forat veilede og beskytte dem mod amerikansk Svindel. De, som ikke forud var bleven advaret mod dem, fæstede derfor meget let Tiltro til dem, medens paa den anden Side Advarslerne gjorde Emigranterne saa mistænksomme, at de heller ikke turde tro de enkelte redelige Mennesker, som tilbød sin Bistand. Selv den senere Tids Tolke, som bestod af en bedre Klasse Mennesker og arbeidede for fast Løn, var ofte udsatte for en haard Mistanke. Det gaar gjerne saa, at Reiseudgifterne som oftest bliver større end forud paaregnet, og for Folk, der ikke forstod hvad der forhandledes, faldt det ganske naturligt at se Bedragerier overalt. Men de Kjæltringstreger, som af og til kom for Dagen, gjorde denne Mistænksomhed meget undskyldelig. Da Runnernes Overgreb i New York havde bragt dette Landingssted for Emigranter i et meget slet Rygte, og da høie Landgangspenge strengt opkrævedes, begyndte den norske Udvandring at tage Veien over Quebeck i Canada, hvor det i Førstningen gik bedre; men det gik her som det gaar overalt: "Hvor Aadselet er samles og Ørnene." Runnerne var ikke sene med at finde Vei til Quebeck og det blev kun lidet bedre førend Udvandringen begyndte at drives med Dampskib og Jernbane; thi da traadte Lovgivningen beskyttende til og en strængere Kontrol førtes med de Transportlinier, som førte Emigranter saavelsom med deres Agenter og Tolke.

Jeg har omtalt denne vor Overreise noget udførligt, dels fordi Beretningen derom støtter sig paa egne Oplevelser, dels fordi Overreisen, saalænge den foregik med Seilskib, hovedsagelig var en Gjentagelse den ene af den anden, saaat meget deraf kan tjene som Exempel paa dem alle.

Det var næsten en ufravigelig Regel hos de første norske Indvandrere, at søge ud paa Landet forat finde et Stykke Land, hvorpaa de kunde bygge og bo. Det var en sjelden Undtagelse, at nogen norsk Bonde med Overlæg nedsatte sig i Byen. Kun naar hans Reisepenge ikke rak længer, tog han Arbeide i Byen, og naar det saa begyndte at gaa godt, forblev han hvor han var. De første Udvandrere kom jo udelukkende fra Landdistrikterne i Norge og deres første Tanke var, at faa et Stykke Jord at dyrke for deraf at udvinde det Fornødne til Livets Ophold. Med Sømænd og Haandværksfolk var det anderledes; deres Næringsvei førte dem naturlig til Byen. Den eneste Undtagelse jeg kan erindre, var Vossingerne i Chicago. Allerede blandt de første af dem nedslog enkelte sig i Byen, ja jeg kjendte endog dem, som vendte tilbage fra

Koshkonong til Chicago forat bo der, og det lykkedes for alle, som ikke drak for meget Brændevin.

XXIX.
De første Norske i Wisconsin Byerne.

Blandt de første Norske, jeg ved at fortælle om i Byen Racine, var en Vestlænding ved Navn Farbjørn Gunleiksen med Familie. Han holdt et lidet Boardingshus, hvor de Norske fra Muskego og Yorkville altid tog ind, naar de kom til Byen, og det skal siges til hans Ros, at der aldrig fandtes berusende Drikke i hans Hus. De Gamle ere nu døde, men to Døtre bo der endnu, og en Søn bor i Chicago. Racine havde for en Tid en ikke saa liden norsk Befolkning, men da daarlige Arbeidsforholde indtraf, flyttede mange ud paa Landet. Nu er Racine voxet sig op til en blomstrende Fabrikby paa 20,000 Indbyggere, og det siges at næsten en Trediepart er Danske.

Milwaukee havde tidligere en ikke saa liden norsk Befolkning, mest Sømænd og Haandværksfolk. Blandt de ældste, jeg kan erindre, var Kaptein Saveland. Han selv er død for mange Aar siden, men hans Efterkommere udgjør en talrig Slægt, hvoraf flere er Velstandsfolk. En Mand ved Navn Nordbo, som pleiede at modtage Logerende, havde tidlig nedsat sig der, og hos ham tog Farmerne fra Muskego og Yorkville, saavelsom fra Pine Lake og Rock River ind, naar de kom til Milwaukee. Da jeg i 1843 kom til Milwaukee, kunde jeg ikke finde nogen bosatte Norske, men Svenskeren, den velbekjendte Mr. Lange i Chicago, havde da et Hotel over paa Vestsiden. James D. Reymert og, tager jeg ikke feil, ogsaa John Thorson, var dengang unge Handelsbetjente. John Thorson er nu en af Byens ledende Forretningsmænd. Familien Kildal var vist ogsaa blandt de første, som nedsatte sig der. Reinertsen var en af Byens gamle Settlere og hans Boardingshus paa Clinton Street, som endnu staar paa sin gamle Plads under Navn af "Scandinavian House," var gjerne Samlingsplads for Byens norske Søfolk, saavelsom det Sted, hvor de norske Farmere altid fandt en venlig Modtagelse og Husly for sig og sine Trækdyr, naar de kom til Byen med sine Varer. En Bergenser, som kaldte sig Frøiseth, forsøgte sig der som Handelsmand, men blev der ikke længe. Hos ham traf jeg første Gang den bekjendte Dr. [Johan Christian Brotkorb] Dass (Dundas), som senere bosatte sig i Koshkonong. De første Norske, som nedsatte sig i Milwaukee, bestod hovedsagelig af Sømænd og Skibstømrere. Nu tæller Byens norske Befolkning flere Tusinder af alle Samfundsklasser, med tre norske Kirker og flere Foreninger til gjensidig Understøttelse o. s. v. Jeg tror det er et Særkjende blandt vore Landsmænd i Byerne, at de ikke liker at bo tilleie, men søger snarest muligt at kunne bo i egne

Huse; dette giver dem et godt Fodfæste og en solidere Grundvold, hvorpaa at bygge sig en uafhængig og lykkelig Fremtid—noget, som Efterkommerne vilde gjøre vel i at lægge sig paa Minde. Saavel under Krigen som i de nærmest paas følgende Aar, var Skibsfarten paa de store Indsøer en meget lønnende Forretning, og der var ikke saa faa af Nordmændene i Milwaukee, som i den Tid samlede store Formuer. Mange af dem førte egne Skibe og eiede desuden Part i andre, hvilket saalænge Tiderne var gode bragte en respektabel Indtægt; men saa kom Pengekrisen i 1873 med andre Forandringer i Konjunkturerne, hvoraf fulgte en saa brat Nedgang i Fragter og Priser, at de, som traf til at sidde inde med megen Skibseiendom, led uhyre store Tab; de derimod, som havde anbragt sin Formue i Grundeiendomme, blev uberørte.

XXX.
Erindringer om Nybyggerlivet.

De første norske Settlementer paa Prærierne Jefferson, Rock og Koshkonong er allerede blevne omtalte i Forbigaaende, og da det ikke er Meningen at levere udførlige Settlement-Beskrivelser, hvilket forudsætter ganske andre Kilder at øse af end dem, jeg raader over, faar jeg lade mig nøie med nogle faa personlige Erindringer fra den Tid, jeg besøgte disse smukke og frugtbare Egne. Til Jefferson og Rock Prærie kom jeg ikke før i Foraaret 1849 og da kun paa Gjennemreise. Det var bleven sagt, at Jefferson var et af de smukkeste Landskaber, man havde seet, og det saa ud til at være sandt. Da jeg reiste derigjennem med Pastor Clausen, var næsten alt brugbart Regjeringsland optaget og overalt saaes velbyggede Gaarde ligesom alt vidnede om Flid og Velvære blandt Farmerne. Vi blev over til næste Morgen hos Kristoffer Nyhus, en af de første fra Numedal, som nedsatte sig der. Pastor Clausen var kjendt deromkring fra sine Missionsreiser i de nye norske Settlementer, og hvor han var kjendt, var han ogsaa altid velkommen; overalt hvor han kom, var han agtet og elsket blandt de norske Nybyggere. Paa denne Tur besøgte vi Beloit og Janesville, Stæder, som endda var i sin Barndom, og kom endelig til Luther Valley paa Rock Prærie, hvor Pastor Clausen dengang eiede en velbebygget Farm. Prærien her er et mere storslaget og bakket Landskab end Racine og Jefferson, og jeg havde alt længe hørt, at Egnene omkring Rock River havde Navn for at være meget rige og frugtbare; Landet var derfor tidlig bleven optaget af amerikanske Pionerer. Der var dog allerede dengang Norske nok til at danne en stor Menighed, og de havde faaet sig en rummelig Stenbygning til Kirke. Som hørende til de første Settlere hørte jeg nævne Lars Skavland, Gulleik Laugen, Mr. Gravdal—blandt andre, hvis

Navne nu ikke erindres—; de havde nedsat sig der i 1839 samtidig med dem paa Jefferson.

XXXI.
I Dane County.

Nord for Rock County ligger Dane County med en Fortsættelse af det samme deilige Prærieland og det var naturligt, at disse ivrige Landsøgere fra Klippelandet hinsides Havet følte sig henrevne af disse skjønne Egne. De første norske Indvandrere kom derfor samtidig til Rock og Dane County, nemlig i 1839 og 1840. De var for det meste fra Numedal, Vos og Stavanger. Her som overalt fulgte deres Flid og Sparsomhed dem og bar de samme gode Frugter—de fik sig hurtig hyggelige Hjem og et sorgfrit Udkomme. Det saakaldte Koshkonong Settlement blev snart anset for det største og rigeste norske Settlement i Wisconsin. Da jeg første Gang (1844) kom dertil med et Læs Emigranttøi, hed det overalt, at alt det bedste Land var optaget og at der ikke var Husrum at faa for Nykommere. Ved det bedste Land forstod man dengang, at man maatte have en Skovlund ved Siden af Prærielandet. Men det var dog sandt, at Indvandrerne stuvede sig altfor tæt sammen i de nye Settlementer. En Mand fra Numedal, hvis Navn jeg nu har glemt, var saa god at modtage den Familie jeg kjørte for. Han boede ikke langt fra det saakaldte Christiana og var nok en af de første norske Settlere. Han fortalte om en Mand fra Skien, som havde roet med Baad fra Beloit i Rock County, da han kom derop i '39 for at søge Land. En Mand ved Navn Bjoland fra Stavanger var ogsaa kommen der i 1839 og havde som en af de første taget Land der paa Prærien. En ung Mand fra Saue paa Vos sagdes at være en af de første Settlere nær Cambridge og havde senere Navn for at være den rigeste Farmer blandt de Norske paa Koshkonong. Efterfølgende af Prof. J. Olsen, i Anledning af Prof. Rasmus B. Andersons Moders Død for nogle Aar siden, vil her maaske være af historisk Interesse. Det er dels et Uddrag, dels en fri Oversættelse af en engelsk Artikel i "Madison Democrat":

"Da Abel Cathrine Amundsen var den første hvide Kvinde, som bosatte sig i Town of Albion (Dane County), vil nogle Oplysninger om hendes Liv være af Interesse, især deleshed da hendes Søn, Prof. Rasmus B. Anderson, den nuværende Forenede Staters Minister i Danmark, er saa vel bekjendt. Hun var født i Sandeid i den sydvestlige Del af Norge. Hendes Fader, Bernhardus Arnoldus von Krogh, var Løjtnant i den norske Armee. Hendes Moder var ogsaa af den berømte von Krogh Stamme, som strækker sig i en hel Linie af Militær-Officerer tilbage til en vis Major Bernhardus von Krogh i Lübeck, som i 1644 kom til Bremen med Soldater forat hjelpe Danmark imod Sverige. Han forblev i den danske Tjeneste, og hans eneste Søn, George Frederik von Krogh blev Oberst for et norsk Regiment i 1710. Hans Efterkommere vare talrige og største Delen af dem indtraadte i Armeen som Officerer. I 1830 blev hun gift med Bjørn Anderson, en Bondesøn, født nær Stavanger i 1801. Det er næsten umuligt for Amerikanere at forestille sig med hvilken Bestyrtelse og Forbitrelse dette Ægteskab mellem Officerens Datter og Bondesønnen blev modtaget. At hendes Mand var en Kvæker og hørte saaledes ikke til Statskirken, forøgede ogsaa Uvilien mod det unge Par. De besluttede da at reise til det Land hinsides Havet, hvis Stjerne just nu begyndte at vise sig over Horizonten. Saa forlod de da Norge i Vaaren 1836 med det første store Følge af norske Emigranter, som kom til dette Land. Da de naaede New York, reiste Bjørn Anderson med Kone og nogle andre Familier til Rochester, N. Y., hvor de boede to Aar. Bjørn arbeidede da som Bødker. Ved Udløbet af denne Tid flyttede de til det norske Settlement i La Salle County, Illinois, hvor de ogsaa levede i to Aar. I 1840 gik Bjørn Anderson tilfods med to Kammerater paa en Undersøgelsesreise til Wisconsin for at finde et passende Sted for et nyt Hjem. Han valgte en Strækning Land nær Lake Koshkonong og vendte saa tilbage til La Salle County. Den følgende Vaar, med Kone og fire smaa Børn og de samme to Reisefæller, drog han afsted til sit nye Hjem i Wisconsin. De vare det første Par, som bosatte sig i det nuværende Town of Albion, og de Besværligheder og Lidelser, som de da maatte udstaa, synes nu kun som en Roman for den yngre Generation. Men igjennem hele denne haarde Tid mistede de aldrig Modet. Begge havde en sjelden Viliekraft; han var driftig, rastløs og virksom, hun var blid, stille og udholdende. I de første to eller tre Aar var 6 Cents alle de rede Penge de eiede. Med de faa Produkter, som de kunde spare, reiste han 70 Mile over den vilde udyrkede Egn til Milwaukee for at kjøbe Livsnødvendigheder. Da han var borte blev hun hjemme i Loghytten med sine Børn, og havde nu og da en Indianer som Gjest. Deres Bestræbelser lønnedes tilsidst og i ti Aar havde de første 40 Acres formeret sig til 230 Acres frugtbart Land. Men netop da Pionerlivets Strid var endt, kom en ny Fiende. I Sommeren 1850 rasede Koleraen i Settlementet og Bjørn Anderson og en Søn døde deraf. Ni Børn efterlevede ham, af hvilke otte endnu er ilive. Hans ældste Søn, Andrew A., er en velstaaende Farmer i Goodhue County, Minn.; Abel B., er Præst i Muskegon, Michigan; Brown Anderson er Handelsmand i Spring Grove, Minn.; Prof. Rasmus B. Anderson er, som allerede sagt, Minister i Danmark. Deres fire Døtre ere alle gifte; tre bor i Minnesota og den fjerde i Iowa. Enken blev gift i 1854 med Ingebrigt Amundsen. Han døde i 1861 efterladende en Søn."

XXXII.
Tollefsons Erfaringer.

En Farmer, G. Tollefson, som kom til Amerika i 1843 og nu bor i Dane County, skriver en Artikel i et engelsk Blad om sin Erfaring ved Ankomsten til Amerika, hvoraf her hidsættes følgende: Ankomne til New York gav en Mand ved Navn Bakke Fripas for Tollefson-Familien og Følget til Milwaukee, hvorhen de kom i god Behold. Denne By var da paa Udkanten af Civilisationen og der var kun faa Norske i Wisconsin. Tollefson og hans Familie reiste med Lars Dommerud til Muskego, hvor de mødte iblandt andre Landsmænd, Even Heg, Reymert og Bakke. En Tid derefter drog han længere vestover og arbeidede for en Sherwood, der boede nær Clinton, i Rock County. Tollefson siger: "Jeg splittede 600 Rails forat faa laane Sherwoods Oxer og Vogn, saaat jeg kunde bringe mine Forældre til Rock County. Da jeg ikke var vant til at drive Oxer og da jeg ønskede at se mine Forældre snarest muligt, drev jeg Teamet for fort. Det varede ikke længe før Oxerne blev trætte og saa lagde de sig ned og jeg formaaede ikke at faa dem at røre sig fra Stedet. I denne Forlegenhed gav jeg dem Maisax og efter en Tid stod de op og gik fremad efter mig. Dette gjentoges flere Gange, indtil det blev saa tilsidst, at naar de vilde have Mais lagde de sig blot ned og førend de fik det kom de ikke af Stedet. Jeg kom saa paa den Ide, at hænge et Maisax paa Ryggen og gaa foran Dyrene. Paa denne Maade lokkede jeg dem fremad og endelig kom jeg til mine Forældre. Paa Hjemreisen drev vi mere langsomt. Jeg har ofte tænkt, at Sherwood havde usædvanlig Tillid til mig, en Fremmed og dertil en Nykommer, idet han laante mig Oxespandet for saa lang en Reise, uden at vide om jeg kunde drive dem eller ikke.

"Da jeg ønskede at eie mit eget Land saa snart som muligt, reiste jeg til Primrose i 1849. Her mødte jeg Niels Einarson. Der var nok af Land, men hvorledes at finde Numer for det jeg valgte, var Spørgsmaalet. Efter megen Undersøgelse fandt vi et stort Egetræ, et kort Stykke Øst fra der hvor Norman Randal bor. Paa dette Træ var tydelig at se de følgende Bogstaver og Nummere: N. W. ¼, S. 23, T. 5, N. R. 6 E. Der var hverken Pen eller Papir at faa uden at gaa mange Mile, og noget maatte strax gjøres. Jeg laante en Øxe af Einarson, huggede ned et lidet Aspetræ, og efterat have gjort det fladt paa begge Sider saaat det blev ganske tyndt, tog jeg min Lommekniv og skar i det Bogstaverne og Numerne akkurat som de vare i Egetræet. Med denne Aspestok under min Arm gik jeg til Landkontoret og lagde Stokken og Pengene paa Disken til Embedsmændenes store Moro, De forstod Beskrivelsen og jeg fik Landet."

XXXIII.
Den første Præstestrid.

De første Settlere i Dane County pleiede at gjøre sig lystige over en Tildragelse mellem deres første Præst [J. W. C.] Dietrichson og en Bonde ved Navn [Halvor Christian Pedersen] Funkelien. Denne Funkelien synes at have været en Spøgefugl og en Nar. Han fandt sin Fornøielse i at forarge Præsten, hvem han stadig laa i Strid med. Præstens svage Side var, at han snart blev vred og tabte sin Selvbeherskelse. Tilsidst kom det saavidt, at han forbød Funkelien at komme i Kirken. En Søndag opfordrede han derfor Medhjelperne til at kaste Funkelien paa Dør, da denne trods Forbudet var kommen i Kirken. Medhjelperne forholdt sig imidlertid rolige. Dette bragte Præsten ud af Fatning, og han gik selv ned paa Kirkegulvet for at kaste Funkelien ud. Denne modsatte sig og der blev stort Spektakel i Kirken. Funkelien sagsøgte Præsten, og den før omtalte Bjørn Anderson, der var en Slags Sagfører, optraadte som Funkeliens Advokat, og Præsten maatte finde sig i at betale Mulkt. En anden Nykommer, som jeg kjendte personlig, kunde ogsaa fortælle, at han engang havde sendt sin Kone over til Præstegaarden i et Ærinde, som forargede Præsten. Han greb hende saa haardt i Armen for at jage hende paa Dør, at der viste sig fire blaa Mærker efter hans Fingre paa Konens Arm. Derfor blev han ogsaa sagsøgt og maatte bøde 50 Dollars. Man ser heraf at "Præstestriden" mellem de Norske i Amerika begyndte tidlig, og det anføres her som formodentlig den første Ytring af denne Slags iblandt dem.

XXXIV.
En Nybyggers Hytte i Columbia County.

Det var i Sommeren 1845, at Forfatteren reiste sin Nybyggerhytte i det nuværende Columbia County og var maaske den nærmeste Anledning til at de herlige Landomraader—Springprærie, Bonnetprærie, Lodi og Omegn kom i de Norskes Besiddelse, thi den amerikanske Indflytningsstrøm var begyndt at sprede sig mod Nord med stærke Skridt. Hermed gik det saaledes til: Da jeg i 1843 kom til Yorkville Prærie, Racine County, var det bedste Land optaget, de 80 Acres Prærie jeg kjøbte, ansaas for at ligge for lavt og jeg var ikke tilfreds med det. Jeg og en anden ung Mand, Niels Torstensen, for hvem jeg havde betalt Overreisen, besluttede derfor at reise vestover for at søge Land. Med et Par staute Oxer og Vogn, forsynet med en liden Kogeovn, Proviant, Sengklæder og andet nødvendigt Tilbehør for Leirlivet, drog vi afsted i August Maaned, 1845, og satte mod Vest veiledet af et Kort over Wisconsin og et Lommekompas. Vi kjørte direkte til Koshkonong Prærie, hvor vi havde været et Par Gange før, og det var egentlig derfra Landsøgningen skulde begynde. Jeg havde nemlig faaet den Ide, at den samme Præriestrækning fortsatte sig længer mod Nord. Vi fulgte den slagne Landevei til Madison, hvor der intet indbydende var for en Præriefarmer. Madison havde intet mærkeligt undtagen sin Naturskjønhed, og den store Territorial-Bygning der saa meget røselig ud blandt de smaa Træhuse—nu derimod vilde den tage sig meget forladt ud ved Siden af den prægtige Capitol-Bygning, Staten eier.

Vi kjørte en Mil fra Byen, men skræmtes af de bratte Bakker, hvor Statsuniversitetet nu ligger, og vendte om mod Øst, hvor vi slog ind paa den gamle Vei til Fort Winnebago. En Landsmand ved Navn Amund [Endresen] Rosseland, som kom herover i 1837 og med hvem jeg var kjendt fra Norge, havde jeg hørt var flyttet herud tidligere og jeg vilde nu besøge ham. Han skulde have nedsat sig i Nærheden af "Dells" ved Wisconsin River, nogle Mil fra Fort Winnebago. Landet omkring Fortet var i flere Mils Omkreds lavt, sumpigt og uhyggeligt. Efter en høist besværlig og kjedelig Vandring over Sandrygge med Skrubeg og Sumper naaede vi endelig en Eftermiddag frem til Stedet. Vi traf en halv Mil fra Huset, en norsk Mand som holdt paa at rage Hø, og han var saa lidet meddelsom, at vi neppe kunde faa mere at vide af ham, end at Amund var reist bort og ventedes ikke hjem paa nogle Dage. Dette, tilligemed Landets Beskaffenhed, bestemte os til at vende om; men da baade vi og Oxerne var trætte, slog vi Leir for den Dag, et Stykke nedenfor, hvor der fandtes Vand. Vi var jo som hjemme hos os selv i Vognen og det samme var Oxerne paa den rige Græsmark. Vi bagede vore Kager, stegte vort Flesk, kogede vor Kaffe og spiste med en Appetit, som en Fyrste kunde misunde os. Vi tog samme Vei tilbage, omkring 20 Mil til et Sted, hvor en intelligent Amerikaner, ved Navn Young, netop holdt paa at bygge sin Hytte. Han sagde os, at naar vi bøiede af nogle faa Mil mod Østen, vilde vi finde hvad vi søgte, nemlig godt Prærieland ved Siden af Skovland. Vi fulgte hans Raad og kom snart til et Landskab afvexlende med Skov og Prærie. Vi traf her et Par Amerikanere, som ogsaa holdt paa at bygge sine Huse. Den ene af dem, en gammel Pioner, ved Navn Gilbert, vilde sælge os sin Claim, men da vi nu fandt, at vi havde frit Valg af ligesaa godt Land som hans, og tillige besad den samme Ret til at tage Claim, kjørte vi et Par Mil længer Syd, og vor største Vanskelighed bestod i at træffe et Valg, da der var Overflod af tilfredsstillende Steder at vælge imellem. Vi traf endelig vort Valg, begyndte at bygge vor Loghytte og snart kunde vi med Digteren Sagen synge:

"I Dalens Skjød en Hytte laa
Ved Bredden af en Kilde,

Dens Væg var Ler, dens Tag var Straa,
Dens Hegn var Roser vilde."

Det led nu ud i September Maaned og vor første Omsorg var at slaa Hø og bygge Stald mod Vinteren for vore Oxer. Saaledes blev Begyndelsen lagt til de rige og blomstrende norske Settlementer paa Springprærie, Bonnetprærie, Lodi, og de andre omliggende deilige Præriestrækninger. Der kom ikke nogen andre norske Nybyggere til Stedet den Høst. Vi syslede med at sætte istand for Vinteren indtil første November. Vi hørte, at der var kommen en norsk Mand, som hed Kleppen, og havde taget Land noget Syd for det Sted, hvor vi nedsatte os, men vi saa ham aldrig. Han var et Slags folkesky Eneboer, som ikke pleiede Omgang med andre Mennesker. Det næste Foraar havde han solgt sin Claim. Da jeg senere paa Høsten reiste til Milwaukee for at udtage Pre-emption Papirer paa Landet, omtalte jeg Stedet for Folk paa Koshkonong, som jeg kjendte, og da Indvandringen fra Norge paa den Tid var meget stor, kunde det forudses, at Nykommerne den næste Sommer vilde strømme indover de norske Settlementer i Dane County. Jeg skrev ogsaa Breve til Venner og Bekjendte i La Salle County, Illinois, hvilket havde tilfølge, at et Par af dem flyttede derud det næste Foraar. Den næste Sommer blev en travl Tid i det nye Settlement. Ved Besøget i Milwaukee bragte jeg med nogle af de nødvendigste Redskaber, saasom Plov, Harv og lignende. Tidlig om Foraaret kom en personlig Ven af mig, Peder Frøland, som var kommen over til La Salle County i 1837, derud og bragte med sig to Par Oxer med Vogn og andre Redskaber. Vi to slog os da sammen om Arbeidet. Da det led udi Juni Maaned begyndte norske Emigranter at ankomme i Skarer over Koshkonong. Et Selskab af dem havde leiet Ole Trovatten, en gammel bekjendt Mand paa Koshkonong, til at komme med dem for at udtage Land. Jeg var allerede før bleven bekjendt med denne Mand, og da han fandt, at ogsaa jeg kunde udtage Land, blev han snart kjed af at trampe om over Skov og Prærie, uden anden Erstatning end Tak for Hjelpen, og han gik glad tilbage til sit Hjem, og overlod mig Strævet. Alt det Land, man ansaa værdt at tage i hele Egnen, kom snart i Nybyggernes Hænder. Jeg og Per Frøland havde nu et Team paa 4 Par Oxer og pløiede den Sommer omkring 100 Acres Prærieland for Nykommerne.

XXXV.
Et Indianerbesøg.

Her havde jeg min første og sidste Erfaring mellem Indianerne. En varm Sommerdag, da jeg var ude paa en Myr for at slaa Hø, fik jeg se en Hob

Hjorte komme i flyvende Fart henover en Høide paa Prærien og strax efter fulgte nogle vilde Jægere tilhest. Hjortene syntes dog denne Gang at have altfor stort Forsprang til at komme dem paa Skudvidde. Snart efter viste der sig paa Prærien, i samme Retning, en lang Række Hestfolk og Fodfolk. Det var en Bande Winnebago Indianere, som havde forladt sin Reservation og gjort et Streifetog til de sydlige Countier i Staten. Her havde de gjort sig skyldige i nogle Overgreb, og Authoriteterne havde befalet dem at vende tilbage til deres Hjem. Det var denne Bande som nu, paa Veien nordover til deres Reservation, kom her forbi. Et Par af deres unge Mænd kom hen til mig og gjorde Tegn til at de var tørstige. Jeg havde en liden norsk Kaffekjedel med Drikkevand staaende i Græsset, og de pegede paa den og gjorde Tegn til at ville drikke. Heldigvis var der en prægtig Kilde henne ved Myrkanten, en halv Mils Vei fra os. Jeg viste dem derhen med Tegn saa godt jeg kunde. Derpaa drog de fornøiet derhen, slog Leir og forblev der i tre Dage. De farvede Amerikanere behandle deres Kvinder ligesaa haardt som de hvide Amerikanere behandler dem godt og bærer dem paa Hænderne. Mændene red stolte i Spidsen for Følget, med Riflen over Knæerne, medens Kvinderne fulgte efter tilfods, belæssede med Proviant, Leirekvipering, o.s.v. Da jeg gik hjem om Aftenen, ledte min Nysgjerrighed mig gjennem Indianernes Leir, for at se hvorledes de stelte sig. Der var i Banden en Halvblodsindianer, som talte lidt Engelsk. Han lod mig forstaa, at jeg ikke maatte komme i Leiren. Jeg lod mig ikke dette sige to Gange, da jeg var alt andet end vel tilmode over disse vilde Naboers Nærværelse. Et Par af deres Kvinder kom dog den næste Dag til vor Hytte, og vilde bortbytte Dyrekjød for Brød og Poteter. Indianerne tilbragte de tre Dage, de opholdt sig paa Stedet, med at jage i Skoven og paa Prærien og opførte sig forresten fredeligt.

XXXVI.
En ubehagelig Reise.

Her endnu en Episode fra det andet Aar, jeg boede paa Stedet: En Dag, sent om Høsten, skulde jeg gjøre en Tur til Madison, som laa 16 Mile borte og var en stiv Dagsreise frem og tilbage med Oxeteam. Jeg havde faaet mange Smaaærinder af Naboerne, og jeg tilbragte mere Tid i Byen end paaregnet. Paa Hjemreisen, som gik over en stor ubanet Prærie, blev jeg overfaldt af et voldsomt Tordenveir. Natten var kulsort, og jeg maatte lide paa Oxerne, for at finde Veien hjem. Dette slog imidlertid feil, thi jeg vidste ikke af før de standsede midt i et langt Græs, som gik dem over Ryggen. Jeg havde nu intet andet at gjøre, end at komme op paa Prærien og spænde fra for at afvente Dagslyset. Regnen begyndte at falde i Strømmevis, og jeg lagde mig under Vognen, men her blev det snart saa koldt, at jeg ikke kunde sove. Oxerne havde lagt sig ved Siden af Vognen, med Aaget paa. Jeg greb da den fortvivlede Udvei, at lægge mig saa lang jeg var mellem Oxerne. Dette hjalp, thi jeg blev snart varm og sov den Uskyldiges Søvn indtil Dagslyset. Jeg har anført disse Smaatræk, for at vise vore Efterkommere, hvorledes det ofte gik til i Nybyggerlivets første Dage.

Alt det gode Land var nu bleven optaget og der var mange Nykommere med Familie, som foretrak at kjøbe Claims af dem, som havde bygget Huse og var villige at sælge. Jeg solgte da min Claim tilligemed Oxer og andre Kreaturer, som jeg imidlertid havde anskaffet, og flyttede tilbage til Racine County.

I den Tid her omtales, anlagdes ogsaa norske Settlementer ved Pine Lake, Rock River, Wiota, Mineral Point og andre Steder, men da jeg her kun omtaler personlige Erindringer, kan jeg ikke fortælle Noget specielt om dem, uden for saavidt, at den bekjendte norske Storthingsmand Hans Gasmann var en af de første, som (1843) nedsatte sig i Rock River Settlementet, og levede der med sin Familie til sin Død.

XXXVII.
Indvandringen til Texas og Cleng Peersons Død.

Den bekjendte Redaktør [Johan Reinert] Reiersen fra Kristiansand, som var paa en Reise gjennem Veststaterne i en tidlig Periode af den norske Indvandring, kom ogsaa til Texas, som da netop var kommen ind i den amerikanske Union som Stat, og tilbød Indvandrerne meget fordelagtige Betingelser. Hans Skildring af Landet og Forholdene i Texas ledte til, at enkelte Udvandringsselskaber gik direkte fra Norge over New Orleans til Texas. Efterfølgende Brev fra O. Canuteson i Waco, Texas, giver nogle nærmere Efterretninger om de første norske Settlementer, og Cleng Peersons Ophold og Endeligt dersteds:

"Cleng Peersons Færd iblandt os i de 13 à 14 Aar han tilbragte her, kjender jeg saa godt som Nogen, da han tilbragte sin meste Tid med mig og Fader. Han var en Olding paa 83 Aar da han døde, og saa kunde han ikke virke med den Kraft som en yngre Mand, men hans Landsmænds Interesser og Velfærd var hans Livs Opgave til hans Dødsdag. Jeg hjalp til ved og lukkede selv hans Øine i Dødens Blund. Han fortalte os om alle Settlementer og Tildragelser, som han havde oplevet, og det hele kunde have været paa Papir, men i den Tid havde jeg ingen Anelse om, at noget saadant nogen Tid vilde blive efterspurgt, og desuden laa Madstrævet os som næsten alle Nykommere saa nær, at der ikke var Tanke om nogen sammenhængende Beretning om disse

Tildragelser. Fader og jeg kom fra Norge i 1850 og under vort Ophold hos vore Slegtninger i Illinois, kom gamle Cleng der. Vi kjendte ham før, da han var i vort Hus i Norge paa et af sine Besøg. Han var nu just kommet tilbage fra sin første Tur til Texas. Han tilraadede os at gaa herned, da vi her kunde kjøbe deiligt Land for 50 Cents pr. Acre, og saa drog vi afsted. Han blev med os, da han troede dette Klimat bedre passede ham paa hans gamle Dage. Han var født paa Gaarden Hesthammer, i Tysvær Sogn, Stavanger Amt. Reiersen maa ansees som den Mand, som anlagde det første norske Settlement i Texas. Hans yngste Broder lever endnu i Bosque Settlement. Alle andre af hans Brødre her i Staten er døde, saavidt jeg ved, dog tror jeg han har en Broder, som bor i Chicago. Jeg har ikke selv været i de to Settlementer i det østlige Texas, da gamle Cleng ikke vilde vi skulde stoppe, før vi kom vestenfor Trinity Elven, thi han paastod, at Landet og Sundhedstilstanden, begge Dele vare daarlige i østlige Texas, sammenlignet med længere mod Vest, og heri havde han storligen Ret, som senere Erfaring har fuldkommen godtgjort. Han havde nemlig paa sin første Tur været saa langt Vest som til Johnsons Station, omtrent 30 til 40 Mile Vest for Dallas i Udkanten paa det bekjendte Cross Timber, og kun nogle faa Mile fra den nu blomstrende Jernbaneby Fort Worth. Vi har altsaa Cleng at takke for, at vi kom ind i det bedste Strøg som Staten præsterer. Hvad Settlementet i Bosque County angaar, var jeg den første Nordmand, som gik did, dog ingenlunde i den Tanke, at anlægge Settlement, men kun at finde vakant Land for mig og Fader og en Nabo. Land kunde da faaes af Staten for Ingenting, kun at have samme maalt og betale 10 til 20 Dollars for en halv Sektion af det bedste uopmaalte Land, som kunde findes inden Statens Grændser. Snart kom flere Landsmænd fra det østlige Texas og Norge og det blev saaledes det betydeligste norske Settlement i Staten. Jeg boede der i 15 Aar og drev for det meste med Jordavl og nogle Kreaturer. Jeg boede i Dallas County 3 Aar, før jeg gik ud til Bosque og har nu boet her i Waco County 15 Aar. Jeg maa ikke forglemme at fortælle, at den første Nordmand, som nedsatte sig i Texas som virkelig Settler, er udenfor al Tvivl Johan Nordbo fra Østerdalen eller Gudbrandsdalen i Norge. Han var dengang en meget gammel Mand og var nok tidlig kommet til Amerika, da han havde været i Settlementet ved Lake Ontario og kjendte Cleng Peerson fra den Tid. Han havde ogsaa været i Iowa og Missouri, men drog saa tilsidst til Texas paa Grund af de liberale Landgrants til Settlere. Vi kom til hans Hus, 6 Mile Syd for Dallas, i December 1850 og han havde da boet der, saavidt jeg husker, 12 til 15 Aar. Han kom saa tidlig, at han fik en Sektion Land af Staten og en halv Sektion for hver af sine Børn, flere i Tallet, endog for en Datter, som da boede i Illinois. Hun agtede at komme her, men døde. Hendes Børn kom med os og fik Landet som Arv efter sin Moder."

Henimod '50 Aarene var de Norske ogsaa begyndt at flytte ind i Iowa og Minnesota; men da dette, som ovenfor bemærket, ligger udenfor min personlige Erfaringskreds, overlades Beretningerne om Indvandringen dertil til andre Hænder.

XXXVIII.
Ole Rynnings Skrifter.

Den Mand, som efter de første Udvandrere fra Stavanger Amt har udøvet den største Indflydelse paa den norske Emigration, er udenfor al Tvivl Student Ole Rynning fra Snaasens Præstegjæld i Trondhjems Stift. Hvad han i 1838 skrev hjem fra Amerika, cirkulerede i tusindvis udover alle norske Landsbygder. Som et Bevis for, hvorledes han røgtede dette Kald, anføres her nedenstaaende forkortede Uddrag af hans Skrifter:

De første to Spørgsmaal, Rynning besvarer, er med Hensyn til, hvorledes Landet blev bekjendt. Det tredie er: "Hvordan er dette Land i det Hele beskaffent, og hvad er Aarsagen til, at saa mange Folk reise did og vente at finde Levebrød der?" Hertil svarer han, at de Forenede Stater er et meget stort Landskab, den meste Del fladt og dyrkbart, men at dets Udstrækning er saa stor, at der ogsaa er stor Forskjel med Hensyn til Veirets Mildhed og Jordbundens Godhed. I de østligste og nordligste Stater er Klimat og Jordbund ikke bedre end i det sydlige Norge; i de vestlige Stater derimod er Jorden for det meste saa fed, at den bærer ethvert Slags Korn uden Gjødsel; og i de sydlige Stater avles endog Sukker, Risengryn, Tobak og flere Ting, som udfordre en stærk Varme. Rynnings fjerde Sprøgsmaal er: "Er det ikke at befrygte, at Landet snart vil blive formeget opfyldt med Folk? — Er det sandt, at Regjeringen der vil forbyde flere Folk at komme?" Som Svar udpeger han, at de Forenede Stater i Udstrækning er mere end 20 Gange saa stort som Norge, at den største Del af Landet ikke engang er paabegyndt at dyrkes, og at det er saa frugtbart, at det kan modtage mere end 100 Gange saa mange Mennesker som der findes i hele Norge. Det er ikke at befrygte, mener han, at Landet vil blive opfyldt i de første 50 Aar. Rygtet om, at Regjeringen i de Forenede Stater ikke vilde tillade Flere at indvandre did, er, siger han, falskt. Den amerikanske Regjering ønsker netop, at arbeidssomme, driftige og sædelige Folk ville indvandre til dem, og derfor har den heller ikke ladet noget Forbud udgaa i denne Henseende.

Det femte Spørgsmaal er: "I hvilken Del af Landet have de Norske nedsat sig? Hvilken er den bekvemmeste og billigste Vei til dem?" I sit Svar hertil siger Rynning, at de Norske findes omspredte paa mange Steder i de Forenede Stater. I New York, Rochester, Detroit, Chicago, Philadelphia og New

Orleans skal man træffe enkelte Norske. "Dog ved jeg," tilføier han, "kun 4 til 5 Steder, hvor flere Norske paa en Gang have nedsat sig. Disse Steder ere: 1) Morri Town, Orleans County, New York State, hvor det første Indvandringsselskab af Norske nedsatte sig i 1825. Der er nu kun 2 til 3 Familier tilbage; de øvrige ere dragne længere ind i Landet, hvor de have nedsat sig i 2) La Salle County, Illinois State, ved Fox River, omtrent 1½ norsk Mil nordøst for Byen Ottawa, og 11 til 12 Mile vestenfor Chicago. Her bor 16 til 20 Familier af Norske. Denne Koloni stiftedes i 1834. 3) White County, Indiana State, omtrent 10 norske Mile Syd for Michigan Sø ved Tippecanoe River. Her bor endnu kun to Norske fra Drammen, som tilsammen eie henved 1,100 Acres Land. 4) Shelby County, Missouri State, hvor en Del Norske fra Stavanger nedsatte sig om Vaaren 1837. Jeg ved ikke hvormange Familier der er. 5) Iroquois County, Illinois State, ved Elvene Beaver og Iroquois. Her nedsatte sig en stor Del af dem, som kom over sidste Sommer. Der er nu 11 til 12 Familier." Spørgsmaal No. 6 er: "Hvorledes er Landets Beskaffenhed, hvor de Norske have nedsat sig? Hvad koster en god Jordvei der? Hvilke ere Priserne paa Kreaturer og Levnetsmidler? Hvor høi er Daglønnen?" Rynning beskriver i sit Svar Præriernes Herligheder og Frugtbarhed. "Prisen paa Regjeringsland," siger han, "har hidtil været 1¼ Dollars pr. Acre, hvad enten Jorden har været af bedste Sort eller af ringere Godhed. Prisen vil nu nedsættes og Jorden inddeles i tre Klasser efter dens forskjellige Godhed, hvorefter ogsaa Prisen vil rette sig. Saaledes har jeg hørt, at der for Jord af tredie Klasse alene skal fordres ½ Dollar pr. Acre." Her giver Rynning klar Underretning om, hvorledes Land var beskrevet og udtaget. Det følgende Uddrag af Svaret angaaende Priserne paa Kreaturer og Levnetsmidler i den Tid vil være af Interesse: "Her ved Beaver Creek koster en taalelig god Hest 50 til 100 Daler; et Par gode Arbeidsoxer 50 til 80 Daler; en Firehjulsvogn 60 til 80 Daler; en Melkeko med Kalv 16 til 20 Daler; en Sau 2 til 3 Daler; et middels Svin 6 til 10 Daler; Flesk 3 til 5 Skilling Marken; Smør 6 til 12 Skilling Marken; en Tønde fineste Hvedemel 8 til 10 Daler; en Tønde Kornmel (Mel af Mais) 2½ til 3 Daler; en Tønde Poteter 1 Daler; et Pund Kaffe 20 Skilling; en Tønde Salt 5 Daler. I Wisconsin Territory ere Priserne 2 til 3 Gange høiere. Ti Mile Syd for os og i Missouri ere Priserne paa de fleste Ting billigere. Daglønnen er ogsaa meget forskjellig paa de forskjellige Steder og staar temmelig nær i Forhold til Priserne paa andre Ting. Heromkring kan en duelig Arbeider om Vinteren fortjene fra ½ til 1 Daler om Dagen og om Sommeren næsten det dobbelte. Aarslønnen er fra 150 til 200 Daler. En Tjenestepige har 1 til 2 Daler om Ugen og intet Udarbeide undtagen at malke Køerne. I Wisconsin Territory er Daglønnen 3 til 5 Daler; i New Orleans og Texas er den ogsaa meget høi, men i Missouri er den igjen mindre. Her ved Beaver Creek kunne vi faa Folk til at brække Prærie for os for 2 Daler pr. Acre, naar vi alene holde dem med Kosten."

Til det syvende Spørgsmaal: "Hvad Slags Religion er der i Amerika? Er der nogen Slags Orden og Regjering i Landet, eller kan enhver gjøre, hvad han lyster?" svarer han, at her kan enhver have sin egen Tro og dyrke Gud paa den Maade, han anser for den rette; men han tør ikke forfølge nogen, fordi han har en anden Tro. Til Trøst for de Kleinmodige forsikrer han dem, at her er Love, Regjering og Øvrighed ligesaavel som i Norge, men at alt her er beregnet paa at haandhæve Menneskets naturlige Frihed og Lighed. Om Slavehandelen siger han: "De nordlige Stater arbeide ved hver Kongres paa at faa Slavehandelen afskaffet i de sydlige Stater; men da disse altid modsætte sig og beraabe sig paa deres Ret til selv at ordne deres indre Anliggender, vil der sandsynligvis enten snart blive Skilsmisse mellem de nordlige og sydlige Stater eller ogsaa blodige indvortes Stridigheder." Da dette blev skrevet 22 Aar førend Krigen begyndte, maa det ansees for mærkværdigt.

Spørgsmaal No. 8 er: "Hvordan er der sørget for Børnelærdommen og for de Fattige?" Som Svar til dette fortæller han om det frie Skolevæsen og Amerikanernes Omsorg for sine Børns Undervisning og Dannelse. Blandt de Norske ved Fox River, siger han, er der oprettet frie Skoler, hvor Børnene lære Engelsk; men det norske Sprog synes der at ville uddø med Forældrene. Fattigvæsenet roser han som ypperligt. Det niende Spørgsmaal, som han besvarer er: "Hvilket Sprog tales i Amerika? Er det vanskeligt at lære?" Han siger, at formedelst Immigrationen findes mange forskjellige Sprog, men at det engelske Sprog er overalt det herskende. Man kan, tilføier han, ved daglig Omgang med Amerikanerne snart lære saa meget, at man hjælper sig godt. Spørgsmaal 10 er: "Er det farligt med Hensyn til Sygdomme i Amerika? Har man noget at befrygte for vilde Dyr eller af Indianerne?" Rynning fordølger ikke Sandheden, men siger, at det uvante Klimat almindelig foraarsager Nybyggerne en eller anden Sygelighed i det første Aar, saasom Diarrhoe og Koldfeber. De er dog ikke meget farlige. Af farlige Rovdyr fandtes der ingen paa de Kanter, hvor de Norske havde bosat sig. Af Slanger var der mange, men kun faa, som var giftige. Indianerne vare allerede transporterede langt mod Vest, og ingensteds i Illinois var man udsat for Overfald af dem. Det ellevte spørgsmaal er: "For hvad Slags Folk er det raadeligt at reise til Amerika, og for hvem er det ikke raadeligt? Advarsel imod urimelige Forventninger." Han raader den norske Bonde, Haandværksmand og Handelskarl at komme. Smede, Skræddere, Dreiere, Snedkere, Vognmagere og lignende Haandværksmænd kunne let faa lønnende Arbeide; men for Drankere og de, som hverken kan arbeide eller som ikke have Penge til at udføre Spekulationer, er der ikke Plads. "Den, som ikke kan eller vil arbeide," siger han, "maa aldrig vente, at Rigdomme og Vellevnet her staa aabne for ham. Nei, i Amerika faar man intet uden Arbeide ; men sandt er det, at man ved Arbeide her kan vente engang at komme i bedre Kaar. Mange af de Nykommere have stødt sig over de usle Hytter, som ere Nybyggernes første Boliger; men de gode Folk skulde dog betænke, at de ved at flytte ind i et udyrket Land ikke kunne finde Huse færdige for dem. Førend man har sat sin Jord i en saadan Stand, at det kan føde sin Mand, er det neppe klogt at lægge sin Formue i kostbare Husbygninger."

"Hvilke Farer kunne især møde paa Havet? Er det sandt, at de som føres til Amerika bliver solgte som Slaver?" Disse ere de sidste Spørgsmaal, som han besvarer. Om Havets Farer siger han, at de ikke ere saa forfærdelige, som mange forestiller sig. Naar man har et godt Skib, en duelig Kaptein og flinke, paapasselige Søfolk, mener han, at saa faar man forresten slaa sin Lid til Herren. Om Slaverygtet siger han: "Et taabeligt Rygte troedes af mange i Norge; nemlig, at de, som vilde udvandre til Amerika, bleve førte til Tyrkiet og solgte som Slaver. Dette Rygte er aldeles grundløst. Derimod er det sandt, at mange, som ikke selv kunde bekoste sig over Søen, alene paa den Maade er komne over, at de have solgt sig selv eller deres Tjeneste paa visse Aar til en Mand her i Landet. Mange skulle derved være komne i slette Hænder, og have ikke havt det bedre end Slaver. Ingen Norsk, saavidt jeg ved, er kommen i saadanne Omstændigheder, heller ikke er det at befrygte, naar man gaar med norske Skibe og sine egne Landsmænd."

XXXIX.
"Nordlyset," det første norske Blad i Amerika.

Det var allerede i Aarene 1844 og 1845 kommen paa Tale mellem de mere oplyste af de indvandrede norske Bønder, at vi her, i dette Avisernes Land, ogsaa burde have en norsk Avis, og det var to Aar senere, nemlig i Aaret 1847, at D'Hrr. Heg og Reymert, begyndte Udgivelsen af "Nordlyset," den første norske Avis i Amerika, i deres Hjem i Norway, Racine County. Even Heg var en velstaaende Mand, nylig kommen fra Norge, og var nok den, som egentlig gjorde Pengeudlægget til Presse og Trykkeri. James D. Reymert, som blev Redaktør, var en oplyst ung Mand, med store Begavelser og var bleven opdraget dels i Skotland, dels i Norge, da han fra Modersiden nedstammede fra Skotland. Den mindeværdige Free Soil Bevægelse mod Slaveriets Udbredelse, var paa den Tid meget levende i Wisconsin. Reymert havde optaget dette Partis Principer og "Nordlyset" skulde være Partiets norske Organ. Det gik i Begyndelsen godt med at faa Abonnenter paa Bladet, saaat deres Antal i Aarets Løb voxede op til 200 eller derover, men det var trange Tider for Indvandrerne, og da Betalingstiden kom, forekom Sagen dem ikke fuldt saa romantisk og mange af dem glemte at indsende sin Kontingent. Det demokratiske Parti havde ogsaa et stærkt Anhang mellem de norske Indvandrere, og "Nordlyset"s Free Soil Politik modarbeidedes af mange. Da Bladet havde været holdt gaaende i næsten to Aar med betydelige Pengetab, blev Trykkeriet nedlagt. "Nordlyset" var et firesidet Blad med fire Spalter paa hver Side. Det blev udgivet inde i et Landdistrikt og kunde ingen Støtte faa ved Avertissementer. En af Even Hegs Sønner besørgede for det meste Sætning og Trykning, og da det lille Blad kun udkom engang om Ugen, var Udgifterne vistnok ikke saa betydelige, men med et stadigt Pengetab kunde det dog ikke holdes gaaende. Foretagendet var øiensynligt kommen for tidligt. "Nordlyset" kom dog Reymert til Fordel forsaavidt, at det bragte ham ind paa den politiske Bane. Han blev nemlig sit Partis Elektor ved Præsidentvalget i 1848, blev Medlem af Konstitutionskonventionen i 1847, samt valgt til Medlem af Legislaturen i flere Aar efter hinanden og spillede idetheletaget en ikke ubetydlig politisk Rolle i Wisconsin.

XL.
"Demokraten."

Det var i Slutningen af Aaret 1849, at jeg begik den Daarskab at kjøbe Trykkeriet af Heg og Reymert, og med O. J. Hatlestad som Medeier flyttede vi det til Racine, og begyndte i 1850 paany at udgive "Nordlyset." De demokratiske Blade i Wisconsin havde været skaanselløse i deres Kritik over "Nordlyset." De sagde, at dernede i Muskegos Sumpegne var en Lygtemand, som vandrede omkring og vildledte de norske Vælgere ud i ufremkommelige Free Soil Moradser. Dette var en Satire over Bladets Navn og havde i Grunden intet at betyde, men vi kjendte den Gang intet til Partipolitikens Skik og Brug, og skræmtes over at Bladets Navn blev gjort Nar af. Havde vi havt nogen politisk Erfaring, maatte vi vidst, at saadant hører til Dagens Orden i de politiske Blade. Som det var, førte dette til, at vi forandrede Bladets Navn fra "Nordlyset" til "Demokraten". Vi brugte dog ikke det sidste Navn i sin Partibetydning, da det skulde vedblive at være en Free Soil Demokrat, et Folkestyrets Organ. I Begyndelsen gik alt over Forventning godt. Subskriptionslisten forøgedes til 300; men vi gjorde snart den samme Erfaring som vore Forgjængere, at Bladet ikke kunde udgives uden Penge. Venligsindede og oplyste Landsmænd skrev og opmuntrede os og udtalte sig vel tilfreds med Bladets Virksomhed; men Penge var ikke at opdrive. Med en dygtig Forretningsfører er det muligt, at vi kunde have slaaet os igjennem; men da vi selv besørgede Arbeidet ved Redaktion og Trykkeri, og ingen af os var Finantsmænd, blev Indkasseringen overladt til velvillige Agenter rundt om i Settlementerne. Det begyndte snart at gaa op for mig, at vi havde anskaffet os en Elefant, som kun fortærede og intet gav tilbage. Med andre Ord: som politisk Blad var det kommet for tidlig.

XLI.
"Maanedstidende."

Jeg havde imidlertid indgaaet Overenskomst med Præsterne Clausen, Preus og Stub om at trykke deres kirkelige Organ, "Maanedstidende," og da Hatlestad ogsaa ønskede at udgive en Kirketidende, blev vi enige om at dele Trykkeriet. Der var nemlig Udsigt for, at religiøse Tidender vilde finde bedre Understøttelse, da den første Indvandrerbefolkning hovedsagelig bestod af Folk fra Landsbygderne, som for en stor Del ikke var vant til at læse andet end deres Religionsbøger, og mange af dem ansaa det endog for en Synd at læse politiske Blade. Det var i '50 Aarene, at den mindeværdige Kamp gik for sig i den amerikanske Kongres angaaende Loven om bortrømte Slaver og Slaveriets Udbredelse i Territorierne Kansas og Nebraska. Vort lille norske Blad tog en levende Andel i disse Forhandlinger. En Række Taler af Mænd som Seward, Giddings, Durkee, Hale, Chase og flere, hvis Navne ere skrevne med udødelig Skrift paa den amerikanske Histories Blade, bleve oversatte og tilsvarende Redaktionsartikler meddelte. Det var Selvstyret og Folkefriheden i Kamp med Slaveriets Overmagt, det her gjaldt at forsvare. Det er sandsynligt, at jeg behandlede denne Sag altfor udførligt og maaske ensidigt; thi det var en Materie, som stemte overens med min personlige Tilbøielighed. Nok er det, "Demokraten" fik ikke den fornødne Understøttelse og blev derfor, efter at være holdt gaaende et og et halvt Aar, nedlagt.

XLII.
En gammel Abonnentliste.

Vi giver nedenfor en Liste over Abonnenter paa "Nordlyset" og "Demokraten". Denne Liste vil være af Interesse for disse Mænds mange Efterkommere omkring her i Vesten. Det er en Liste over oplyste og frisindede Fremskridtsmænd, hvis Minde fortjener at opbevares, saalænge deres Efterkommere bor i Amerikas Vesten. Mange ere nu samlede med deres Fædre, men der er ogsaa mange endnu ilive og erindrer vore første Forsøg paa at grundlægge et norsk Blad i Amerika, og det vil maaske ogsaa glæde dem, at de var med om at fremhjælpe en god Sag, nemlig den norske Literaturs Opbevarelse i dette Land.

Wisconsin.

Norway og Muskego, Racine County.

Anders Kløve.
G. Larsen.
Johannes E. Skoftestad.
Mathias Heimo.
Helge Torsen.
Ole Haagensen.
Niels Nærum.
Jens O. Hatlestad.
Peder Jacobsen.
Bjørn Hatlestad.
Ole Tollefsjorden.
Halvor Lonar.
Niels Brownson.
Ole Mikkelsen.
Thron Thordsen.
Thorkild Hansen.
Thorsten Sjøgaarden.
Knud B. Pedersen.
Syvert Ingebretsen.
Thorsten Hougaasen.
Gunder Goutesen.
Gitle Danielson.
Svennung Johannesen.
Christian Hallofsen.
Christian Christiansen.
Thormod Thorstensen.
Rev. H. A. Stub.
Niels Hansen.
Tyke Hendriksen.
Gudmund Samuelsen.
Halvor Guttormsen.

Rochester, Racine County.

Dr. Blood.
Herbrand Anstensen.
R. E. Ela.
Syvert Johnson.

Beloit, Rock County.

Rev. C. L. Clausen.
T. Tollefsen.
Tollef Numland.
Paul H. Gallager.
H. Ommested.
Hans Christophersen.
Hans Smedrud.
Knud Skjerve.
Hans H. Hansemoen.
Svend Larsen.
Peter Halvorsen.
Peder H. Gaarden.
Gisle Halland.
Gullik O. Gravdal.
C. Halvorsen.
David Anderson.
T. G. Fladeland.
Halvor H. Folkestad.

Cambridge, Dane County.

Windberg & Jørgensen.
Knud Eriksen.
Ole Lawrence.
Ingebret Homstad.

Christiana, Dane County.

Lars Johannesen.
Niri Herbjørnsen.
Iver H. Leimle.
J. Hoff.
Brynhild H. Lønne.
Johannes L. Hole.
John Olson.
Ole Christiansen.
Peder L. Svartskul.
C. Corneliusen.
Niels A. Berg.
Stad Sivertsen.
Anfind Storksen.
Andrew Ellingsen.
O. T. Torgesen.
Lars P. Haugelia.
Ole K. Frovattn. [Trovatten]
Dr. Madsen.
Rev. Dietrichson.

Clinton, Rock County.

Ole Knudsen.
Elling Eielsen.
Ansten Knudsen.
Knud Nielsen.
Gullik Knudsen.
H. Poulsen.
Christ Newhouse.
Jens Gulbrandsen.
Peder Thomsen.
Thorsten Nielsen.
O. A. Haadtvet.
Erik Gulbrandsen.

Columbus, Columbia County.

Lars Johansen.
Anders Dælan.
Mons Johnsen.
Peder Langeland.

Deerfield, Dane County.

Ole K. Bakketun.
Ole Olsen Tveten.
Ole Syvertsen.
Aslak Olsen Lie.

Delafield, Waukesha County.

Hans Gasmann.
Hans Rasmusen.
Ellef Bjørnsen.
Chr. Olsen.

Dodgeville, La Fayette County.

John Lie.
Niels Arneson.
Syvert Tallerssen.

Door Creek, Dane County.

Niels Saem.
Osmund Lunde.
Christian O. Holo.

Fulton, Rock County.

Johan Niels Luuraas.

Cedar Grove, Sheboygan County.

Endre Michelsen.
Ole Michelsen.
Knud Aaberg.

Madison, Dane County.

Erik Andersen.
Lars Johnson.
William Andersen.

Manitowoc, Manitowoc County.

C. Andersen.
Ole Andreasen.
Jacob Madsen.
L. Nordboe.
Hans M. Hansen.

Milwaukee, Milwaukee County.

C. E. Jenkins.
Lars Bæver.
P. L. Morin.
Jens Lund.
Abraham Sørensen.
Tønnes Sæveland.
S. Gabrielsen.
C. Sørensen.
M. N. Olsen.
R. Reinertsen.

Mineral Point, Iowa County.

Peder Stenerson.
Ole Thorsen.

Neenah, Winnebago County.

John Nielsen.
Anders J. Dalen.
Aslak Brynildsen.
Søren Wilson.
Ole P. Klokkerengen.
Svend T. Husetoft.

Oconomowoe, Waukesha County.

H. B. Paus.
David Førre.
Thron Thronsen.
Amund Aamodt.
Ole Iverson.
Johs. Lie.
Gunder Naas.
Ole Olsen.
Jørgen Olsen.

Palmyra, Jefferson County.

Sjur Flettre.
Tollef Brynildsen.

S. S. Berkorg.
Rasmus Jacobsen.
Lars Johnsen.
Iver W. Grintland.

Pine Bluff, Dane County.

Thor J. Spaanem.
Halvor Halvorsen.

Sun Prairie, Dane County.

Sjur Johnson.

Spring Valley, Rock County.

Halvor Monson.
G. Guttormsen.
John E. Solem.

Tolands Prairie, Washington County.

Niels Lønningen.
Jørgen Lüberg.
Hans Christophersen.
Halvor Halvorsen.
Christian Moen.
Martin F. Sørensen.

Utica, Dane County.

Bottel Lunde.
K. S. Okere.
Niels Drougsvold.
John O. Herredal.

Port Washington, Washington County.

Amund Olsen.
Salve Tallaksen.

Racine, Racine County.

Andrew Johannesen.
H. Rasmussen.
O. Hedejord.
Knud Lunden.
H. Hansen.
John Larsen.

Yorkville, Racine County.

Mons K. Aadland.
Aslak S. Aa.
Elias Stangeland.
Arentz Wigeland.
Johannes Bjøs [? Njøs].
Ole J. Landsværk.
Peter M. Andsjøn.
Knud A. Aarethun.
John C. Spellum.
Gunder Lunden.
Hans Landsværk.
Steen Sanderson.

Wiota, La Fayette County.

Knud Knudsen.
Niels L. Finne.

Niels Nielsen.
Arne Anderson.
Ole Andersen.
Erik Ingebretsen.
Peter Davidsen.
Helge Olsen.

Illinois.

Amazon, Boone County.

Thor Trahjem.
Kittil K. Moland.
Knud Tveten.
Niels Johannesen.
Kittil O. Blomhaugen.

Belvedere, Boone County.

Hans Anderson.

St. Charles, Kane County.

John Anderson.

Chicago.

Knud Larsen.
Niels Sjursen.
Regina Wigeland.
Lars Dygestien.
Torger Olsen.
Iver Lawson.
Rev. Paul Anderson.
Anders Pederson.
Magnus Nordboe.
Ole Nordhuus.
Jens Gulbrandsen.
Haagen Paulson.
N. P. Løberg.
Lars A. Bryn.
S. G. Bøe.
John Ammundsen.
S. Arentz.
Jacob Hodnefjeld.
Bernt Abrahamson.
E. Stephenson.
Bjørn Nielsen.
Endre Nielsen.
Anders N. Brække.
Niels Johnson.
John Johnson.

Dorr, McHenry County.

Andreas A. Schjeie.
Erik Knudsen.
Mikkel J. Bryn.

Lisbon, Kendall County.

Erik Skjeldal.
Thorkild Henrysen.
K. A. Bouge.
Lars Skjeldal.
John Hill.

Freedom, La Salle County.

Hellik C. Furlie.
Tjerran Osmundsen.
Kittil Kittilson.
Ole Andersen.
Geo. Pedersen.
Helge Olsen.
Made Madesen.
Knud Thomson.

Mission Grove, La Salle County.

Ole Olsen.
Ole Pearson.
Osmund Tuttlie.
Hermand Osmunsen.
Halvor Pedersen.
Christian Olsen.
Ole Knudsen.
Knud Williamson.
Gunlik Johnson.
Peder Ormsen.
Niels N. Nielsen.
Ole Anderson, Jr.
Anders Knudsen.

Norway, La Salle County.

Gudmund Hougaas.
Niels Nielsen.
Halvor Nielsen.
Nels Andersen.
Niels Thomsen.
Rev. Ole Andrewson.

Ottawa, La Salle County.

Henry L. Hellmann.
Mr. Thomson.

Rock Run, Stephenson County.

Ole Olsen Sunne.
Lars O. Andersen.
Ole Andersen.

Wilmoth, Boone County.

Ole Pehrsen.
Peder Torkelsen.
Ole Torkelsen.

Iowa.

Keokuk, Lee County. Jacob Olsen.

Indiana.

Monticello, White County. Peter B. Smith.

Missouri.

St. Louis. Hans Sandberg.

New Washington, Franklin County. L. A. Hansen.

New York.
Kendalls Corner, Orleans County. Ole Osland.
New York City.
F. Knauft. A. Løvenskjold.
John Holfeldt. Chr. Hansen.

Rhode Island.
Providence. N. B. Schubarth.

Efterfølgende er en Liste over de amerikanske og tydske Blade som byttede med "Nordlyset" og "Demokraten": New York Weekly Sun, New York; Christian Advocate and Journal, New York; Western Citizen, Chicago, Ill.; Daily Wisconsin, Milwaukee, Wis.; The National Era, Washington, D. C.; The New York Weekly Tribune, New York; Ohio State Tribune, Columbus, O.; Racine Advocate, Racine, Wis.; Wisconsin Argus, Madison, Wis., Wisconsin Free Democrat, Milwaukee, Wis.; Wisconsin Express, Madison, Wis.; Southport Telegraph, Southport, Wis.; Buffalo Telegraph, Buffalo, N. Y.; "Volksfreund," Milwaukee, Wis.; Wisconsin Banner, Milwaukee, Wis.; Western Star, Elkhorn, Wisconsin.

XLIII.
Andre norsk-amerikanske Blade.

Efterat vi havde delt Trykkeriet, begyndte Hatlestad at udgive sin "Kirketidende" og sled sig igjennem for en Tid i Racine og flyttede derpaa til Leland i Illinois, hvor Udgivelsen fortsattes, indtil Bladet gik over i Ole Andrewsens Hænder. Han flyttede det til Norway, La Salle County, hvor det endelig nedlagdes efter flere Aars møisommelig Kamp for sin Tilværelse.

Paa Pastor Clausens Foranledning besluttede jeg at flytte mit Trykkeri til Janesville for der at fortsætte Trykningen af "Maanedstidende". Vor Overenskomst var nemlig, at Præsterne selv skulde læse Korrektur, og Clausen mente, at dette meget lettere kunde ske i Janesville end i Racine. Korrekturlæsningen havde nemlig foraarsaget os mange Ubehageligheder saalænge vi var i Racine. Saavidt jeg nu erindrer, var det i Sommeren 1852, jeg flyttede til Janesville. Denne Flytning faldt ud til at være en Feiltagelse; thi istedet for at faa større Understøttelse, fik Trykkeriet fordoblede Udgifter. For at kunne sætte "Maanedstidende" trængte jeg flere Typer. En Landsmand i

Madison, Ole Torgerson, havde i nogle Maaneder udgivet et norsk Blad i Whig-Partiets Interesse, men været saa forstandig at nedlægge det, førend det ruinerede ham. Jeg gik derfor derned og kjøbte hans Typer og bragte dem til Janesville. Foruden en ung Dreng, som vilde lære Bogtrykkerkunsten, og som senere er bleven en fremragende Præst iblandt sine Landsmænd, havde jeg en norsk Bogtrykker, som hed Conradi, en Broder til den bekjendte Professor af samme Navn. Denne Conradi var en snild og godslig Mand, men offrede altfor meget af sin Tid til Bachustjenesten. Der var dengang stor Mangel paa norske Bogtrykkere, og denne Mangel gav os ofte meget Bryderi.

XLIV.
"Emigranten."

Da den første Aargang af "Maanedstidende" var udkommet, ønskede jeg at sælge Trykkeriet, og da Præsterne skulde have sit Organ trykt, slog de sig sammen om at oprette et Aktieselskab. Dette kom snart istand, og jeg solgte Trykkeriet til dem. Det blev derpaa flyttet til Inmansville i Rock County, hvor Pastor Clausen da boede. Præsterne havde den bedste Anledning til at samle Støtte for Trykkeriet, da de stadig færdedes blandt Folket omkring i Settlementerne. Det nye Aktieselskab besluttede derfor foruden deres kirkelige Organ ogsaa at udgive et politisk Blad, "Emigranten". Pastor Clausen skulde være Redaktør for "Emigranten", og Trykkeriet skulde staa under den bekjendte Emigrantagent John Holfeldts Bestyrelse. Jeg blev hos dem i Inmansville et Par Maaneder for at faa Trykkeriet igang, og flyttede derpaa tilbage til min Farm i Racine County. Begyndelsen i Inmansville blev gjort i Januar Maaned 1853, og Trykkeriet dreves i en kort Tid under Holfeldts Bestyrelse. Pastor Clausen blev snart træt af Arbeidet, og Holfeldt var meget upopulær blandt den norske Emigrantbefolkning paa Grund af sin Virksomhed som Emigrantagent. Senere kom Trykkeriet i Konsul K. Fleischers Hænder, og det syntes at bære sig taalelig, indtil det efter nogle Aars Forløb flyttedes til Madison, hvor det senere gik over i C. F. Solbergs Hænder som Privateiendom. "Emigranten"s senere Historie ligger os for nær til her at behøve Omtale. Den blev endelig forenet med "Fædrelandet" i La Crosse og existerer nu under Navnet "Fædrelandet og Emigranten" og udkommer i La Crosse og Minneapolis.

Mindes jeg ikke feil, var det i 1850 at et norsk Blad, kaldet "Frihedsbanneret", begyndte at udkomme i Chicago. Det gik nogle Maaneder, men maatte standse, efterat Finantserne vare komne i Uorden. Dette Blads Venner sendte en Mand til Racine for at faa mig derned og tage fat paa Sagen; men da jeg netop var draget ud paa min Farm, undgik jeg heldigvis at falde i en ny Fristelse.

XLV.
"Den Norske Amerikaner."

I 1856 begyndte den bekjendte Elias Stangeland at udgive "Den Norske Amerikaner" i Madison, Wis. Han havde som Handelsmand erhvervet sig nogle Penge, men var kommen i Forlegenhed for en Redaktør for sit Blad. Da jeg var personlig bekjendt med ham, formaaede han mig til at komme derud og hjælpe ham med Redaktionen. Dengang James Buchanan af det demokratiske Parti i Baltimore blev nomineret til Præsident, var Stangeland tilstede ved Konventionen. Politikerne havde lovet ham Guld og grønne Skove, hvis hans "Norske Amerikaner" vilde understøtte deres Kandidat. John C. Fremont var Republikanernes Kandidat og alle mine Sympathier hørte hjemme i dette Parti. Jeg kunde derfor ikke redigere Stangelands Blad, da han besluttede at understøtte den demokratiske Kandidat. Jeg forlod ham derfor i al Venskabelighed, og da Politikerne holdt deres store Løfter paa sædvanlig Vis, gik Stangelands "Norske Amerikaner" snart al Kjødets Gang og samledes med sine Fædre.

Det er Avertissements-Forretningen, som for en stor Del støtter vore nuværende gigantiske norske Aviser her i Landet, og derfor ser vi dem hovedsagelig at samle sig i Storbyerne Chicago og Minneapolis. Store Byer betinges af Handelen, Handelen igjen af en stor Befolkning ud over Landdistrikterne. Disse Betingelser manglede under vore første Forsøg med norske Aviser. Ogsaa udlærte Bogtrykkere og erfarne Forretningsførere manglede. Det Billede, jeg her har udkastet af den norske Avissags Barndom i Amerika, er derfor ikke smilende, men sandt. Avisforretningen har nu voxet sig stor og mægtig, og der er ingen Fare for en heldig Opposition mod vore kjæmpestore norske Blade.

Det var de ovenanførte Betingelser i Chicago, som i Begyndelsen gav "Skandinaven" det bedste Fodfæste og gjorde, at de Ligtaler, som tidlig blev lovet den, aldrig kom til at blive holdte. Med "Skandinaven"'s Udgivelse begyndte en ny Æra i vor Avisliteratur, og det er stadig gaaet fremad dermed til, hvad den nu er.

XLVI.
De Norskes Fremtid i Amerika.

At den norske Indvandrer-Befolkning har været ualmindelig heldig med

Hensyn til det Strøg, hvorpaa den har nedsat sig, vil fremgaa tydeligere af efterfølgende Fremstilling: En Amerikaner skrev for et Par Aar siden en Artikel, hvori han anførte nogle interessante Beregninger angaaende Mississippi-Dalen og Antallet af Indbyggere, som der kan finde Hjem i Fremtiden. At denne Del af Amerika vil blive tæt befolket, kan Ingen betvivle, da Landet er næsten overalt meget frugtbart, og af Kul er der i Illinois alene tre til fire Gange saa meget som i hele Storbritannien. England har idag 500 Personer pr. Kvadratmil; Belgien har omtrent det samme Antal og nogle af de kinesiske Provindser har 700. Det store Hvedeland paa dette Kontinent kan ansees for at strække sig fra det østlige Ohio til det vestlige Nebraska og fra det sydlige Kentucky til Peace River i Britisk Amerika. Beregnende dette Distrikt til 1,500 Mile fra Øst til Vest og 2,000 Mile fra Syd til Nord faar vi et Areal af 3,500 Kvadratmile af godt og frugtbart Land. Noget lignende findes ikke andetsteds paa Jorden. Dersom vi nu antager, at 1,000,000 af disse 3,000,000 Kvadratmile er kun en Trediedel saa tæt befolket som i de ovenanførte Exempler, eller at der er omtrent 200 Personer pr. Kvadratmil, saa har vi en Befolkning af to Hundrede Millioner. Naar man betænker, at de Forenede Staters Befolkning nu blot er sexti Millioner, kan man faa en nogenlunde klar Ide om Mississippi-Dalens store Fremtid. At denne Del af Amerika vil i Tidens Løb overgaa Østen og Stillehavskysten ikke alene i Folkemængde, men ogsaa i Rigdom og Indflydelse, kan ikke betvivles. Skulde nu dette Fremtidsbillede realiseres, er der stor Sandsynlighed for, at Chicago vil blive for Nordamerika, hvad London nu er for Europa, Handelens og Pengeomsætningens Midtpunkt, en myldrende Verdensstad med mange Millioner Indbyggere, som det pulserende Forretningslivs Centrum. Hermed være det nu som det vil. Tiden fører ofte uventede Forandringer med sig, som omstøder de bedste Beregninger; men vist er det, at de første Indvandrere var mærkværdig heldige med Hensyn til Valg af Tid og Sted for deres Kolonisation, ligesom de og deres nærmeste Efterslægt har vist sig denne Lykke værdig ved den Fremskridts- og Foretagsomheds-Aand, de allerede har lagt for Dagen, saavel paa Økonomiens, Industriens og Handelens som paa de videnskabelige og kirkelige Omraader, saa at Tusinder af dem i Velstand, Oplysning og Dannelse nu kan stilles i Række og Geled med Jordens bedste Mænd og Kvinder.

Som et Middeltal mellem de forskjellige Angivelser af vor Befolknings Antal i Amerika sættes 500,000 (en halv Million). Dette forudsætter, at hver ti Indvandrere har forøget sig med syv siden de kom hertil. Der er ingen sikre Data at holde sig til, men dette Tal er neppe for høit. Mange af disse er indkomne i de senere Aar og kunne ikke regnes med som bidragende til de Fremskridt, vi her omtale. Hvad deres Velstand angaar, kan Farmer- og Haandværksklassen antages at eie fra $5,000 til $30,000 for hver Familie, medens Kjøbmænd og Fabrikanter hver eier mere end dobbelt saa meget. Hvad Opdragelse og Intelligents angaar, da finde vi deres unge Slægt vel repræsenteret som Præster, Læger, Advokater, Redaktører, Ingeniører, Telegrafister og andre vigtige Stillinger, som forudsætter en omhyggelig Forberedelse og et langt Fagstudium. Ligeledes er de talrigt repræsenterede som Skolelærere og Professorer ved høiere Læreanstalter. Selv i den amerikanske Kongres har vi to Repræsentanter og en anden i Landets diplomatiske Korps, som alle gjør deres høie Stilling Ære. Naar man betænker Vigtigheden af det Landomraade i Mississippi-Dalen, som er givet dette vort Folks Efterkommere til Tumleplads gjennem mange kommende Tider, da vil det visseligen indrømmes, at det er gaaet godt for vore første Indvandrere, og at de endnu gjenlevende af dem med Tilfredshed kan se tilbage paa Resultatet af det vovelige Skridt, de gjorde, da de kastede løs fra gamle Norge og reiste til Amerika.

I kirkelig Henseende er det dog især at Fremskridt har været forbausende. Med runde Tal kan de lutherske Præster blandt de Norske ansættes til noget over 400 med et Medlemsantal af 125,000. Hele Norge har ikke over 600 Præster for en Befolkning af næsten 2,000,000. Efter disse Angivelser skulde vi derfor her i Amerika være langt bedre forsynet med Præster i Forhold til Medlemsantallet end i Norge, og dog klages der stadig over Præstenød, og der oprettes alt flere og flere Præsteskoler. Dette maa være et tilstrækkeligt Bevis for vort Folks store Interesse og Offervillighed for kirkelige Anliggender. De Tal, vi her har angivet, udgives ikke for at være nøiagtige, men de komme Sandheden nær nok som Bevis paa de store Fremskridt, vort Folk gjør i kirkelig Udvikling.

Anden Del.

I.
En Udvandrers Erindringer fra Livet i Norge og Amerika.

Da jeg paa Opfordring af en Del trofaste Venner begyndte efterfølgende Skildring, henlaa jeg ved et Tilfælde arbeidsløs i Chicago. Førend jeg var rigtig færdig med det, som angaar Livet i Norge, kom jeg atter i Arbeide, og disse Erindringer blev lagt tilside, og siden har jeg hverken havt Tid eller Tilbøielighed til at fortsætte dem. Det er derfor alene paa Forlæggerens indstændige Opfordring, at jeg nu i Korthed har fortsat for at bringe Sammenhæng i Fremstillingen. Dette forklarer da ogsaa den Omstændighed, at meget af Erindringerne fra Livet i Amerika fremkommer spredt paa flere Steder foran i denne lille Bog. Den Del, som angaar Amerika, er blevet meget kort og ufuldstændigt behandlet paa Grund af min Helbredstilstand i den senere Tid. Jeg har nemlig ikke selv kunnet føre Pennen, men har maattet bruge en Amanuensis.

Det er en usmykket og troværdig Fremstilling af Hverdagslivet i Norge og Amerika, dels saaledes som jeg selv har oplevet det og dels saaledes, som det iøvrigt i disse 60 Aar har vist sig for mine iagttagelser, jeg her agter at nedtegne. Jeg har modtaget mange Opfordringer fra mine Venner om at gjøre dette, da man troede, at saadanne Livserindringer ikke blot vilde læses med Interesse, men at der ogsaa i et langt og bevæget Livs Erfaringer kunde være adskillige nyttige Lærdomme at hente, medens der ved samme Anledning kunde vindes et lidet Udbytte for den norske Udvandrings Historie. Naar jeg nu imødekommer disse Opfordringer, sker det ikke, fordi der i mine Erindringer ligger noget mere særegent eller usædvanligt end i saamange andre af mine udvandrede Landsmænds, men dels for at udfylde nogle ledige Timer, hvoraf jeg hidtil har havt meget faa, dels for at yde et lidet Bidrag til den norske Udvandringshistorie.

Den Unges Liv inde i Fjordene i det vestlige Norge kunde vist for mange være behageligt og romantisk nok, i den yndige, grønne Vig, i det frugtbare lille Dalstrøg, ved den venlige Fjord, ved den end venligere stille Indsø, ved den skummende Fos, i de bratte Birkelier, i Stenuren, ved den steile Klippevæg og paa den skyhøie Fjeldtinde—overalt i Klippelandets herlige Natur, hvor Plantelivets Vellugt er saa sød, og hvor Fuglesangen er saa fortryllende, kunde den opvakte Aand ikke være andet end glad og lykkelig og den livsglade Yngling ikke andet end føle sig greben af Beundring for det skjønne og poetiske i denne Natur og af Tilbedelse for Naturens Herre. Men det var her som overalt i Verden: kun den Oplyste kan aabne Naturens Bog og forstaa dens Sprog; for Massen af Landets Børn var den en lukket Bog. Ved Siden af Moderens surrende Spinderok lærte vel Dalens Søn at fremsige sit "Fadervor", i den tarvelige Omgangsskole lærte han vel de fem Parter af sin lille Katekismus udenad paa det han nogle Aar senere kunde komme for Præsten og blive optaget i Kirkens Skjød; men hermed maatte han da ogsaa lade sig nøie. Han var neppe ti Aar gammel, før al hans Tid og alle hans Kræfter maatte anvendes paa legemligt Slid og Slæb—paa et Madstræv, der hver Dag vendte tilbage med lige uforsonlige og uafviselige Krav. Det dyrkbare Jordmaal i de trange Dale var lidet, Befolkningen forholdsvis stor, og dette fattige Land formaaede ikke mere. I Løbet af de sidste 400 Aar havde Landet tillagt sig en talrig dansk-tydsk Embeds- og Handelsstand, som havde Magten i sine Hænder. Lovene havde givet denne importerede Klasse Monopol paa alt undtagen Odelsjorden, og denne blev efterhaanden saa udstykket formedelst Overbefolkning og saa betynget med Skattebyrder til en ødsel Regjering og for at holde den herskende Klasse paa Magtens og Oplysningens Høider, at Armod og Uvidenhed blev den norske Almues almindelige Lod. Den gamle norske Helteaand, som gjennem Aarhundreder knugedes og kuedes under disse Forholde, havde med utrolig Seighed endnu bevaret nogle svage Rester af sin fordums Storhed. I Begyndelsen af vort Aarhundrede bestod den fornemmelig i en mageløs Kamp for det daglige Brød og i en medfødt Modbydelighed for at komme paa Fattigkassen eller gribe til Betlerstaven.

Dette er en haard Skildring, og kun den, der ligesom jeg har maattet gjennemgaa Kampen fra Tiaarsalderen og seet Tusinder Andre gjøre det samme, vil indrømme, at jeg her taler Sandhed uden Overdrivelse. Hvad Under da, om den fattige Bondedrengs Øie var lukket for "det deilige Hardangers" Naturskjønhed, som en Wergelands Begeistring har besunget og en Tidemands Pensel afbildet; hvad Under, om hans unge Sjæl blev sløvet og forknyt under Opvæxten, medens han hver Dag i Armodens lasede Dragt barfodet traskede om for at erhverve noget til Livets Ophold ; ja, hvad Under, om han kom til at leve og dø uden at kjende sin Skjæbnes Haardhed, uden andre Længsler og Aspirationer end at tilfredsstille Bugens skarpe Krav som ethvert andet Jordens Dyr? Jeg voxte op paa et Sted, hvor jeg havde Anledning til at se Præstens, Sorenskriverens, Kompagnichefens og Landhandlerens unge Sønner oplæres under en Huslærer (Kandidaten, som vi kaldte ham), og det var udentvivl Synet af disse velklædte, sorgløse, muntre Drenge, der intet andet havde at bestille end at lege og samle Kundskaber, som først gjorde, at det smertelige Spørgsmaal, lig det skarpe Staal, trængte sig frem til mit unge Hjerte: "Hvad har jeg gjort, og hvad har disse gjort, at der skal være saa stor en Forskjel mellem os?" Og naar de saa haanede mig for mine revne Klæder og lo og pegede Fingre ad mig og raabte: "nei, se han!" naar jeg bøiet og kroget under en svær Byrde gik med Næsen mod Jorden, da græd jeg og bandte og forargedes.

Jeg har ofte senere seet tilbage paa denne Scene som det første egentlige Eftertankens Lysglimt i den mørke forkuede Sjæl, og selv i denne Stund tror jeg fuldt og fast, at Forsynet i sin Visdom vendte til det Gode, hvad disse Herremandssønner tænkte til det Onde; thi uagtet jeg i min Forargelse i mit Hjerte anklagede Gud for Uretfærdighed, bevarede han mig dog fra Fortvivlelse og gav mig Mod og Kraft til i en vis Grad at overvinde og Taalmodighed til at bære en haard og ubarmhjertig Skjæbne. Da jeg var 12 Aar gammel kunde jeg kun maadelig læse indenad i Katekismen og Evangeliebogen, som var de eneste Bøger (foruden ABC'en) jeg havde Adgang til. Udenad kunde jeg foruden Fadervor og nogle Bordbønner de ti Bud og de tre Trosartikler, og naar jeg læste det fjerde Bud, brød jeg ofte mit Hoved over, hvorfor Landhandlerens Søn, der slet ikke var nogen snild eller lydig Dreng mod sine Forældre, skulde have det saa godt, medens jeg, der endnu aldrig havde tænkt paa at sige Nei til det, min Far eller Mor bad mig, skulde have det saa inderlig slet. Min Fader havde i Fædrelandets Tjeneste faaet en Kugle i det ene Knæ og dette var blevet aldeles stivt. Denne Vanførhed, kan jeg godt erindre, var ham til stor Uleilighed; han kunde ikke reise sig med en "Børe" paa Ryggen, og jeg skulde da altid være ved Haanden for at hjælpe ham op. Jeg var den yngste af ti Søskende og det var trangt for os. Fader havde en liden Jordvei til Brug paa Livstid, men eiede den ikke. Efterhvert som mine Søskende voxte op, maatte de ud og foretage noget paa egen Haand, og allerede da jeg var 13 Aar, døde min Fader i en Alder af 53 [62] Aar. Trods al hans Sparsomhed og rastløse Arbeiden sad min Moder nu igjen paa et meget indskrænket Levekaar, der med stor Uvilie og Plageri blev hende tilstaaet af Gaardpartens Eier. I sit sidste Leveaar havde Fader, da han mærkede min store Lyst til Læsning og Skrivning, anvendt en stor Del af Søndagene med at give mig Undervisning; saaledes skrev han ofte Tal og lette Regnestykker med Kridt paa Bunden af en Melkeringe og jeg var nu kommen saa vidt i Indenadslæsning, at jeg kunde læse meget af de for mig dengang saa overordentlig interessante Fortællinger i det gamle Testamente.

Jeg kan ikke sige med Vished, hvor langt jeg mindes tilbage. Den første Begivenhed, som har paatrykt sig Erindringen med et uudsletteligt Præg, er, da jeg blev vænnet fra Moderbrystet, og da var jeg vist omkring tre Aar gammel. Den næste Episode, som jeg klart erindrer fra den Tid, er, da min Søster en Søndag havde vovet at klippe mit lange Haar, som Moder holdt saa meget af; det var nemlig nu kommet paa Mode at lade sit Haar klippe, og Søster likte ikke, at jeg skulde være anderledes end de andre Smaadrenge; men Moder vilde ikke give sit Samtykke. Da jeg hin Søndagaften kom hjem minus mit lange Haar, græd min Moder. Det var første Gang jeg havde seet hendes Taarer, og Indtrykket deraf har Tiden ikke formaaet at udslette af Mindets Tavle. I fire-fem Aars Alderen forsaa jeg mig nok af og til mod Moders strenge Regler (idetmindste syntes jeg de var unødvendig strenge), men saalænge jeg vidste mig skyldig, tog jeg Straffen med Taalmodighed. Ved disse Tider havde jeg en stærk Tilbøielighed til at prøve alskens smaa Haandarbeider og var maaske ikke uden visse mekaniske Anlæg. En Dag havde Moder tabt en af sine Strikkepinder, og da hun vidste, at jeg altid stod i Forlegenhed for saadanne bekvemme Sager, blev jeg uden videre beskyldt for at have taget den, og da jeg bestemt negtede at have begaaet denne Brøde, fik jeg en ret alvorlig Straf. Jeg vilde rimeligvis have glemt dette med saa meget andet fra denne Tid, dersom jeg havde været skyldig; men at blive saa haardt straffet i Uskyldighed, gjorde et dybt Indtryk, hvilket desuden meget forøgedes, da min Moder strax efter fandt sin Strikkepind i Asken ved Ildstedet, hvor hun rimeligvis havde tabt den, og blev saaledes greben af Anger over den Uret, hun havde tilføiet mig, at store Taarer trillede nedover hendes Kinder. Men nok med dette.

II.
Forberedelse til Konfirmation.

Efter min Faders Død skulde jeg endnu forblive hos Moder i det gamle Faderhus et Aar for at gaa til Præsten og af ham forberedes til Konfirmationen, og derpaa drage ud i Verden for at skjøtte mig selv som saa mange Andre af mine forsvarsløse Standsforvandte. Det var endnu ganske maadeligt bevendt med mine boglige Kundskaber; det eneste jeg kan sige derom er, at jeg kunde læse nogenlunde ordentlig i Bog og havde begyndt at regne lidt i hele Tal. Jeg vilde nu ogsaa gjerne lære at skrive, men det var trangt om Undervisningen. En Onkel af mig var i sine Ungdomsaar kommen til Bergen, hvor hans ualmindelige Begavelse havde vakt et Par Skolemænds Opmærksomhed, og de havde gjort sig en Fornøielse af at give ham adskillig Privatundervisning. Han havde derved fattet den dristige Beslutning at gaa den studerende Vei, hvilken han dog senere maatte opgive, da den belovede Pengeunderstøttelse slog feil og han selv intet havde at skyde til. Nogle formaaende Velyndere af den herskende Stand anvendte da sin Indflydelse og forskaffede ham Ansættelse i en ledig Lærer- og Vakcinatør-Post i vort Præstegjæld. Han var en ivrig Oplysningsven og arbeidede med stor Dygtighed i sit Kald som Lærer; men hans Distrikt var ikke i det Sogn, hvor jeg var hjemme, og jeg havde derfor ikke nydt Fordelen af hans Undervisning, hvorimod vor Omgangsskolelærer var en Krøbling baade paa Legeme og Aand, fuld af en jamrende religiøs Fanatisme, der bestyrkede Almuen i dens almindelige Fordomme, blandt andet, at det f. Ex. var Synd for Folk af den tjenende Klasse at ville lære at skrive og regne, eller at læse i andre Bøger end Bibelen og Evangeliebogen, at saadant kun var tilladt Folk, som tilhørte den herskende Klasse — Storfolket, som man kaldte dem — osv. Med disse Anskuelser fremherskende blandt Folket blev naturligvis Skolegjerningen saameget mageligere for dette dovne Menneske, der faldt isøvn hver anden Time paa Dagen, og han vandt desuden derved uendelig meget i sin Foresatte, Præstens, Anseelse, som var en af Standens loyale Mænd, der ikke taalte, at nye Ideer opstod i Faarenes Hoveder, hvilket jo — som den herskende Stand dengang overalt udtrykte sig — kun vilde gjøre dem "næsevise" (plante Visdom i Næsen?). Vor Omgangsskole var altsaa ikke Stedet, hvor jeg kunde lære at skrive og regne. Jeg fandt en hel Masse gamle Papirer og Brevskaber efter min Fader, der med Hensyn til Intelligents og Kundskaber havde været en Undtagelse fra sin Stand — noget, der syntes at have gaaet tilbage gjennem mange Slægtled. Om der i Familien fandtes strivekyndige dengang Fædrene for en fire- til femogtyve Aarhundreder siden kom vestover fra det nordlige Ruslands Skove, drog nedad den norske Kyst og bosatte sig langs Fjordene, skal jeg ikke kunne sige; isaafald maa det vist have været Runeskrift de brugte.

Den gamle gothiske Skrift, min Fader havde brugt, var de eneste Mønstre, jeg havde til min Veiledning; der fandtes desuden ikke et Alfabet, og jeg havde ikke først lært at skrive de enkelte Bogstave. Jeg kunde naturligvis ikke læse Skriften og maatte foreløbig kun lade mig nøie med at kopiere den saa godt jeg kunde. Hermed anvendte jeg da saa meget af Søndagene, at min Moder begyndte at irettesætte mig: "Du ved jo, at Du til Vaaren skal for Præsten, og han spørger nok ikke, om Du kan skrive; saalangt derfra vil det maaske holde haardt, om Du 'slipper frem', dersom han faar høre, at Du forøder din Tid med at skrive. Du faar nu holde Dig til Spørgsmaalsbogen og lære den godt udenad, ellers bliver Du ikke engang indtegnet." Hun tog dog feil med Hensyn til Skrivningen, thi det var den unge Kapellan, som skulde overhøre Konfirmanterne, og han var en langt mere liberal og folkeligsindet Mand end den gamle drukne Sognepræst. Nu vel, med Spørgsmaalsbogen gik det inderlig trangt; Indholdet var for svært for min indskrænkede Forstandsudvikling, og det var tørt som Sand, papegøiemæssigt at lære udenad, hvad jeg ikke forstod, saa jeg faldt rent i Fortvivlelse over den Opgave, som nu forelaa, og jeg troede bestemt, at jeg kom til at gaa for Præsten mindst tre Aar, før jeg kunde blive konfirmeret. Det var ved denne Tid, at min ovenomtalte Onkel kom fra Nabosognet i Besøg til os; min Moder fortalte ham om mine Særegenheder og ytrede megen Bekymring for mig; jeg vilde kun læse Historier i det gamle Testamente og sidde hele Søndagene og kopiere min Faders gamle Breve. Den Skoggerlatter, min Onkel satte i med, da han hørte dette, skal jeg aldrig glemme, saa skamfuld og bange blev jeg. Men han kom hen til mig, lagde Haanden paa mit Hoved og sagde: "Vær ikke bange, min Gut; Du er et Skud af den gode gamle Stamme. Læs ikke formeget i det gamle Testamente; Sproget er jo saa forkjert; det fordærver aldeles Din Smag. Jeg skal laane Dig nogle Bøger, og saa skal Du faa Forskrifter af mig og lære den nyere Skrift." Havde jeg eiet et Kongerige, havde jeg i min Taknemmelighed vist givet ham det. Han havde nu Ferie fra sin Skole, og i sin Hengivenhed for Folkeoplysningens Fremme besluttede han et Par Uger at gjøre et Forsøg med en Skriveskole i vort Naboskab, og trods Almuens Fordomsfuldhed lykkedes det ham ved sindige Argumenter og Overtalelser at faa 7-8 unge Gutter til at deltage i den Skriveskole, som han uden Betaling vilde holde for dem. Han var en af Naturen høit begavet, men noget excentrisk Mand, med en levende Interesse eller rettere en mærkværdig Enthusiasme for Almueungdommens Undervisning. Uagtet han havde en talrig Børneflok at forsørge og levede i den yderste Fattigdom, var han dog saa inderlig glad og lykkelig ved uden Betaling at kunne udbrede Oplysning og vække Folket til Eftertanke, vække dem af den skjæbnesvangre Uvidenheds søde Søvn, hvori Aarhundreders Misregimente og fremmed Aag havde neddysset det. Med Skriveskolen gik det herligt. O, det var lykkelige, men desværre altfor korte Dage. Han havde særegne sjeldne Egenskaber til at gjøre sin Undervisning behagelig og lærerig. En Aften kan jeg især erindre, da han havde modtaget et Brev fra en ung Mand i et Nabosogn, der havde nydt hans Undervisning og nu var bleven Omgangsskolelærer. Han var ingen god Stilist og undskyldte sig derfor i Brevet, men tilføiede endelig, at "jeg haaber at drage mig." Dette var formeget for vor gode gamle Lærer; han udbrød med sin karakteristiske Skoggerlatter, lagde sig paa Maven paa en Langbænk og begyndte at trække sig fremover, sigende: "Jeg haaber at drage mig! Jeg haaber at drage mig!" og saa lo han igjen. Saaledes var det han vilde indprente os rigtige Begreber om Ordenes Betydning og rette Brug.

Da hans Ferier vare udløbne, vendte han tilbage til sit Distrikt. Før han forlod os, foreslog han for dem af Drengene, der maatte ønske at fortsætte sine Skriveøvelser, at sende ham Stiløvelser i Breve, saa skulde han rette Feilene og sende dem tilbage ved Leilighed; thi, sagde han, at lære at skrive Bogstaver og Ord er kun Midlet, men den egentlige Hensigt med Skrivningen er at meddele sine Tanker, og at gjøre dette paa en klar og grei Maade, er langt vanskeligere og udkræver meget større Øvelse og Forstandsudvikling, end den blot mekaniske Færdighed at kunne skrive Bogstaver og Ord. Saavidt jeg ved, var der kun faa af Drengene, som benyttede sig af det venlige Tilbud, maaske af misforstaaet Frygt for, at han skulde le over deres Feil. Jeg for min Del lod mig ikke afholde af nogen saadanne Skrupler og skrev derfor en Masse Stiløvelser over forskjellige lette Hverdagsemner, hvilke jeg noksaa punktlig fik tilbage med Lærerens Rettelser. At se disse Rettelser blive alt mindre og ubetydeligere eftersom Tiden skred frem og øvelserne fortsattes, var ikke lidet smigrende for min Forfængelighed, ligesom jeg vistnok ogsaa deraf med Rette kunde drage en fornuftig Opmuntring til fortsat Arbeide.

Da Vaaren kom skulde jeg, som sagt, til Præsten for at indskrives blandt Konfirmanterne, og jeg tror sikkert, at mangen Forbryder i sit Fængsel imødeser den Dag, han skal hænges, med mindre Frygt og Angst end jeg imødesaa den Dag, jeg første Gang skulde overhøres af Præsten. Mon ikke ogsaa han vilde være meget haard og skaanselløs, ja maaske gjøre sig lystig over mig og pege Fingre ad mig, ligesom de unge Herremandssønner ofte havde gjort, fordi jeg var saa daarlig klædt og var saa dum og klodset og forknyt, naar jeg kom i Nærheden af dem, som hørte til den høiere Stand. Endelig kom den frygtede Dag. De fleste af Konfirmanterne ledsagedes af sin Fader og bragte Foræringer med til Præstens Kjøkken. Jeg, som ingen Fader havde mere, kom alene og havde desværre heller ingen Foræring — en meget pinlig Omstændighed, som næsten berøvede mig den Smule Samling, jeg endnu havde tilovers. Jeg blev opmærksom paa en besynderlig Manøvre blandt flere af de tilstedekomne Fædre under Ventetiden før Indskrivningen begyndte; jeg saa nok, at den gik ud paa at komme først ind, men kunde ikke vide hvorfor. En af vore Naboer, hvis Datter ogsaa skulde indskrives, og som havde lovet min Moder at tage mig med ind til Præsten, hviskede til mig, at disse Mænd vilde alle se at komme først ind, for at deres Sønner skulde komme først paa Listen og derved komme til at staa øverst i Rækken under Overhøringen. Dette havde nu ikke jeg tænkt paa. Af Naturen et lidet frygtsomt Væsen ønskede jeg helst at være blandt de sidste og blive saa ubemærket som muligt. Da Naboens Datter ikke var meget flink i Bogen, brød heller ikke hun sig om at være blandt de Første, og hun mente, at det ogsaa for mit Vedkommende var meget bedre at blive flyttet op end ned paa Konfirmationsdagen. Der var desuden adskillige, som vare selvskrevne at være først, hvoriblandt Handelsmandens Søn, Medhjælperens Søn samt en Søn af Præstegaardens Forpagter osv. Da de mest æresyge havde været inde, kom da ogsaa Turen til os, medens der endnu var nogle tilbage. Heldigvis traf det sig nok saa, at flere af dem, som næst foran os havde været til Overhøring, kun havde bestaaet sin Prøve ganske maadelig, og da vor Nabos Datter, som først blev afhørt, ogsaa læste med en hel Del Ustøhed og Besvær, tog min Indenadslæsning sig formedelst Kontrasten ganske fortrinlig ud, og den Ros, jeg derved høstede, gav mig meget af min Fatning tilbage og støttede mine Nerver i den Grad, at jeg næsten ganske ophørte at skjælve, og kunde nu give saa fornuftige Svar, hvad Udenadslæsningen angik, som om det havde været min egen Moder, der spurgte. Da jeg sagde, at jeg kun havde læst udenad saa langt som den første Tavle i Pontoppidans Forklaring, syntes Præsten nok dette var lidet i Forhold til min raske Indenadslæsning. Jeg maatte gjøre den oprigtige Tilstaaelse for ham, at de Stykker, jeg forstod, kunde jeg erindre, naar jeg havde læst dem et Par Gange; men de, som jeg ikke forstod, glemte jeg igjen, om jeg saa havde læst dem mange Gange. "Det skal vi nok komme over," sagde Præsten venlig og tilføiede, at jeg fik nu tage fat for Alvor, og naar jeg saa kom igjen til Overhøring, skulde han forklare. Ved Indskrivningen anmærkede han de Foræringer, hver Konfirmant havde medbragt, og her blev min Stilling meget pinagtig, thi jeg havde ikke bragt ham

Noget. Hvorfor havde jeg da ikke det? Jeg tilstod, at jeg ikke vidste det; maaske havde min Moder forglemt det. Hun havde kun omtalt for mig, at jeg om Sommeren maatte bort i Arbeide, paa en Tid der ikke hjemme var noget nødvendigt, for at fortjene en Speciedaler, som tilkom Præsten, naar jeg blev konfirmeret. Jeg lovede oprigtig at bede Moder om en Foræring, og jeg haabede, hun vilde tilveiebringe noget. Dermed slap jeg da fra det for denne Gang. Det forholdt sig dog ikke saa, at hun havde glemt Foræringen; hun vidste god Besked om Skikken, da hun allerede havde sendt 9 af sine Børn til Konfirmation; men Sagen var den, at denne Skik, der i sin Tid, før Præsten havde begyndt at faa regelmæssig Pengebetaling for at læse med Konfirmanterne, kunde have været noksaa smuk, betragtet som en kjærlig Paaskjønnelse af den Flid, han anvendte paa Ungdommens Kristendomsundervisning, medens den nu var bleven til en Uskik, der benyttedes af den mere velstaaende for at faa sine forsømte Børn konfirmerede uden den fornødne Forberedelse, hvorimod den fattiges Børn, selv om de læste bedre, fik den Byrde og Tidsspilde at gaa to eller endog tre Aar til Præsten, fordi de ikke havde kunnet bringe ham de fornødne Foræringer — kort at sige: dette Uvæsen var nu ikke andet end ved en Foræring til Præsten at frikjøbe sine Børn fra at lære noget. Min Moder og en ældre Broder, som var hjemme og drev Gaarden med hende, mente derfor, at jeg fik lære min Bog godt, og naar saa Præsten fik sin Daler, fik dette være nok. Ved den næste Overhøring havde jeg den Fornøielse at give rigtige Svar paa et Par Spørgsmaal, som de Andre havde strandet paa; men uheldigvis fik den gode Mand det Indfald med det samme at spørge mig i den hele Forsamlings Paahør, om jeg idag havde bragt den Foræring, jeg havde lovet ham. Denne Ydmygelse gik mig saa nær, at jeg ønskede jeg kunde synke gjennem Jorden, hvor jeg stod. Grædefærdig tilstod jeg, at jeg ikke havde faaet noget med denne Gang; men jeg havde gjort, hvad jeg lovede: bedet Moder om noget til Præsten. Han holdt nu en kort Straffeprædiken for mig, sagde, at vi ikke kunde undskylde os med Fattigdom, flere af mine Søskende hørte blandt de mest velstaaende Folk i Bygden, og at han altsaa ikke kunde taale, at der skede nogen Undtagelse for min Skyld; det var at sætte et slet Exempel og opmuntre andre til Efterligning. Jeg havde først følt mig ydmyget og beskjæmmet; nu løb mit hidsige Blod til Hovedet, og jeg blev forarget, men taug. Kun i Tanken gav jeg min Harme Luft: At De finder det stemmende med Deres Værdighed at tigge, kan maaske have sin Rigtighed; men jeg kan ikke tigge hverken hos mine Søskende eller Andre; kan jeg ved ærligt Arbeide fortjene saameget over, hvad jeg behøver til Føde og Klæder, vil jeg med største Fornøielse give Dem en Foræring, om ikke af Kjærlighed, saa dog for at undgaa Skam og Fortræd.

Konfirmanternes første Fællesmøde havde altsaa for mig været sørgeligt;

jeg var skamfuld og nedtrykt, medens de Andre vare glade og lykkelige, og dog havde jeg ved Katekisationen staaet mig saa godt som nogen af dem; men min Katekisation havde hovedsagelig dreiet sig om Foræringen, og der var jeg kommen bedrøvelig tilkort. En heldig Virkning havde dog den første fælles Overhøring udøvet paa mig: min Ulyst til Udenadslæsning var forsvunden. Jeg havde seet, hvorledes det stod til med de andre, og vi havde nu Alle den samme fastsatte Lektie, som skulde læres til næste Møde; dette var Opmuntring nok. Der var ikke hengaaet to Dage, før jeg havde hvert Ord af Lektien paa mine Fingerender, og jeg kunde ikke forstaa, hvorledes det var gaaet til; det var kommet som af sig selv.

III.
Arbeide og Læsning.

Jordarealet paa vor Gaard hjemme var meget indskrænket; derimod havdes en udstrakt, men fjerntliggende Udmark. Didhen (omkring ¾ norsk Mil) maatte vi ofte gaa, saasnart Sneen var væk om Foraaret, dels for at istandsætte Gjærder, Hesjer, Hølader osv., dels for at gaa længere op til Sætren for at berede Brænde og andre Ting til den Tid Budeierne skulde flytte derop med Buskapen. Paa Veien til og fra denne Udmark læste jeg da bestandig mine Lektier i Pontoppidans Forklaring, saa jeg slet ikke behøvede at spilde den ringeste Tid dermed, og det var forbausende, hvor let dette gik for mig; under Læsningen vidste jeg ikke af, før Veien var tilbagelagt, uagtet jeg bar en svær "Nistetine" paa Ryggen, og under Gangen vidste jeg ikke af, før Lektien var læst. Der var kun en Ubehagelighed ved dette Slags Søvngjængeri; man gik nemlig her bestandig barfodet om Sommeren, og under Læsningen stødte jeg uafbrudt mine Tæer mod de skarpe Stene, som overalt bedækkede Fodstien i disse klippefulde Bjergegne, saa Blodet randt. Værst var det, naar de gamle Saar opreves; men "det Onde med det Gode maa annammes alle Dage." Fordommen havde endnu ikke saavidt veget Pladsen for Fornuftens Lys — Overtroen havde endnu ikke givet den syndige Nutids Ingeniørvidenskab Lov til at rydde Kjøreveien til disse Udmarker, skjønt jeg slet ikke tror, man havde behøvet andet end en Smule Muskelarbeide med simple Hverdagshænder for at gjøre mange af disse Fodstier farbare med Vogn eller Slæde. Den allerstørste Del af Høet for flere Nabogaarde blev samlet oppe i disse Bjergegne, som bestaar af bratte Lier og trange Dale. Lierne har kun lidet Skov, men desto mere Sten, og skjønt Græsset er temmelig frodigt, samles dog Høet med stor Vanskelighed paa Grund af den Mængde Sten. Det Græs, som bliver slaaet i Lierne, maa bæres paa Ryggen ned i Dalen til de smaa Bakkeheld, hvor Hesjerne befinde sig, og naar det nu er Regnveir, hvilket paa disse Kanter er meget almindeligt, har man det hyggelige Arbeide at bære det vaade Græs, medens det kolde Vand løber en nedad Ryggen. Da Veien derop er lang og tager altfor megen Tid, ligger man gjerne flere Nætter i Rad i Høladerne, medens en halvvoxen Gut eller Jente gaar hjem efter mere Proviant, som gjerne bestaar af Havregrød med Fladbrød og Graabensild. Melk bringer derimod Sæterjenten hver Morgen fra den modsatte Kant, hvor Sætren ligger; hun arbeider derpaa den ganske Dag til henimod Solnedgang, da hun vender tilbage til Sætren, og har endda ofte en lang Vei at gaa for at finde Buskapen, malke Kjørene og stelle fra sig i Sætren. Skjøndt alle Bønder paa disse Kanter tilbringe Livet i det yderste Slaveri, hvad angaar Arbeide, Mad og Klæder, saa tror jeg dog, at Sæterjenterne her har det værst af dem.

En af vore Nabokoner havde Navn for at være meget gjerrig, og dersom Eilert Sundt havde seet hendes Husstel, vilde han vist have erklæret hende for en ualmindelig skidden So. En Morgen tidlig, da hun skulde i Marken, kunde hun ikke finde noget Kar til at øse Middagsgrøden i, og da hun tilfældigvis saa en gammel haard Skindbuxe, som tilhørte hendes Mand, fik hun det heldige Indfald at øse Grøden i det ene Buxelaar, bandt for ved den nedre Ende, slængte den derpaa over Skuldrene og drog afsted til Udmarken, hvor Mandfolkene havde opholdt sig i flere Dage. Da man skulde faa sin Middagsmad af den i sig selv ikke meget appetitlige Havregrød, der befandt sig i denne sindrige Beholder, gjorde Tjenestekarlen Revolt og negtede at spise, hvilket man maaske ikke kunde fortænke ham i. Han erklærede ligefrem, at naar han ikke kunde faa spiselig Mad, kunde han heller ikke arbeide, og beredte sig derfor til at tage sig det mageligt paa sin tomme Mave. Det havde været en varm Solskinsdag, og nu begyndte en Tordensky at trække hurtig op fra Vesten med alle Kjendetegn paa en af de for Landmanden saa uheldsvangre Regnstyrtninger, som dette ustadige Klima er saa rigt paa. Tilfældigvis havde man en Mængde tørt Hø liggende spredt over Marken, hvilket man om Eftermiddagen netop skulde til at samle i Hus. Konen stormede naturligvis ivei for at rage sammen paa Liv og Død for at faa bjerget saa meget af det tørre Hø som muligt, før Regnen kom, og hvad der bragte hendes Raseri til det Yderste var, at den ubønhørlige Tjenestekarl blev siddende ganske rolig og saa paa. Forgjæves bad og skjældte og græd og truede hun; han holdt paa sit, at "den, som ikke faar Mad, kan heller ikke arbeide." Endelig begyndte de svære Regndraaber at styrte ned, og Dagens Kamp var afgjort. Kun lidet af Høet var kommet sammen, og i sin Fortvivlelse sank Konen ganske forsprængt ned paa Marken, udbrydende: "Vor egen Magt er intet værd; vi ere snart overvundne!"

Som man ser, var Livet i disse Egne ingen Leg; den, som her skulde slaa sig igjennem, fik ikke vandre paa Roser. Levemaaden var knap og Arbeidet yderst haardt og besværligt; dog var Sommeren her, ulig saa mange andre Steder, ikke at sammenligne med Vinteren i Besværlighed. For at gjøre dette forstaaeligt, behøver jeg blot at nævne, at alt det Hø, som om Sommeren blev samlet i disse Udmarker, maatte om Vinteren bæres hjem paa Ryggen, og naar man ved, at Veiens Længde var fra ¾ til 1 norsk Mil, og at den gik igjennem dybe Bjergkløfter, over store Urer, op og ned over bratte Lier og Aaser, belagte med Is og Sne, som ofte gjorde Vandringen over disse Stier livsfarlig selv for den, som intet havde at bære, vil man let kunne gjøre sig et Begreb om, hvad Livet her var for den, som næsten hver Dag i al Slags Veir maatte gjøre denne besværlige Tur. Det har ofte forundret mig, naar jeg har seet tilbage paa dette Liv, hvorledes det gik til, at jeg ikke blev til Krøbling under denne Disciplin, der allerede begyndte med Tolvaarsalderen. Medens jeg nu vistnok ikke bør undervurdere Værdien af en saadan Livsskole for det unge Menneske, som fra en tidlig Alder skal begynde at bryde sin egen Bane, maa jeg dog bevidne, at der virkelig var stor Fare baade for Liv og Helbred forbundet med dette Vinterarbeide, hvor alvorlige Ulykkestilfælder ikke vare sjeldne, og jeg har ofte senere tænkt paa, hvilken lykkelig Omstændighed det var for mig, at min Moder opgav Gaarden, da jeg var bleven konfirmeret og havde fyldt mit 14de Aar. Derved kom jeg idetmindste bort fra dette Sted, og ihvorvel Lykken ikke altid siden førte mig med kjærlig Haand, tror jeg dog, at det vilde have gaaet mig meget værre, om jeg var forbleven længe paa mit Fødested. Ihvorvel den Egn, jeg her har omtalt, maaske hører til de mere besværlige og uheldigt stillede i Fjorddistrikterne i Bergens Stift, er den dog ikke den værste, og jeg tager ikke meget feil, naar jeg mener, at Bondens Liv deromkring omtrent kan ansættes som Gjennemsnits - Maalestok for Forholdene i Bergens Stift. Mange smukkere, bedre og letvintere Gaarde gives der jo, men paa den anden Side ved jeg ogsaa, at der gives ligesaa mange mindre, fattigere og værre stillede end de, jeg her med faa Træk har søgt at skildre.

Efter denne Exkursion til vore Udmarker, vende vi et Øieblik tilbage til Konfirmationen. Jeg gjorde denne Digression for at give Læseren et Billede af det Liv, jeg ved Konfirmationstiden var underkastet.

Det gjorde et meget nedslaaende Indtryk paa mig, at jeg fremfor enhver anden af Konfirmanterne skulde staa tilskamme som den, der ikke vilde bringe Præsten en Foræring. I mine egne Tanker kom jeg derved til at staa paa et lavere Trin, i en mere foragtet Stilling, og var baade en fattigere og slettere Dreng end alle de andre. Jeg havde ikke før vidst, at alle de øvrige Konfirmanter havde bragt Gaver til Præstens Kjøkken, men da jeg nu var den eneste, som blev vanæret med en offentlig Irettesættelse, blev det mig klart, at jeg var den eneste, som ikke havde udført denne Bodshandling. Jeg gjorde derfor de kraftigste Forestillinger hos min Moder, og med mine Taarers Veltalenhed søgte at gjøre hende det begribeligt, hvor ulykkelig jeg følte mig, og hvor krænkende det var for min lille Æresfølelse, saaledes at blive offentlig prostitueret for en ringe Ting, som jeg dog mente ikke behøvede at koste saa meget. Mine Argumenter, hvor gode jeg end selv syntes de vare, lod dog ikke til at udøve nogen synderlig Virkning, og jeg maatte atter møde frem uden at bringe den saa meget ønskede Gave med mig. Hermed forblev det da, til det led ud paa Sommeren, da min Moder en Dag begyndte at tale til mig omtrent saaledes: "Min Søn, det bedrøver mig meget at se dig saa fuldstændig at forsømme din Forklaring, medens du saa ihærdig tilbringer Søndagene og dine andre Fritimer over disse verdslige Bøger, som din Onkel har laant dig. Jeg føler mig næsten forvisset om, at du ikke bliver konfirmeret iaar, og jeg har derfor bestemt foresat mig ikke at lade dig faa nogen Gave til Præsten; thi jeg vil aldeles ikke have, at det skal faa Udseende af, at jeg kjøber dig frem, da jeg ved, at du kan lære dine Religionsbøger, naar du vil; det vilde jo ogsaa være en Uret baade mod Præsten og mod dig, om jeg saaledes kjøbte dig frem, var du derimod en ret flink Konfirmant, vilde Sagen faa et langt bedre Udseende." "Men jeg har da lært de foresatte Lektier hver eneste Gang, Moder, og de andre ere ikke bedre; De kunde jo høre mig engang imellem for selv at faa Vished i Sagen," svarede jeg. Det havde hun ikke Tid til, og mente desuden, at det var en selvgiven Sag, at jeg ikke kunde lære mine Lektier uden at se i Bogen. Den næste Søndag havde Præsten bestemt at katekisere Konfirmanterne i Menighedens Overvær i Kirken, da fik man da høre, hvorledes det forholdt sig med os allesammen. Paa denne Kant følte jeg mig fuldkommen tryg i min Sag; vi havde nu gjennemgaaet Bogen en Gang og havde begyndt forfra paany; jeg havde ikke blot lært Bogen fra Ende til anden, men havde ogsaa de Forklaringer, Præsten ved hver Lektie havde givet, fuldkommen i Hukommelsen. I alle Ting, som ikke angik Pungen og Kjøkkenet, syntes os Præsten at være en meget retsindig og snild Mand. Under Overhøringen stillede han altid sine Spørgsmaal særskilt til hver især, saaat den høirøstede Skraaler ikke, som jeg ofte har seet, fik tage Ordet af Munden paa den flinkere, men undselige og sagte Elev, naar denne havde begyndt Svaret, men enhver maatte aflægge Regnskab for sig selv; og naar Nogen, efter gjentagne Forsøg og Vendinger i Spørgsmaalet, endelig blev Svaret skyldig, blev Ordet først givet frit. Derved fik da den flinkeste ikke alene Anledning til at svare for sig selv, men ogsaa for andre, og naar det kneb rigtig, havde Præsten tilsidst faaet den Vane med et Vink at henvende sig til et vist Sted nede i Rækken. I Menighedens Paahør var han naturligvis altid taknemlig for et rigtigt Svar, naar alle syntes at staa fast, thi ikke at kunne faa noget Svar, betragtede han i en vis Grad som et Nederlag for sig selv.

Den Søndagaften var min Moder meget glad og tilfreds, og næste Gang vi mødte hos Præsten, fik jeg en prægtig Ost med til ham. Efter at have ventet saalænge syntes han nok det var lidet (Smør var egentlig den rette Gave), og satte op et surt Ansigt, hvortil jeg vovede at bemærke, at Osten var sød. Denne halvskjulte lille Vittighed havde sin Virkning; munter tog han en Kniv for at smage paa Osten og lod til at finde, at jeg havde Ret. Jeg var igrunden i Sommerens Løb kommen til at staa paa en fortrolig Fod med ham, han havde vist forlængst glemt Affæren med Foræringen og givet mig mangt et lille Bevis paa Velvilie, især ved sine udførlige Forklaringer ved Katekisationen, og jeg kan desaarsag, saavelsom for hans senere beviste Godhed, aldrig andet end mindes denne Mand med Taknemlighed. Under Overhøringerne var af og til min Forfængelighed bleven smigret, ved at jeg havde besvaret Spørgsmaal, som vare rettede til Landhandlerens eller Medhjelperens Søn, uden at blive besvaret. Paa Konfirmationsdagen kom jeg derfor til at staa næst efter disse Notabiliteter. Medhjelperens Søn, var igrunden en Dosmer, men hans Fader var en meget ærekjær (rangsyg!) Mand, og det vilde have været en utilgivelig Fornærmelse, at stille hans Søn nedenfor Enkens fattige Søn. Saa smaaligt og indskrænket var Synet dengang, selv blandt Almuens ledende Mænd. Da jeg betalte min Daler for Konfirmationen, havde Præsten den Godhed at spørge, om jeg ikke havde Lyst til at blive Skolelærer. Selv havde han, som Kapellan, ikke den Sag i sine Hænder, men havde faaet Paalæg af Sognepræsten at indberette til ham, hvem as Konfirmanterne han ansaa for passende Subjekter til i Fremtiden at kunne beklæde disse Hædersposter. Jeg havde ikke tænkt paa dette, men svarede, at jeg vilde betænke mig derpaa, efter at jeg først havde hørt min Moders og nogle Venners Raad. Visselig havde jeg megen Lyst til, at lære alle mulige Ting, men al min Tid gik med til at erhverve Klæder og Føde. Søndagene havde jeg vistnok fri, men kunde hverken betale for Bøger eller Undervisning. Hermed forblev det da dengang. Min Tanke var, om muligt at faa min Moder til at udruste mig, saaat jeg den Vinter kunde opholde mig hos min Onkel, for at nyde Fordelen af hans Undervisning; men strax efter Konfirmationen, havde jeg det Uheld at faa et meget farligt Øxehug i det venstre Ben, hvorved Musklerne foran paa Ankelledet var bleven saa beskadigede, at man troede sikkert, jeg kom til at faa en stiv Fod. Denne Ulykke holdt mig ved Huset den største Part af Vinteren, men lykkeligvis lægedes dog det slemme Saar uden at efterlade sig nogen permanent Skade. Den Tid, jeg saaledes ikke kunde være med at bære Hø eller hugge Brænde, benyttede jeg, saa godt jeg kunde, til at fortsætte mine Læse-, Skrive- og Regneøvelser; men desværre kun paa egen Haand. Der fandtes efter min Fader en gammel tydsk Bibel; denne tog jeg nu fat paa, og uden Ordbog, uden Grammatik eller mundtlig Veiledning, arbeidede jeg ufortrødent for at lære det tydske Sprog, ved at sammenholde Vers for Vers, den tydske med den norske Oversættelse.

Til Foraaret agtede Moder at opgive Gaarden, og jeg vilde da kunne drage, hvorhen jeg lystede. Da hun kjendte mit naturlige Hang til Bøger, modsatte hun sig ikke min Forberedelse til at blive Lærer. Hun delte sin Samtids Fordomme og ansaa en Omgangslærers Stilling for en af de allerdaarligste, en Stilling, som kun faa andre end vanføre og uduelige Personer søgte; slet lønnede (10 Spd. om Aaret) og end slettere ansete, vare de et Slags Straf, som Bonden kun fandt sig i at modtage, fordi han maatte, og det var i mangt et Hus tvivlsomt, om Skolelæreren eller Lægdslemmet burde indtage første Rang. Men hun ræsonerede saaledes: Dette Bogvæsen passer for Bonden omtrent som det tørre Land for Fisken; som denne maa opgive Aanden af Mangel paa Vand, saa maa Bonden, mellem sine Bøger, opgive Aanden af Mangel paa Brød. Boglærdommen tilhører Stormanden; alle de lette Næringsveie tilhøre ham og hans Slægt; og naar du, min Søn, vil blande dig i en fremmed Bestilling og pryde dig med laante Fjædre, gaar det dig som det gik Kragen blandt, Paafuglene; du bliver udstødt af de Stores Selskab, medens dine egne Standsbrødre ville foragte dig og nægte at optage dig i sin Kreds. Er der et Lærer- eller Lensmandsombud, som kan føde sin Mand, er en Stormandssøn med en svag Hjerne sikker paa at faa det. En rask Karl kan som Husmand skræbe sammen nok til nødtørftigt Brød, og være agtet blandt sine Ligemænd; men en Omgangsskolelærer maa finde sig i at stilles i Klasse med Svein Lægdslem og ingen rask Pige i Bygden vil dele Armod og Elendighed med ham. Men da du nu maa seile din egen Sø, og jeg ikke mere har Arbeide og Brød at give dig, vil jeg ikke tvinge dig. Jeg ved at din Farbroders Gjerning som Lærer har været ædel og skjøn; jeg ved han har opofret egen Bekvemmelighed og egen Fordel for sine Medmenneskers Bedste, og at en rastløs Arbeidsomhed, Ærlighed og Sparsommelighed altid har betegnet hans Vei; men dette har ikke kunnet redde ham fra Opinionens Magt. Hans gode Villie er bleven upaaskjønnet og hans Arbeide ubelønnet. Alt fordi hans Lærdom og Tænkemaade har fjernet ham fra hans egen Stand, medens hans Herkomst gjorde det umuligt for ham at blive optaget i den herskende Stand. Jeg kan altsaa kun give dig det Raad at lære godt, hvad du begynder at lære, og udføre med Flid og Troskab, hvad du paatager dig at gjøre, og forresten finde dig med Taalmodighed i den Uret og Tilsidesættelse, som vor Samfundsorden synes at paalægge. Mørk som denne Skildring var, og sand som den med Hensyn paa hendes indskrænkede Synskreds var, troede jeg dog, eller idetmindste haabede, at den var en Smule overdreven. Det ungdommelige Syn ser stedse saa meget deiligt og ønskeligt i det, som man har sat sit hele Hjertes

Attraa til. Som det gaar et Par fattige elskende, der ikke ser den Armod og Elendighed, som truer dem, hvis de gifte sig, saa gik det ogsaa mig; jeg var over Ørene bleven forelsket i norsk Stiløvelse og Jordbeskrivelse, og intet kunde afskrække mig fra at kaste mig i deres Arme.

Saasnart jeg var bleven rask, reiste jeg derfor til min Onkel, dels for at raadføre mig med ham, og dels for at forhøre mig hos ham, om han ikke vilde lade mig arbeide for min Kost, medens han i Fritimerne gav mig Undervisning. Det bør her bemærkes, at mine ældre Brødre havde altid fraraadet mig og ofte drevet en bitter Spot med min afsindige Lyst til Bøger, saaat jeg stundom blev greben af en bange Anelse om, at jeg maaske spillede en Rolle ligesaa latterlig som Don Quixote, da han gav sig i Kast med Vindmøllen, om jeg ellers dengang havde kjendt hans Heltebedrifter.

IV.
En haard Skole.

Det var imidlertid ikke Skolelærer jeg ønskede at blive. Udsigterne paa den Vei vare altfor mørke og lidet lovende. I Grunden havde jeg slet ikke nogen vis Bestemmelse i saa Henseende. Hvad det var, som drev mig til boglige Sysler, ved jeg ikke; jeg vil kalde det en naturlig Tilbøielighed; maaske var det en endnu ubevidst ærgjerrig Stræben efter at blive, hvad den sunde Fornuft maatte tilsige, at jeg ikke kunde blive, eller en svag Afsky for at være, hvad Stand og Fødsel havde bestemt mig til at blive; nok er det, jeg maatte og vilde sysle med Læsning og Skrivning, hvor haardt min Moder og mine Brødre end irettesatte mig for det. Min Onkel havde nu forladt Skolegjerningen, havde faaet sig en liden Husmandsplads, paa hvilken han kunde holde et Par Kjør og avle nogle Poteter, men drev et Snedkerverksted som sin egentlige Næring. Han var et af disse Mennesker, som man i Amerika kalder Public Spirited Men, og besjæledes af en inderlig Længsel efter at indføre nyttige Reformer blandt Landmændene. Ligesom han tidligere, som Lærer, havde arbeidet ad den intellektuelle Vei ved Almenoplysning og Aandsudvikling at bortrydde Fordomme, vilde han nu ved Indførelsen af forbedrede Redskaber og Arbeidsmethoder fjerne mange skadelige Fordomme og gamle bagvendte Vedtægter ved Agerbruget og Landbovæsenet i Almindelighed. Til den Ende havde han indrettet en Smedje ved Siden af sit Snedkerverksted, skjønt han selv ikke var Smed, forat kunne levere Plove, Harve, Kjærner, Spader, Hakker og en Mangfoldighed af Sager, som endnu ikke var kommen i Brug paa disse Kanter af Landet og ikke engang var at faa, uden at forskrives fra et eller andet Fabrik paa Østlandet. Da jeg om Foraaret besøgte ham, havde han Hænderne fulde med Forberedelser til den egentlige

Drift, som endnu ikke var kommen i Gang. Han sagde mig, at jeg kunde faa nok af haardt Arbeide og en simpel Kost, men anden Undervisningstid kunde han ikke ofre for mig, end den han nødvendig maatte anvende til sine egne Børns Undervisning, og selv denne maatte han for Øieblikket meget indskrænke, men haabede dog, at det hermed vilde blive bedre, naar Værkstedet var kommen istand. Jeg gik naturligvis ind paa enhver Betingelse, thi her var dog idetmindste noget at lære, som ikke forekom hos den almindelige Jordbruger; hvad der hos denne var at lære, syntes jeg nok at jeg havde lært altfor vel. Han nærede endnu, som før, en varm Interesse for Undervisningsvæsenet, og skjønt han selv var bleven lønnet med stor Utak for sine Opofrelser i Almueskolens Tjeneste, vilde han dog ikke fraraade mig at slaa ind paa denne Vei, dersom jeg senere hen kom til at finde for godt at vælge den. Der var nemlig, i 1827 tror jeg, udkommet fra Storthinget en ny Skolelov, som noget forbedrede Lærernes Lønning, og søgte at hæve dem i Samfundets Stilling ved at kræve en større Dannelse og Dygtighed af dem. Under denne Lov skulde de tidligere Klokkerembeder inddrages, efterhvert som Indehaverne døde, og den bedst skikkede blandt Sognets Lærere skulde blive Kirkesanger, for ved denne lille Indtægtskilde at bøde paa hans usle Løn, samt ved den med denne Post formentlig forbundne Ære at hæve Lærerstanden en Smule i Almuens Agtelse, noget der rigtignok var en høist fornøden Betingelse, saavel for at gjøre dens Virksomhed gavnlig, som for at formaa flinke, begavede unge Mennesker til at vælge denne Stand. Denne Lov gjorde nu foruden Læsning ogsaa Skrivning og Regning til faste Undervisningsfag; men Hovedsagen var og forblev dog, som hidtil, Religionsundervisning, og Folkelærerens Gjerning bestod i Katekismus-Overhøring, der forudsatte nøie Bekjendtskab med Troslæren efter de fem Parters Inddeling.

Efter at have givet mig denne Forklaring, fortalte min Farbroder, hvor uheldig det var gaaet ham, da han ved den gamle Klokkers Død havde søgt Ansættelse som Kirkesanger og Lærer ved Hovedsognets faste Skole. Det var blandt Bønderne da som nu en almindelig Skik at diskutere om Troslærdommene ved deres selskabelige Sammenkomster. Den, som var mest belæst i Bibelen og kunde bedst forklare de vanskelige og tildels hemmelighedsfulde Steder i Skriften, gjaldt for den klogeste Mand. Farbror var en Menneskeven, fuld af Kjærlighed og Medlidenhed for Andre, og fandt derfor i Kristus et herligt Mønster for sine Ideer, men kom altid i Forlegenhed overfor de Extra-Orthodoxe, naar de fremholdt deres hjerteløse Trostheori uden Gjerning og Menneskekjærlighed. Han var et Slags Henry Ward Beecher, der helst vilde se Frugter af en kjærlig Kristentro i Menneskets daglige Omgjængelse og vilde, for at være konsekvent, ikke hænge sig fast i de vanskelige Knuder, hvorefter han kom til at fordømme gode Kristne og retsindige Mennesker, der i et eller andet Punkt kunde tænke anderledes end ham — med et Ord: han var for liberal i sin religiøse Anskuelse for den Tids mørke Livsanskuelse. Nogle ubetænksomme Udtalelser angaaende den hellige Skrift havde bragt ham et Par Fanatikeres Fiendskab paa Halsen, hvoraf den ene var en gammel afskediget Skolelærer. Disse Mænd forfulgte ham med den uforsonligste Bitterhed, hvilken de naturligvis kaldte Nidkjærhed for den "rette Tro" eller hvad man nu kalder den "rene Lære". Hans Ord bleve i deres Mund fordreiede og mistydede og de udbredte snart de forfærdeligste Rygter om hans Vranglærdom og Kjætteri. Den talrige Ungdom, der havde nydt godt af hans fortræffelige Undervisning og kjærlige Omgang, vare ham inderlig hengivne, og de allerfleste af Forældrene havde ham kjær og agtede ham langt anderledes end sædvanligt var med de usle Omgangslærere; men hans Fiender gik frem med megen Trædskhed og fik i al Hemmelighed udfærdiget en Klage imod ham, som de forsynede med en Del Underskrifter, hvoraf dog flere tilhørte Mænd, som intet Begreb havde om, hvad de egentlig underskrev. Denne Klage blev indleveret til Sognepræsten, der var en gammel fordrukken Mand, som levede i Dovenskab og Overdaadighed og principielt helst ønskede at se Almuen saa uvidende og overtroisk som mulig. En Søn af den netop afdøde Klokker var den anden Ansøger om Kirkesanger- og Lærerposten under den nye Skolelov. Han var omtrent ligesaa vel skikket til at lede Kirkesangen som Farbror, men i Kundskab, Dannelse, Lærerdygtighed saavelsom i varm Interesse for Undervisningsvæsenet var han kun som et Barn i Sammenligning med ham. Sognepræsten ønskede naturligvis Klokkersønnen, hvis Fader havde tilhørt Rumpen af Herrestanden. Da de to Ansøgere samtidig skulde møde hos Provsten for at blive prøvede, afsendte Sognepræsten foruden en varm Anbefaling for Klokkersønnen ogsaa hin Anklage mod Farbror for Kjætteri. Klagen var bleven saa fuldstændig hemmeligholdt, at sidstnævnte intet vidste derom, før Provsten, efterat Exrminationen var forbi oplæste den for ham og forklarede, at han ved sine Kundskaber og sjeldne Lærerdygtighed vilde have været selvskreven til den Post, han søgte, men formedelst dette Vidnesbyrd imod ham var han bleven umulig som Folkelærer. Onkel følte sig bittert skuffet over denne Tilsidesættelse for en doven og uduelig Lærer; men mest krænkende var det dog, at han af sine egne Standsfæller var bleven overlistet paa en saa foragtelig Maade ved en hemmelig Klage, for hvis Falskhed og Ondskab han kunde have bragt et Hundrede respektable Mænds Vidnesbyrd for hver af de inkompetente Mennesker, som havde underskrevet den, dersom han havde vidst af Klagen. Det var dog hverken første eller sidste Gang Bigotteriets misforstaaede Iver havde forført Folk til at give sine egne bedste Interesser et farligt Saar. Næsten hvert Blad af Kristendommens Historie har Exempler af dette Slags efter en langt større

Skala at opvise. I næsten nitten Hundrede Aar har Forfølgelser for religiøse Meninger fortsat sig. I vor Tid brænder man ikke Kjættere paa Baalet eller stener dem som i de forbigangne Tider; i vor Tid og i vort Land sker Forfølgelser mere i Ord end i Gjerninger. Indbildte Vildfarelser ere saalænge blevne forfulgte med Ild og Sværd, at de religiøse Fanatikeres blodtørstige Hevn har frembragt en almindelig Afsky hos Folkene, og de mildere Sæder har forandret den offentlige Opinion, indtil det er blevet umuligt for det religiøst Rethaveri at bringe Nogen paa Baalet. At strække Vranglærere paa Pennens Pinebænk, eller sætte dem i Prædikenens Gabestok, er nu det høieste, man kan bringe det til.

Naar det var gaaet saaledes til med det grønne Træ, hvad skulde der saa blive af det tørre, tænkte jeg ved Slutningen af hans Fortælling; thi som Lærer var han dengang i mine Øine virkelig det grønne Træ overfor det tørre, imod hvad jeg nogensinde turde haabe at blive. Havde jeg før havt Ulyst til Lærerfaget, fik jeg det endnu mere nu. Jeg blev nu i tre Maaneder hos Onkel og fik virkelig gjøre Ret for min Kost, thi han var et ualmindelig arbeidsomt, tarveligt Menneske. Med al sin Hjertensgodhed kunde hans Filosofi undertiden bringe ham til en ren Urimelighed baade mod sig selv og dem, som arbeidede med ham. En Morgen tidlig, før Solen stod op, drog vi saaledes afsted før Frokosten, roede en Fjerdingvei over Fjorden, gik derpaa nok en Fjerding ind i Skoven for at hugge en Del Materialier, som Manden, der eiede Skoven, skulde kjøre ned til Søen. Dette Arbeide bleve vi ikke færdige med før udpaa Eftermiddagen og kom ikke hjem før det var bleven mørkt, medens vi den ganske Dag havde arbeidet af alle Kræfter. Da jeg blev udmattet af Hunger og ofte var færdig at segne til Jorden, lo han med sin sædvanlige egne Latter og sagde, det vilde gjøre os godt baade paa Legeme og Sjæl; thi Hvilen er ikke sød, uden man er træt, og Maden smager ikke, uden man er hungrig; heller ikke kan man tænke klart med en Mave fuld af sletfordøiet Føde. Jeg mente dog, at det vilde have været menneskeligt, om vi havde faaet lidt Frokost, før vi tog hjemmefra. Arbeidede og svedede man haardt hele Dagen uden Middagsmad, kunde jeg ikke skjønne, at Tankens Klarhed vilde fordunkles af en med ufordøiet Føde overfyldt Mave, om vi havde faaet en Ske kold Havregrød med lidt sur Melk til om Morgenen, før vi tog ud. Men jeg var jo kommen i Skole og maatte ikke vise Insubordination mod min Lærer. En anden Gang havde vi med en stor Baad roet udad Fjorden til nogle bratte Skovlier for at hugge Almetræ til Vognmateriale. Passende Trær for hvad vi søgte fandtes kun høit oppe i Lien, hvorhen man ikke kunde komme med Hest. Det var en varm Foraarsdag; vi arbeidede haardt, og Skjorten blev gjennemvaad af Sved; vi havde intet at drikke, og Tørsten var næsten utaalelig. Dengang havde vi rigtignok Middagsmad med, men den bestod af salt

Fisk og Brød uden Mælk eller Vand. Da vi skulde spise, foreslog jeg derfor at ville løbe ned til en Elv, som rigtignok fløď en halv Fjerdingvei nedenfor os i Dalen, forat hente Drikkevand, ellers kom vi til at sætte Livet til, om vi nu spiste den salte Fisk. Min Læremester var dog af en anden Mening. Mennesket er lykkeligvis saaledes indrettet, at det ved Vanen næsten kan lære Alt; vi burde vænne os til Udholdenhed, lære at overvinde Vanskeligheder i vor Ungdom, saa vilde slige Ting ikke besvære os, naar vi bleve ældre; ved en stærk Viliekraft skulde vi styrke de legemlige Svagheder og holde Lidenskaberne i Tømme. Saa rigtig denne Filosofi var, kunde jeg dog ikke efterleve den i den urimelige Udstrækning, han vilde give den. Jeg brød dennegang gjennem alle Skranker og løb ned til Bækken efter Vand. Uden dette er jeg næsten vis paa, at vi ikke den Dag kunde have fuldført det herkuliste Arbeide, som endnu stod tilbage. Efter at vort Materiale nemlig var hugget og opkløvet i svære Blokke, skulde de rulles eller trækkes nedover de steile Lier til Søen, der lastes i Baaden og derpaa ro næsten en norsk Mil tilbage om Natten. Havde jeg ikke allerede fra Tolvaarsalderen været hærdet i en lignende, skjønt mindre urimelig Skole, hvad Mad og Drikke angik, vilde jeg naturligvis ikke kunnet udholde Prøven.

Da de tre Maaneder var omme, kunde jeg saavidt bruge Bilen, Sagen og Høvlen, at han tog mig med til en rig Bonde, hvor han havde paataget sig at opføre en Saugmølle og gav mig Anledning til at arbeide for Dagløn. Nu syntes jeg da, det allerede saa smaat begyndte at lysne. Den Kost, vi her fik, forekom mig kongelig imod, hvad vi før var vant til, og det var desuden en ret interessant Familie, med hvem Omgangen var meget behagelig. Opholdet paa dette Sted staar endnu som et Lyspunkt i min Erindring fra denne halvmørke og vaklende Tid af mit Ungdomsliv. Jeg led nu ofte af Melankoli og Modløshed, der satte et forstemt Præg paa mit hele Væsen. Inden i mig var der en stærk fremadstræbende Aand, hvis Flugt hindredes og hemmedes saa aldeles af ydre haarde Kaar, at jeg kom til at staa mellem disse to Kræfter som et nedtrykt og vaklende Væsen. Jeg har derfor stedse siden vedblevet at mindes den venlige Deltagelse og Opmuntring, jeg fandt blandt de unge Medlemmer af den Familie, jeg her var kommen i Berøring med.

Da Slaataannen begyndte, drog jeg tilbage til min Hjembygd og arbeidede hos min Svoger, der havde en god Gaard. Ved Arbeidet paa Saugmøllen havde jeg havt en større Løn end jeg efter min Alder kunde vente, og min Svigerbroder var god nok til at give mig den samme Løn for Sommerarbeidet, saa at jeg om Høsten havde sparet sammen nogle Dalere, og min Moder vedblev endnu at forsyne mig med det nødvendigste til Klæder. Min Formynder lod nu bortsælge ved offentlig Auktion det Løsøre, som ved Skifteretten tilfaldt mig, da min Moder opgav Gaarden; hun havde nemlig indtil da siden min Faders Død siddet i uskiftet Bo, som man kaldte det. Ved denne Auktion blev Varerne solgte for en høi Pris og udbragte 80 Spd. istedetfor 54 Spd., som var den af Retten udlagte Vurderingssum. Denne lille Arv kunde jeg ikke modtage, før jeg var 18 Aar gammel, og den blev derfor hensat paa Renter i Overformynderiet. Om Høsten kom jeg atter tilbage til Farbroder, der nu havde faaet sit Værksted i fuld Gang og slog sig saa vidt igjennem, at han kunde opoffre lidt mere Tid paa sine Børns Undervisning og jeg fik da samtidig lidt Undervisning. Jeg skulde nu betale noget for min Kost og tillige forrette en Del Arbeide. Paa denne Maade tilbragtes Vinteren. Min Lærer sagde mig nu rentud, at det vilde være forgjæves for mig at lægge mig efter Skjønskrivning, da jeg dog aldrig kuude bringe det til nogen stor Fuldkommenhed i den Henseende. Selv havde han ved Tegning og Skjønskrivning vundet stor Beundring dengang han frekventerede den bergenske Søndagsskole, som da var en Slags polyteknisk Anstalt for fattige Haandværksdrenge, og han maatte derfor ansees for en god Authoritet i saa Henseende. Jeg beskjæftigede mig derfor den Vinter især med Regning samt norsk og tydsk Sproglære, i hvilke Fag han fandt stor Tilfredshed med min Fremgang.

V.
Paa Bergens Vexelskole.

Jeg var nu 15 Aar gammel, og om Foraaret maatte jeg fatte en bestemt Beslutning for Fremtiden. For at hjælpe mig til at komme til en Beslutning, reiste Farbror med mig til Bergen og havde den Godhed at tage mig med til flere af sine gamle Velyndere blandt Bergens fremragende Skolemænd, hvoriblandt den bekjendte Digter Lyder Sagen. Jeg havde ytret stor Tilbøielighed til at komme paa Handelsskolen for at blive Kontorist og derfra at arbeide mig frem til Handelsstanden. Da gamle Sagen hørte dette, spurgte han hvormange Penge jeg kunde regne paa at faa, naar jeg blev myndig. Ikke over firsindstyve Speciedaler, var Svaret, og der vilde udkræves langt mere end det for at kunne absolvere Kjøbmandsexamen under det da gjældende strenge Reglement. Jeg kan aldrig glemme, hvor knusende hans Svar faldt over mig: "En Kjøbmand uden Penge og en Violin uden Strenge ligne hinanden meget." Han vilde raade mig alvorlig fra at tænke paa Handelsstanden; et Haandværk, f. Ex. Kunstdreier, mente han vilde passe noksaa bra for mig. Nu havde jeg hørt hans Mening, og jeg maa oprigtig tilstaa, at den var i fuldt Maal nedslaaende for ikke at sige afskrækkende. Hos Hr. Winding, som dengang var Lærer ved Realskolen, gik det ikke meget bedre. Han var nok villig til at give mig privat Timeundervisning i de til Handelsexamen fornødne Fag

(Regning, Bogholderi og tydsk Handelskorrespondance), men gav mig en ligesaa mørk Skildring af den pengeløse Kontorists forlorne Stilling som Hr. Sagen havde gjort, og for ret at faa mig i Fortvivlelse, som han troede, spurgte han, om jeg kunde bruge Dixlen og arbeide som Sjouer med at paafylde og tilslaa Sildetønder, efterat jeg havde taget Examen, fordi det var saa uhyre vanskeligt at faa Plads som Bogholder. Omtrent paa samme Maade gik det mig hos et Par andre af min Onkels Bekjendte, med hvem vi søgte at raadføre os, og det blev mig nu klart, at Døren var lukket for mig, og at man instinktmæssig, som om man var kommen overens om det, paa alle Kanter udestængte mig paa Grund af min Stand. Hr. Winding var dog saa artig, paa Grund af Kjendskabet til min Farbror, at paatage sig for 70 Spd. at forberede mig til Examen. Jeg indgik paa dette, skjønt jeg ikke raadede over saa mange Penge, endsige det dobbelt saa store Beløb, som var fornødent til et saa langt Ophold i Byen. Jeg vilde nu engang prøve Lykken og trøstede mig med den Tanke: Kommer Tid, kommer Raad.

Men da jeg et Par Maaneder senere kom tilbage, for at begynde mine Forberedelser, og allerede havde leiet et lidet Værelse, hvor jeg agtede at besørge min egen Husholdning, medens en gammel Kone, der var Husholderske hos den Politiofficiant, der eiede Huset, paatog sig for en meget liden Betaling at besørge min Vask—havde den gode, gamle Hr. W. glemt den hele Akkord, lod ikke til at kjende mig igjen, og spurgte meget naivt, hvem min Onkel var, om han ogsaa var Bonde o.s.v., og erklærede endelig, at jeg maatte tage feil, og at han ikke var Manden, skjønt han jo vidste, at det var plat umuligt for Nogen, der engang havde seet den særegne lille pukkelryggede Mand at tage feil af ham. Her stod jeg da atter, ligesaa forlegen og raadvild som nogensinde, ja var i en vis Grad værre faren, thi jeg kunde ikke slippe fra at betale den omakkorderede Leie for mit Værelse, der rigtignok kun udgjorde 6 Spd. for sex Maaneder, men selv dette var for et ungt Menneske i min Stilling ikke saa lidet at kaste bort, især da mit hele Foretagende i Bergen havde mødt den mest afgjorte Misbilligelse hos min Moder og mine Sødskende, af hvem jeg altsaa slet ikke kunde vente nogen Hjelp, uagtet flere af dem stod sig ganske godt. De ansaa min hele Stræben for en ungdommelig Daarskab, en Vildfarelse, der sent eller tidlig, efter deres Mening, ufeilbarlig maatte lede mig i Ulykke. Midt i denne min Forlegenhed traf jeg en Dag paa Gaden den Landhandlers Søn, som var bleven konfirmeret sammen med mig. Med faa Ord forklarede jeg ham min Stilling og hvor ærgerligt det forekom mig at maatte opgive mit Forehavende og vende tilbage til Hjembygden, skuffet og ydmyget, med uforrettet Sag. Han var meget forekommende og ytrede megen Deltagelse for mig, bad mig følge ham hjem til hans Logis, hvor han da fortalte mig, at han netop havde faaet sin Examen fra Handelsskolen, og tilbød sig, da han ikke havde synderlig at bestille, at overtage min Information for de 70 Spd. og dimittere mig til Examen. Jeg takkede forbindtligt for dette venlige Tilbud, og udbad mig Betænkningstid til den næste Dag, da jeg atter skulde lade høre fra mig. Sagen var, at jeg nærede stærk Mistillid til hans Evne til at give mig den fornødne Forberedelse; thi hvorvel han selv netop havde bestaaet sin Prøve, fulgte dog ikke deraf, at han var kompetent til at lære fra sig saaledes, at jeg i en given Tid kunde opnaa den fornødne Dygtighed i alle Fag. Ved det forrige Besøg i Bergen, sammen med min Onkel, havde vi besøgt en Lærer B., som var Lærer ved den saakaldte Vexelskole, det vil sige, i en af Byens Friskoler for fattige Børn, hvor den saakaldte Vexelmethode var indført ved Undervisningen. Dette vil igrunden ikke sige andet end at Skolen var inddelt i mange Klasser, med en af de bedste Elever i hver Klasse som Lærer for sin Klasse, og hvori hver Elev ved Læseøvelserne fra en paa Væggen ophængt, med store Bogstaver trykt Tabel fremsagde hver sit Bogstav i Ordet og hver sit Ord i Sætningen, samt oplæste vexelvis hver sin Paragraf paa de forskjellige Tabeller, der selvfølgelig vare indrettede efter Klassens Fremskridt. Denne Lærer B., der var kommen fra Nordfjord i Bergens Stift, og mærkeligt nok tilhørte Bondestanden, uagtet han nu havde faaet Frakke og blanke Støvler paa, havde vist sig særdeles forekommende, da min Onkel og jeg besøgte ham. Erindrende mig dette, besluttede jeg mig nu til at raadføre mig med ham i min Tvivlraadighed og tog derfor Veien til "Krybben," som hans Skole (der oprindelig, saavidt jeg erindrer, havde været en eller anden velgjørende Stiftelse) almindelig kaldtes. Ganske beleilig traf jeg ham netop da Skolen sluttede, og han hørte med deltagende Opmærksomhed paa Fortællingen om min Skuffelse hos Hr. W. og om mine Tvivl angaaende min unge Vens Tilbud. Førend et lykkeligt Tilfælde havde ført ham ind i den vellønnede Post, han nu indehavde, havde han et Par Aar været Skolelærer og Kirkesanger i sin Hjembygd, havde stedse fra Skridt til Skridt havt Lykken med sig—en gunstig Vind havde altid fyldt hans Seil, og han var, som det lod til, derved bleven en Smule stolt og forfængelig, men var dog ogsaa af Naturen en glad og godmodig Fyr. Han fortalte mig, hvorledes flere unge Mænd fra Landet vare blevne sendte ind til hans Vexelskole, dels for at lære denne nye Undervisningsmethode, dels for at uddanne sig videre for at modtage Skolelærer- og Kirkesanger-Poster paa Landet; han gjorde sig i det Hele taget megen Umage for at stille Lærerfaget i et saa fordelagtigt Lys som muligt og endte med at raade mig til at frekventere hans Skole i sex Maaneder for at uddanne mig for dette Fag, og havde derhos den Godhed at tilbyde sig at give mig et Par Timers Undervisning i Tydsk hjemme i sit Logis. Det behøvede ikke at koste mig mere, end hvad jeg selv fandt for godt at give ham, naar Tiden var omme. Hvad enten det nu var et høiere Forsyns Styrelse, det blinde Tilfælde eller Tingenes uundgaaelige Logik, som her greb ind og forandrede min Livsretning, skal jeg ikke her befatte mig med at undersøge. Nok er det, jeg gik ind paa denne Mands Forslag og begyndte under hans Veiledning af alle Kræfter at forberede mig for en Almuelærers Gjerning.

Mit sex Maaneders Ophold i Bergen denne Gang bar neppe den Frugt, som jeg havde ventet; de Fremskridt, jeg gjorde, havde jeg mit flittige Selvstudium at takke for mere end den Hjelp, min Lærer kunde yde mig. I norsk Sprog og Regning var jeg ham fuldkommen voxen; i Tydsk hjalp han mig ikke saa lidet, da han netop selv holdt paa med dette og var kommen lidt længere frem end jeg; men det var egentlig i Sang og den praktiske Undervisningsmaade jeg i hans Skole gjorde mest Fremgang, og som jeg ikke ret vel kunde have tilegnet mig ved privat Undervisning. Han havde sat sig i Hovedet at gaa den studerende Vei og holdt nu paa at forberede sig for at komme til Universitetet. At blive Student var det store Maal, han nu sigtede til, og som ofte opfyldte hans Sind med den mest overdrevne Indbildning om Fremtidsstorhed. Havde han først faaet Examen Artium, var der, lod det til, intet, som kunde hindre ham fra at blive Statsraad eller hvad det skulde være. For Tiden var det Latinen, som satte ham graa Haar i Hovedet. En ung Mand ved Navn Sexe (fra mit Nabopræstegjæld), hvem Lyder Sagen, paa Grund af en Skjæppe Hardangeræbler, havde skaffet Adgang til Latinskolen, kom til ham om Aftenerne for at læse en Timestid med ham. Denne Sexe, der senere som Mineralog har tiltrukket sig adskillig offentlig Opmærksomhed — især da han paa Grund af Intriger var bleven afsat fra sin Post ved Kongsberg Sølvværk og derfor af Storthinget blev tilstaaet 800 Spd. aarlig for at kunne fortsætte sine Studier i Bergvidenskaben — var en med sjeldne Evner udrustet ung Mand, som, dengang jeg saa ham give Privatundervisning hos Lærer B., snart skulde afgaa til Universitetet for at læse til Artium. Jeg kan erindre, hvorledes han undertiden gjorde sig lystig over Hr. B.'s Forfængelighed og Dumheder, men paa en saa fin Maade, at denne ikke mærkede den bittre Ironi, som laa deri. En Dag, ret som jeg paa det alvorligste stod og underviste en af de øverste Klasser i Skolen, medens Hr. B. sad fordybet over sin Latin, kom en af Skolens Inspektører, Hr. Pastor Flotman, Sognepræst til Nykirken, for at holde Visitats i Skolen. Forbauset over at se en fremmed beskjæftiget med Undervisningen — en fremmed i en fremmed Gjerning — kom han lige hen til mig og med en rigtig Herskermine spurgte, hvem jeg var og hvad jeg havde at gjøre her. Jeg, der ikke kjendte ham og ikke vidste, at han stod i noget særegent Forhold til Skolen, svarede ham ligefrem, at jeg agtede at blive Lærer paa Landet og var kommen herind for at gjøre mig bekjendt med Vexelmethoden. Det lod til, at den gode Mand, uagtet han havde lært saare meget, endnu ikke havde lært at lægge Tømme paa sin egen Sindsbevægelse, thi han blev formelig vred og befalede i en barsk Tone: "Væk, unge Mand; vi oplærer ikke Bønder til Skolelærere her!" Og derpaa søgte han Læreren, som uheldigvis sad bag Disken og pugede over Badens latinske Grammatik. Jeg skjønnede nu, at det maatte være en af Skolens Foresatte og fjernede mig saa ubemærket som muligt, da jeg begyndte at faa en Anelse om, at Lærer B. ikke var bemyndiget til at gjøre, hvad han gjorde med mig og adskillige andre, som dels havde været der og dels ventedes. Hvorledes Hr. B. kom fra det med den bistre Præstemand, ved jeg ikke; han beklagede sig senere over den uheldige Affære, og jeg hørte ikke mere derom. B. blev i flere Aar ved Skolen og var ialfald heldig forsaavidt, at han ved sit Ægteskab gjorde et fordelagtigt Parti og kom derved i Besiddelse af en smuk Eiendom i Byen; men jeg hørte senere, at han faldt igjennem til Examen Artium. For ikke oftere at overrumples af Inspektøren brugte vi senere større Forsigtighed, men fortsatte dog som før vort Arbeide i Skolen. En Skolelærer fra Sogn kom nu ogsaa derind for at øve sig i Sang og gjøre sig bekjendt med den nye Undervisningsmethode. Vi skiftedes nu om at holde Vagt, men Hr. Pastoren kom ikke igjen, saalænge jeg var der.

VI.
Skolelærerlivet.

Hvad jeg under mit 6 Maaneders Ophold i Bergen havde seet og erfaret, og det nærmere Indblik, jeg havde faaet i Forholdene, selv blandt dem, som kunde kaldes den studerende Ungdom, havde mere og mere forliget mig med Tanken om at blive Lærer og den Fremtid, jeg paa denne Vei gik imøde — jeg havde, for at bruge et gammelt Ordsprog, seet med egne Øine, at det ikke alt er Guld, som glimrer. Selv i min endnu saa indskrænkede Erfaringskreds og med mine saa lidet udviklede Begreber om Livets Alvor, begyndte det allerede nu at opgaa for mig, at det beroede mindre paa, hvad vort Kald i Livet var, end paa, hvorledes vi opfyldte dette Kalds Pligter, hvorvidt vi kunde være glade og lykkelige her i Verden. Hemmet og atter og atter kastet tilbage hver Gang min ivrige Stræben efter Kundskaber havde bragt mig for nær Kastevæsenets skarpttrukne Grændse, gik det mig maaske noget nær som det gik Ræven, der opdagede, at Rønnebærene vare sure, da han saa, at han ikke kunde naa dem: jeg begyndte at opdage, at Standspartiet paa mange Steder lignede kalkede Grave, der udenpaa ere deilige at se til, men ere indenfor fulde af Raaddenhed og døde Ben. Det var dog flere Aar efter denne Tid, at jeg først klart lærte at anvende det Skriftsprog, som siger: "Lader os ikke forlade vor egen Forsamling, som nogle have for Skik," paa de borgerlige

Forholde, lærte at se, hvor bagvendt man handlede, naar man skræmt af det haarde Tryk, hvorunder Almuen sukkede, søgte at komme op i den herskende Stand for at faa det bedre, uden at tænke paa, at Trykket derved forøgedes. Man redder ikke Skibet ved at forlade det; det er Forræderi under Kampens Hede at gaa over til Fienden. At stille sig i Rækken med sine egne, ved Ord og Daad, ja ved Arbeide, Miskjendelse og Lidelser at søge at opmuntre, trøste, udvikle og løfte dem og sig selv alt høiere og høiere opad til den Selvstændighedsstilling, hvor det store Lighedsprincip gjælder som ufravigelig Lov for alle Samfundsklasser, er hvad Pligten byder, og her kan den simple Folkelærer ogsaa høste Laurbær. Et Folk, som i 400 Aar fra den ene Generation til den anden havde levet og døet i en forkuet, nedtraadt og forholdsvis retsløs Tilstand, kunde ikke under den i 1814 indtraadte Forandring i Forfatningen hæve sig til nogen almindelig Bevidsthed om sine Rettigheder; de faa ædle Mænd, som paa Eidsvold havde nedlagt i den nye Forfatning den Sæd, hvoraf de engang i Tiden haabede at se Folkefrihedens Træ fremspire, vare selv konservative og ønskede, at Frihedens Væxt skulde være langsom, og endmere konservative (nogle endog frihedsfiendske) vare deres nærmeste Efterkommere i Styrelse og Lovgivning. Paa den Tid, jeg her omtaler, nemlig omkring 1830, havde den nye Forfatning endda ikke i den Del af Landet, hvor jeg var hjemme, frembragt nogen synlig Forandring i Forholdene. Folkets økonomiske Tilstand, Oplysning, Tænkemaade, Sæder og Skikke vare omtrent de samme, som de havde været ved det 18de Aarhundredes Slutning. Den herskende Stand bestod, som jeg tidligere har paavist, af importerede tydske og danske Embedsmænd og Handelsmænd og deres Afkom i nedstigende Linie og tilhørte saaledes ikke den norrøne Stamme, hvorfra det egentlige norske Folk nedstammede. Allerede den i vor Tid lovpriste (Tyran) Harald Haarfager fratog i det 9de Aarhundrede den norske Bonde en af hans fornemste Rettigheder, Beskatningsretten, og med sine blodtørstige Sønner drev han de bedste og mægtigste Slægter til at gaa i Landflygtighed hellere end at gjøre sig til Slaver af Kongemagten. Den Rest af Folkeretten og Minderne derom, som herskesyge Høvdinger og langvarige Borgerkrige ned til det 14de Aarhundrede ikke havde formaaet at tilintetgjøre og bringe i Glemsel, det fuldførte den under Foreningen med Danmark hidsendte tydske Junkerstand og dens Efterkommere noksaa trolig. Med Love, som fra Ende til Ende vare tilskaarne efter denne Stands Ønsker og Farve, med Embederne, Handelen og Magten udelukkende i sin Haand, var det intet Under, at deres firehundredaarige Herskervælde havde bragt det engang saa mægtige og selvstændige norrøne Stamfolk til en Umyndighedstilstand, som de første halvhundrede Aar efter den nye Forfatning ikke formaaede at bortrydde. Naar man saa erindrer, at den herskende Stand endnu med nogle faa mærkværdige

Undtagelser holdt trolig sammen i Styrelse og Lovgivning fra øverst til nederst for at bevare sine Privilegier og Forrettigheder mod den folkeligere Tendents, som smaaningom begyndte at ytre sig, kan man gjøre sig et Begreb om den Betydning, Almuelærerens Gjerning dengang maatte have i hans egen Bevidsthed, om han ellers forstod den og var den voxen. At en 16 Aar gammel Dreng, for hvis Blik kun enkelte Hovedtræk af dette Forhold begyndte at vise sig dunkelt som i et Halvmørke, ikke var den voxen, er unødvendigt at tilføie. En Lykke er det dog maaske, at neppe nogen af den Tids Folkelærere havde et klart Blik paa sin Gjernings umaadelige Betydning fra denne Side betragtet, thi ellers vilde Ansvaret og Bevidstheden om egen Svaghed skræmt dem bort alle tilhobe.

En Kirkesangerpost havde været ledig i et af Annexsognene i vort Præstegjæld ligesiden den gamle Klokkers Død, og Sangen under den offentlige Gudstjeneste var imidlertid bleven ledet af en af Præstens Medhjælpere, da ingen af Sognets tre Skolelærere kunde synge. Da jeg opholdt mig ved Vexelskolen i Bergen, havde jeg skrevet til den Kapellan, som læste med mig til Konfirmation, og sagt ham, at jeg nu havde besluttet at søge Ansættelse som Lærer og Forsanger og ønskede helst at forblive i vort Præstegjæld, hvis der var nogen Vakance. Han havde underrettet sin Sognepræst derom, og man havde Plads i Beredskab for mig i omtalte Annexsogn. Da jeg var forsynet med Attest og en noget overdreven Anbefaling fra Lærer B., drog jeg paa Hjemreisen til Sognepræsten for at melde mig som Ansøger og udbede mig en Skrivelse til Provsten, til hvem jeg da agtede at henvende mig for at underkastes den fornødne Examination. Det led udpaa Eftermiddagen, og Sognepræsten var nu kommen saa dybt i Glassene, at der ikke var nogen Greie paa ham; men han havde nylig faaet sig en Personelkapellan, og denne unge, venlige lille Mand viste mit Andragende al fornøden Opmærksomhed. Forsynet med Sognepræstens Anbefaling og et meget fordelagtigt Konfirmations-Vidnesbyrd fra min Ven Kapellanen, drog jeg afsted til Provsten, der boede over fire norske Mil derfra. Den nye Personelkapellan kjendte nok ikke Affæren med Klagen for Kjætteri mod min Farbror, vidste heller ikke, at jeg var en Nevø af den anklagede Lærer, ellers kan det nok hænde, at han havde anseet det for sin Pligt at give Provsten et Vink i saa Henseende. Den sidste lod det dog til ikke trængte noget saadant Vink, thi han underkastede mig en efter hvad jeg senere erfarede af Andre ganske uberettiget streng Examen i Religion. Bibelhistorien havde jeg paa Fingerspidsene, og hvad forøvrigt Læsning, Skrivning, Regning, Grammatik, Geografi, Historie og Sang angik, da var hans Spørgsmaal lette og ubetydelige undtagen Prøven i Sang, som han syntes at være personlig interesseret i. Ved Prøven i Regning og Grammatik syntes Svarene flere Gange at vække hans Forundring, uden at det blev mig klart, om det var til min Fordel eller anderledes. Den egentlige Troslære havde jeg siden min Konfirmation ikke læst over, men havde den dog saavidt i Hukommelsen, at jeg ved en almindelig Katekisation kunde have klaret mig med Lethed, men han lagde an paa at gjøre sin Spørgen saa indviklet og utydelig som muligt. Min Onkel havde slet ikke undervist mig i Religion, og den gode Lærer B. havde Hovedet saa fuldt af Deklinationer og Konjugationer, at han nok aldeles glemte, at Hr. Provsten maaske kunde falde paa at føre mig ned i Dogmatikens mystiske Dybder for at se, om jeg var smittet af Datidens Fritænkeri, og jeg vil gjerne tilstaa, at jeg paa dette Felt var mindre vel forberedt end i de andre Fag, skjønt mit Vidnesbyrd fra Konfirmationstiden syntes at vise det modsatte. Provstens Spørgen var dog meget vidtgaaende, og jeg blev ham flere Gange Svaret skyldig, medens jeg ogsaa et Par Gange svarte galt. Hans Aasyn blev meget mørkt, og jeg saa nu tydelig, at han nærede Mistanke til min Rettroenhed. Efter en kort Betænkning sagde han: "Du har i de regulære Fag givet nogle forbausende Svar, og nu staar Du fast; jeg ved ikke, hvad jeg skal tænke om dette." Jeg spurgte, om jeg maatte faa Lov til at forklare mig, og gav derpaa en kort Resumé af Troslæren efter de 5 Parter og erklærede, at dette var min Børnelærdom, paa denne Tro og Bekjendelse var jeg bleven et Medlem af den lutherske Kirke, og dersom heri var noget Falsk, havde jeg lært det hos Pastor X., som havde forberedt mig til Konfirmationen, og til hvis Vidnesbyrd jeg maatte tillade mig at henvise. Rimeligvis havde jeg her vist formegen Varme; thi uagtet han slet ikke paapegede noget som afvigende i min Bekjendelse, vedblev dog det karakteristiske Mørke at hvile over hans Aasyn. Jeg sluttede derfor, at min Forklaring havde været rigtig, men mit Slutningsargument havde givet Fornærmelse. Jeg fik en ganske kold Afsked. Jeg spurgte ikke, og han værdigede ikke at svare enten Ja eller Nei til min Ansøgning, men sagde tørt, efterat jeg havde bukket og sagt Farvel, at han skulde tilskrive Sognepræsten. Jeg uddrog heraf den Slutning, at "min Onkels Nevø", trods Anbefalinger og gode Vidnesbyrd, var bleven forkastet, og med mørke Skyer til Kammerater tiltraadte jeg den lange Tilbagereise.

To Uger efter min Hjemkomst (jeg betragtede endnu stedse min gamle Moders Hus for mit Hjem) modtog jeg skriftlig Befaling fra Sognepræsten om at indfinde mig ved angjældende Annexkirke den paafølgende Søndag for at blive indført i Ombudet og begynde mit Arbeide som omgaaende Skolelærer. Disse omgaaende Læreres Løn var egentlig 10 Spd. om Aaret og Undervisningstiden 38 Uger, men den af Sognets tre Lærere, som fik Kirkesangerposten, med hvilken den saakaldte Klokkertiende var forenet, skulde i Betragtning heraf kun faa 6 Spd. aarlig som Skoleløn. Dette var allerede tidligere af Præstegjældets Skolekommission bleven fastsat; men for den saakaldte Klokkertiende existerede ingen faste Bestemmelser, og det beroede ganske paa, hvorledes den nye Kirkesanger forstod at vinde Gaardbrugernes Yndest og Velvilie, hvorvidt denne Tiende blev Noget eller Intet. Jeg skulde altsaa i 38 Uger om Aaret gaa omkring fra Gaard til Gaard for at holde Skole og ved Aarets Slutning modtage 6 Spd. i Løn samt dagligt Brød i de Huse, hvor jeg holdt Skole. Om Søndagene var jeg tilpligtet at være ved Kirken og lede Sangen samt føre Lister over Kommunikanterne, Barnedaabs- og Vielseshandlinger osv., og hvorvidt jeg kom til at faa noget for dette Arbeide, der ikke var saa lidet byrdefuldt endda, derom var der ingen Vished. Det var altsaa ikke noget fedt Embede, jeg var kommen i; men jeg havde nu engang begyndt at se Syner og var fast besluttet paa at søge min Lykke i den glade Bevidsthed, som efter min Mening skulde være Frugten af en almennyttig Virksomhed, og jeg trøstede mig med, at jeg i de 14 Uger, som jeg om Sommeren havde fri, skulde oparbeide nok til Klæder og Sko — Kost skulde jeg jo faa omkring i Husene. I Skolen gik det bedre end jeg ventede. Vel kunde jeg ikke gjennemføre Undervisningen fuldstændig saaledes som jeg havde lært den i Bergen, fordi jeg manglede det dertil fornødne Inventarium, og de forskjellige Lokaler, hvori jeg kom med min Skole, tillod det heller ikke. Men da jeg sjelden i nogen af de fire Roder, hvoraf Distriktet bestod, kom til at have over 20, oftest kun 10 til 15 Elever, var det heller ikke nødvendigt at anvende Vexelmethoden; i Grunden viste det sig snart, at den i sig selv ikke var nyttig, men kun en Nødhjælp, hvor en Lærer havde omkring 100 Børn at undervise. Klasseinddelingen kunde jeg anvende med Nytte ved Læseøvelserne, idet hver Klasse fik sin egen Lektie at indstudere og hver Elev i Klassen forelæste den efter Tur. Det samme kunde ogsaa til en vis Grad gjennemføres ved Skrive- og Regneøvelserne, saa at der kom mere Orden og System saavelsom større Liv, Virksomhed og Kappelyst i Skolen, medens man ogsaa fik Fordelen af en delvis Vexelvirkning mellem Eleverne i hver Klasse. Jeg havde forresten under mit Ophold i Bergen allerede gjort mig saavidt fortrolig med Undervisningen og Skoledisciplinen, at jeg i saa Henseende ingen Vanskelighed mødte, og fra Børnenes Side var det saa langt fra, at jeg havde nogen Grund til at beklage mig, at jeg tvertimod i deres Flid, Lydighed og gode Opførsel mod mig fandt min bedste Trøst under den ellers saa prøvende og ofte ubehagelige omvankende Skolegjerning. De ældre Mænd og Kvinder i Distriktet erklærede ofte, at de aldrig havde seet nogen Lærer, der saaledes kunde tilvende sig Børnenes Fortrolighed og Kjærlighed og paa samme Tid blive saa fuldstændig agtet og adlydt. Den stadige Afvexling mellem Læsning, Skrivning, Regning, Sangøvelser og Katekisation gjorde Undervisningen behagelig og tiltrækkende; alt kjedsommeligt Pugeri søgtes undgaaet; de unge Hoveder holdtes i stadig Virksomhed ved Fremstillingen af en uafbrudt Række af nye Begreber og Tanker, som fremsattes og udvikledes altid i opadstigende Retning, eftersom Fatteevnen styrkedes og tiltog. Sognepræsten var et ligegyldigt Menneske, der forsømte Alt, som kunde forsømmes, og havde saaledes aldrig i den lange Tid, han havde været i Kaldet, ført nogetsomhelst Opsyn eller Kontrol med Skolegjerningen, hvis lovlige Værge han dog var; derfor var Almueskolen i hans Præstegjæld ogsaa kommen i stort Forfald, og jeg fandt snart, at den stod betydelig tilbage for, hvad den var i andre Præstegjæld. Den residerende Kapellan var en virksommere Mand, der interesserede sig for min Skole. Han benyttede flere Gange Leiligheden til at besøge Skolen, naar han kom for at holde Gudstjeneste i vor Kirke. Ved disse Leiligheder gjorde jeg ham opmærksom paa, hvad der egentlig stillede sig som mine største Vanskeligheder, nemlig Mangelen paa passende Læsebøger, Tabeller, Regnebøger osv., og lagde især Vægt paa, hvor nødvendigt det vilde være, at Børnene i hver Klasse havde lige Bøger, og at jeg troede, de fleste af Forældrene vilde være villige til at kjøbe Bøgerne, men at jeg ikke kunde paatage mig at indføre Bøgerne uden Bemyndigelse fra rette Vedkommende. Dette ledede til, at Henvendelse blev gjort til Sognepræsten, og hans Personelkapellan, som nylig var ankommen, fandt da en Masse authoriserede Tabeller og Bøger omdelte af Departementet for Undervisningsvæsenet, men som den gode gamle Præst havde henlagt i sit Rustkammer og forglemt — desværre havde han ikke, som Digteren, gjenfundet dem paa Bunden af sit Krus, hvor ofte han end havde tømt det. Personelkapellanen fik ved denne Leilighed sin Opmærksomhed paa en særegen Maade henledet paa Almueskolen og blev fra denne Stund af min oprigtige Ven og Forsvarer, da jeg senere kom i Kamp med Bigotteriet. Jeg fik nu, hvad jeg hidtil saa meget havde savnet: Tabeller med Stave- og Læseøvelser, Grøgaards Læsebog osv. Af Religionsbøger havde vi allerede den gamle ABC, Luthers lille Katekismus og Pontoppidans Forklaring, som alle brugtes ved Religionsundervisningen og lagdes til Grund ved den kateketiske Undervisning. Af Regnebøger, Tavler, Grifler, Papir, Blæk og Penne anskaffede jeg et godt Forraad for egen Regning og solgte til dem, som kunde kjøbe, og gav til dem, som ikke kunde.

VII.
En forbuden Frugt.

Jeg var nu kommen paa gode Veie og syntes det allerede begyndte at lysne. Jeg begyndte saa smaat at tænke paa at give de flinkeste blandt Drengene lidt Undervisning i Retskrivning og Grammatik samt Geografi; men desværre var dette en forbuden Frugt, som ikke fandtes i Skolekommissionens Kramkiste. At Gutterne lærte at skrive og regne, syntes en Del af de mere konservative Forældre var at gaa temmelig vidt, men de kunde dog ikke godt bortforklare den deri liggende praktiske Nytte og Nødvendighed for det daglige Liv, især naar jeg kunde overbevise dem om, at de ved denne Afvexling i Undervisningen lærte mere Religion i en given Tid, end om de den hele Skoletid blev lænket fast til Religionsbogen alene; men naar Smaapigerne ogsaa begyndte at ville skrive og regne, og jeg ogsaa sagde Ja dertil, da blev det formeget. En slig Skandale kunde ikke taales. Dersom jeg ikke ophørte med dette Uvæsen — dersom jeg vedblev at ville indføre denne nye Vildfarelse, vilde jeg blive anklaget for Præsten. Jeg vilde, mente man, have godt af at mindes, hvorledes det var gaaet min Onkel. Jeg vilde nu engang slet ikke indrømme, at det var Vildfarelse eller Kjætteri at undervise Ungdommen af begge Kjøn i at skrive og regne, og dersom man endelig vilde anklage mig for dette, fik man saa gjøre. At blive afsat for en saadan Aarsag kunde jeg ikke have stort imod, og dagligt Brød med 6 Spd. om Aaret i Løn kunde jeg sagtens opnaa i en anden Livsstilling. Da Sognepræsten var Ex-Officio Formand i Skolekommissionen, vilde jeg i Forening med Sognets Medhjelpere forelægge ham Sagen til nærmere Overveielse. Førend dette kom til Udførelse, kom imidlertid en mere alvorlig Sag paa Bane. Grøgaards Læsebog, som blev brugt i min Skole, var ikke retlærende — den var kjættersk. Der stod ikke alene at læse om de fem Sandser og andre Naturlærdomme, men der stod endog, at Troldkvinden i Endor ikke havde formaaet at mane Samuel op fra de Døde, da Kong Saul vilde raadføre sig med ham, men bedrog ham ved at lade en, som hun havde skjult i Nærheden, agere Samuel og svare paa Sauls Spørgsmaal. Ja, dette var rigtignok slemt, men jeg var da ikke Bogens Forfatter, og det var desuden Øvrigheden og Præsten, som havde anskaffet denne Bog til Brug i Skolen, og jeg skulde bruge den, indtil rette vedkommende fandt for godt at ombytte den med en anden.

Al denne Bevægelse førte ikke til noget Resultat; den unge Personelkapellan var afgjort paa min Side, og desuden havde jeg ved Flid og Arbeidsomhed i Skolen saavelsom ved en vindende Omgang, baade med Børn og Forældre, vundet et stort Flertals Bifald og Velvilie. Ved Kirkesangen indfandt der sig adskillige Vanskeligheder, hvilket saavel Præsten som jeg indsaa, at det vilde kræve lang Tid og megen Taalmodighed at overkomme. Flere af de gamle i Menigheden vilde ikke vide af de nye Koralmelodier, hvilke Overlærer Bohr i Bergen havde udgivet for at befordre en ordentlig, taktmæssig og ensartet Sang i Kirkerne, hvor de gamle Melodier efterhaanden vare blevne forvanskede og blev nu sunget høist forskjelligt i de forskjellige Kirker. Man vilde raade Bod paa dette, men stødte paa mange Vanskeligheder, som, da der viste sig Uvilie i Menighederne, ikke kunde ryddes af Veien paa anden Maade end ved at oplære Ungdommen i et Par Generationer, saaledes at Fordommene forsvandt uformærket. I vor Kirke var der næsten altid tilstede en kjæmpestor Mand med en Stentorstemme. Denne Mand var en rigtig gammelnorsk Viking, fuld af Stolthed og Trods. Han var blandt Andet meget forhippet paa de forandrede Salmemelodier, og naar nogen af disse Forandringer forsøgtes i Kirken, tog han saaledes i med sin "egen Melodi", at Kirkevæggene formelig rystede, og det var ikke alene forgjæves, men vilde jo være en ren Latterlighed at trodse ham. Vi maatte altsaa i dette Stykke temporisere. — Paa denne Tid havde jeg stadig i min Erindring den Sætning: "Den, som gjør Venner af sine Fiender, er større end den, som indtager en Stad." Jeg lagde an paa at komme i personlig Berøring med dem, som jeg ansaa for de værste Modstandere, for i en venlig Omgang at komme til at samtale med dem, læse med dem, synge med dem og uformærket at faa dem interesseret i de foreliggende Spørgsmaal; paa denne Maade vandt jeg ad Venskabets og Overbevisningens Vei efterhaanden saa meget Terræn i mit Distrikt, at jeg sommetider smigrede mig med, at jeg maaske snart kunde tillades at virke uden Modstand i Folkeoplysningens Tjeneste.

Med Sangen i Skolen og blandt den konfirmerede Ungdom, hvoraf mange nu fik isinde at komme i Skolen om Vinteren forat lære at skrive og regne, gik det langt bedre end i Kirken. Mange anskaffede sig de saakaldte Salmodika med de af Organist Bohr i Tal udsatte Koraler, og ved Hjælp af disse og ved flittige Sammenkomster om Vinteraftenerne i den Rode, hvor Skolen holdtes, havdes ved Enden af det første Aar et Sangkor, som med Takt og Præcision kunde synge enstemmig Sang efter den nye Methode. Ved enkelte Leiligheder gaves dem Anledning til at optræde i Kirken, men jeg vovede aldrig at drive det videre end til at give Prøver, medens de for Dagen bestemte Salmer ved Gudstjenesten stedse blev overladt til Menigheden at synge paa sin gamle Vis. Jeg saa nok, at det paa denne Maade vilde gaa meget langsomt med Kirkesangens Forbedring, ja at Forsøget ganske vilde mislykkes og mit Arbeide i den Retning være spildt, dersom ikke mine Eftermænd i Ombudet besjæledes af den samme Aand og fortsatte Værket; men da der ikke for Tiden viste sig nogen kortere eller sikrere Vei til Maalet, vedblev jeg dog taalmodig at gjøre min Gjerning, saa godt jeg kunde.

Hvad der ovenfor er bleven bemærket, om Modstand mod Skrive- og Regneøvelserne, mod Grøgaards Læsebog og mod Kirkesangen, maa ikke forstaaes derhen, at denne Modstand var almindelig blandt Folket i mit Distrikt eller i Sognet. Dette vilde være at gjøre dem en skammelig Uret. Tvertimod var min Stilling som Lærer efterhaanden bleven langt hyggeligere, end jeg fra først af havde turdet haabe. Kun med Undtagelse af nogle enkelte, meget fordomfuldes Misnøie, mødtes jeg overalt med den største Venlighed og Agtelse. Uagtet der ikke var saa liden Uleilighed forbundet med at have Skolen samlet i sin Dagligstue (og den var man om Vinteren næsten overalt henvist til) kappedes man dog om at faa mig til at komme i deres Huse. Saalænge Vinterkulden ikke gjorde en varm Stue nødvendig, fik jeg gjerne overladt mig en eller anden lys og rummelig saakaldet Storstue, hvor Skolen da vedblev at samles for flere af de omliggende Gaarde saaledes, at jeg vel gik til hver især af Gaardbrugerne for at spise i det bestemte Antal Dage, medens Skolens Samlingssted ikke forandredes. Man indsaa, at Bekvemmeligheden derved blev meget bedre for Undervisningen, da der jo i Bondens Dagligstue foregaar alskens forskjellige Arbeider, saavelsom Samtaler mellem Husets Folk, hvilket er til megen Hinder for Undervisningen, og fandt sig derfor i denne min Indretning, uagtet en Omgangslærer ikke havde Ret dertil. Det var nu kommen dertil, at man satte sin Ære i, at Skolen samledes hos dem, og man var tildels lidt misundelig paa den Nabo, som overlod mig sin Storstue til Skolens Brug. Om Vinteren derimod kom jeg næsten i Hvermands Hus, uden forsaavidt man havde Forfald, og selv traf Overenskomst om en Forandring. Det var sædvanligt i denne Del af Landet, at ikke blot Kvindfolkene stadig drev sit Husflidsarbeide i Dagligstuen, saasom at spinde, væve, binde, sy, o.s.v., men ogsaa Mandfolkene drev her et eller andet Haandarbeide, især paa de Dage da de ikke kunde bestille noget udenfor. En kunde saaledes lave Tøndebaand, en anden kløve og hugge Stav, en tredie forarbeide Slæder eller Kjøretøier, en fjerde drive Skomagerarbeide, en femte Snedkerarbeide, o.s.v. Det er let at indse, hvor forstyrrende dette maatte være for Skolens Virksomhed og hvor ønskeligt det fra denne Side betragtet vilde være, om man overalt kunde have oprettet de saakaldte Rodestuer, hvor det ikke lod sig gjøre at indføre det i de fleste andre Lande brugelige Fastskolesystem. Men jeg for mit Vedkommende begyndte alt mere og mere at anse Omgangsskolen for meget anbefalingsværdig for den Lærer, som virkelig af Hjertet elskede sin Gjerning og betragtede den som noget ganske andet og høiere end et blot og bart Madstræv. Han kom nemlig derved i en langt anden venskabelig og fortrolig Omgang med Forældre, Børn og Sødskende i enhver Familie i Distriktet. Derved lærte man at forstaa hinanden bedre; man kom i Samtale, begyndte at tænke og udvikle for hinanden sine Meninger, Forhaabninger og Ønsker. Var Læreren ved sine Kundskaber, Dannelse og en forædlet menneskekjærlig Tænkemaade hævet over sin Omgivelse saaledes, som han efter sit Kalds Medfør burde være, fik han her en rig Anledning til ei alene at bortrydde gamle indgroede Fordomme mod et bedre og tidssvarende Undervisningsvæsen; men ogsaa paa tusinde forskjellige Maader at bearbeide Landboens Sindsstemning overfor nyttige Reformer i de økonomiske, sociale og politiske om ikke ogsaa kirkelige Forhold. Han kunde benytte de lange Vinteraftener paa en overmaade underholdende og belærende Maade, i den lune Dagligstue omgivet af den hele Familiekreds, ved at fortælle eller forelæse af gode Bøger om Agerbrug, Kvægavl, Husstel o.s.v. Han kunde til andre Tider benytte Reisebeskrivelser med de forskjellige Landes Folk, Sæder og Skikke, eller historiske Skildringer fra Fortid og Nutid o.s.v., og derved vække Sandsen for Læsning, Tænkning og Viden hos den yngre Slægt, som snart skulde indtage den gamles Plads paa Livets Skueplads. Traf han paa den modnere og mere tænksomme Landmand, kunde Aviser og statsøkonomiske Spørgsmaal give rigt Stof til hans Aftenunderholdning. Fastskolen tilbyder aldrig Læreren nogen saadan Anledning til en gavnlig Virksomhed. I de Lande, hvor Massen af Folket er naaet frem til et saadant Dannelsestrin, at Lærerens Overlegenhed indskrænker sig til hans Fagdannelse alene, som f. Ex. i de Forenede Stater, er det anderledes. Men i Norge paa den Tid, vi her har for os, kan jeg ikke tænke mig nogen Stilling saa fuld af Interesse og saa rig paa den skjønneste Anledning til med Kraft at anvende Løftestangen for at lette Folkets Opreisning fra Aarhundredernes Kastevæsen og Undertrykkelse. Det vilde være umuligt i Livet at kunne glemme den Glæde og den Længsel, hvormed Bygdens unge Mennesker imødesaa den Tid, jeg atter ventedes til deres Huse med min Omgangsskole, eller den hjertelige Beklagelse, hvormed de igjen imødesaa den Tid, jeg skulde drage bort. Det Baand, der paa denne Maade var knyttet mellem den unge Lærer og hans jevnaldrende i Distriktet, var ganske anderledes helligt og varigt end det, som knyttedes i Dansestuen og i Bryllypslaget. Det førte med sig, at Husmødre og Fædre droges med af det samme Baand, og man vidste aldrig, hvor venligt man skulde behandle Læreren og gjøre ham Opholdet behageligt hos sig. Hvor ofte dvæler ikke Tanken med Velbehag ved hine, den unge Lærers lykkelige Tider, selv nu, da Alderens Sne har farvet hans Lokker hvide, hvor klart staar ikke Billedet af hine hengivne, elskelige Mennesker afspeilet paa Erindringens Tavle! Jo, der er Rigdom i dette, at kunne gjøre med Glæde, Troskab og Flid det, man tror, at Livets Pligt har paalagt os. I et Liv saa fuldt af Omskiftelser, af Glæder og Sorger, af Lykke og Ulykke, er der intet, som under Tilbageblikket saaledes kan vække Glæde og Trøst som Minderne fra denne Tid.

I pekuniær Henseende gik det da heller ikke saa daarligt til, som det i Begyndelsen tegnede til, takket være den Velvilie og Paaskjønnelse, hvormed man overalt i Bygden betragtede min Lærervirksomhed. Den gamle Klokkertiende, som i det Aar ikke beløb sig til 5 Spd., gik i det andet og tredie Aar op til 20 à 25 Spd. Aaret, foruden det meget liberale Offer, hvormed man nu aldrig glemte mig, ved de kirkelige Forretninger. Ganske uventet fik jeg efter en 3—4 Aars Forløb en anden ganske god Indtægtskilde. Min Farbror havde nemlig været ansat som Vaccinatør for det hele vidtstrakte og folkerige Præstegjeld, men fandt nu, at hans Forretning led altfor meget ved den lange Fraværelse i den bedste Sommertid, da denne Gjerning skulde udføres. Han tilbød sig derfor at overgive den til mig, eller rettere, at fratræde i min Favør, anbefalende mig til sin Efterfølger. Saavel for at lære at bruge Lancetten rigtig og med den fornødne Færdighed, som for at lære at bedømme Vaccinationens Ægthed, opholdt jeg mig en Maanedstid i Bergen hos den bekjendte Dr. Wisbeck. Forsynet med hans Attest afsendte jeg i al Stilhed min Ansøgning til Kirke- og Undervisningsdepartementet. Da min Farbror i de Par sidste Aar havde forsømt dette Gjøremaal og ganske undladt at foretage sine sædvanlige Vaccinationsreiser, var det kommen stærkt paa Tale at dele Forretningen sognevis, saaat hver Kirkesanger fik Vaccinationen i sit Sogn at forestaa. Jeg frygtede altsaa meget for, at hvis man fik at vide, at den gamle Vaccinatør var fratraadt, vilde man indgaa til Regjeringen med Ansøgning om den paatænkte Deling, og jeg ventede igrunden slet ikke at blive ansat for det hele Præstegjeld. Heldigvis var Tanken om en Deling nok ikke kommet til Regjeringen, rimeligvis fordi Amtet ikke ønskede at faa med saa mange vankundige Menneskers Regnskab at gjøre, og jeg modtog ganske rigtig Bestalling som Vaccinatør for hele Præstegjeldet. Lykken havde denne Gang staaet mig bi. Saasnart denne Ansættelse blev bekjendt, afgik Protester mod min Ansættelse for mere end mit eget Sogn, men det var nu for sent, Regjeringen vilde ikke kuldkaste sin egen Ansættelse. Da min Forgjænger i denne Befatning, som sagt, ikke havde røgtet sit Kald, havde jeg de to første Aar en temmelig rig Høst, idet mine Regninger, Skydsgodtgjørelse iberegnet, gik op til omkring 100 Spd. aarlig. Iøvrigt naaede jeg senere aldrig over 40 til 50 Spd. om Aaret for Vaccinationsforretninger. Dette var dog en stor Hjelp. Mine Sommerferier, som jeg hidtil havde anvendt i Arbeide hos en eller anden Gaardbruger, for at hjelpe lidt paa min ringe Løn, blev nu fuldstændig optaget med Vaccinationsreiser. Paa disse Reiser fik jeg atter Anledning til at stifte mange interessante Bekjendtskaber, og for flere af Præstegjeldets mest oplyste og fremseende Landmænd at fremsætte mine Yndlings-Theorier om Folkeoplysningen og hvad dermed kunde staa i Forbindelse. Jeg har Grund til at tro, at den Sæd, som saaledes nedlagdes, heller ikke blev ganske uden Frugt. Idetmindste mindes jeg med stor Tilfredshed, hvorledes ledende Bønder kom lange Veie til de Steder, hvor mine Møder skulde afholdes, for at tale med mig om Ting, som det var en stor Glæde at høre dem omtale med saa megen Interesse.

VIII.
Reise til England.

I Foraaret 1835, efter at jeg var bleven myndig og havde modtaget min Arv og tillige sparet sammen det meste af min Fortjeneste, undtagen hvad jeg kjøbte Bøger for, fandt jeg mig i Besiddelse af nogle Hundrede Spd., hvoraf jeg saa smaat kunde gjøre mig bred, da ingen af mine jevnaldrende, saavidt bekjendt, kunde opvise saa mange Kontanter. Jo mere min Videbegjærlighed næredes ved nye Bøger, jo større og stærkere blev den. Bøger kunde ikke længer tilfredsstille mig, jeg længtede efter at komme ud i Verden for at se og erfare noget af det, som gjennem Beskrivelsen var kommet til mig i altfor tynde og ubestemte Træk. Jeg fik en gammel Lærer til at indtage min Plads i Skolen, og en af Medhjelperne til at paatage sig Kirkesangen og henvendte mig derpaa til Sognepræsten om Tilladelse at være borte i 6 Maaneder. Personelkapellanen var mig altid en tro Ven, og da jeg forklarede ham, at en god Ven i Bergen, der i disse Dage agtede at afsende et Skib til Shields i England, havde tilbudt mig fri Reise derover i Selskab med hans Søn, som skulde derbort for at lære Sproget, udvirkede han uden stor Vanskelighed den fornødne Tilladelse hos den gamle Sognepræst, der iøvrigt var saa godslig af sig, at man næsten kunde overtale ham til hvad det skulde være, saalænge det kun gjaldt Pligtforsømmelser. Jeg erindrer engang paa et Visitatsmøde, da Biskoppen med Strenghed insisterede paa, at Sognepræsten skulde besøge Omgangsskolerne, at han i al Underdanighed spurgte om ikke Kapellanen maatte gjøre det for ham: "Nei!" svarede Biskoppen opbragt, "Du skal gjøre det!" "Det skal ske, det skal ske, Deres Høiærværdighed," svarede Sognepræsten, men tænkte forresten vist ikke i fjerneste Maade paa at lade det ske, thi det skete idetmindste ikke saalænge han levede.

Jeg havde allerede for et Aars Tid siden begyndt at læse Engelsk, hvortil de reisende Englændere, som allerede da havde begyndt at besøge Fjorddistrikterne i Norge, havde givet den største Anledning. Under mit Ophold i Bergen, før Afreisen til England, skulde jeg hos en af Byens Boghandlere kjøbe et Par engelske Bøger, i hvilken Anledning jeg kom til at sige, at jeg netop stod i Begreb med at foretage en Reise til Shields, Newcastle og nogle andre Steder i det nordlige England og derfor ønskede at gjøre mig lidt bedre bekjendt med Sproget. Han havde ikke de Bøger, jeg spurgte efter, og maaske var det dette, som satte ham i ondt Lune, men jeg frygter meget for, at det var den gode Mands Kastestolthed, der blev ubehagelig berørt; nok er det, han blev meget opbragt og udbrød i retfærdig Harme: "Du til England! Hvad skal du gjøre i England? En norsk Bonde til England—lære Engelsk! Din Næsevished gaar dog altfor vidt. Hold dig til Katekismen og Salmebogen, det passer dig bedst." Manden følte sig meget indigneret over, hvad han i Lighed med de fleste af sine Standsfæller ansaa for en ren Skandale, at høre slig Tale af en Bonde. Jeg anfører enkelte af de mange Tilfælde af dette Slags, som mødte mig under mine 30 Aar i Norge, og havde ikke saa liden Indflydelse paa min Tankeretning og senere Livsskjæbne, for det viste, hvorledes Stemningen paa den Kant af Norge dengang var mellem den herskende og den underordnede Klasse; thi nu er jo Alt saa uendelig meget forandret i denne Henseende, takket være den yngre studerende Slægts og Maalmændenes heltemodige Bestræbelser for at udjevne Kløften mellem de to Klasser, uden hvilket man endelig har opdaget, at det er umuligt for Norge at følge med Tiden. Skade kun, at man et Par hundrede Aar for sent synes at have opdaget den Sandhed, at det kommer an paa Grundvolden om Bygningen skal staa fast og blive varig, at de manges Armod tilsidst vil fortære de faas Rigdom og, lig en prægtig Bygning paa en raadden Grundvold, falde sammen i en fælles Ruin.

Englandsreisen havde, saavidt jeg kan forstaa, en vigtig Indflydelse paa min Fremtidsbane; den blev den første, skjønt ikke eneste Aarsag til en radikal Vending i mit Livs Forsætter for Fremtiden. Vel havde jeg, som tidligere berettet, helst ønsket at komme i Handelen, men havde dog ikke vovet at se længere frem end til at blive Kontorist. Nu kom jeg derimod i en direkte Berøring med Skibsfarten og Udenlandshandelen, og her aabnede sig for mig nye Scener, Stillinger og Forholde, hvorom jeg før kun havde havt meget dunkle og ufuldstændige Forestillinger. Et Parti Ryper og andet Vildt fra Hardangerfjeldene, som jeg havde faaet Tilladelse at tage med, gav et meget opmuntrende Resultat, idet de solgtes i det engelske Marked for mere end dobbelt af hvad Prisen var i Bergen. De Klædesvarer, jeg kjøbte og bragte tilbage for Beløbet, gav ogsaa et meget tilfredsstillende Resultat, og tjente derfor end mere til at bestyrke mig i en (som jeg senere fandt) overdreven Mening om Fordelen med Farten og Handelen paa Udlandet. Udreisen foregik under meget gunstige Omstændigheder. Havet var forholdsvis roligt og med en vedvarende nordøstlig Vind kom vi over Nordsøen i tre Døgn. Det var første Gang, jeg befandt mig paa Havet; det var første Gang, jeg saa mit Fædrelands Klippekyst hurtig forsvinde og skjule sig bag Nordsøens "puklede Ryg." Alt var herligt og skjønt og bekræftede Sandheden af den norske Digters Ord: "Havet er skjønt, naar det roligen hvælver staalblanke Skjold over Vikingers Grav." Jeg havde naturligvis min Køie forud hos Skibsmandskabet og fik saaledes en herlig Anledning til at blive bekjendt med Sømandsstandens Liv og Væsen, der hidtil havde været mig næsten fuldkommen ubekjendt. Det første Indtryk, jeg fik af Sømandens almindelige Karakter, har ved senere Erfaringer i det Hele taget bekræftet sig, og Wolf [Simon Olaus Wolff] har Ret naar han siger: "Havet er herligt og herlige Sønner, stedse det fostred i kraftfulde Favn."

Om Opholdet i England kan jeg fatte mig meget kort. Næsten alt det, som her mødte Øiet, var nyt og forskjelligt og lagde uafladelig Beslag paa min Opmærksomhed. En Vildthandler i Newcastle ved Navn James Pape viste mig megen Godhed og gik med mig til de fleste Seværdigheder i Byen, hvoriblandt Musæet var det vigtigste og havde for mig overordentlig Interesse, saa jeg ofte senere tilbragte et Par Timer om Dagen her. Man var dengang nylig begyndt med Jernbaner i England, og jeg fik her Anledning til for første Gang at prøve Farten med Jernbane fra Newcastle til Shields og tilbage. Det flade, herlige Land i Tyneflodens Dalstrøg kunde ikke andet end have overordentlig Interesse for et Menneske, som aldrig før havde været udenfor det bjergrige og klippefulde Bergens Stift. Mine Udflugter, dels tilfods og dels med Postvognen, ud i Landdistrikterne, med Opholdet i de saakaldte Inns ved Veikanten, vare de behageligste af den Tid, jeg tilbragte i England. Sproget gav mig ingen Vanskelighed forsaavidt, at jeg godt kunde gjøre mig forstaaelig for Folket og fortælle dem, hvor jeg var fra, hvad jeg vilde osv.; men at forstaa dem, naar de, som det forekom mig, begyndte at lade Tungen løbe i Gallop, det havde desværre store Vanskeligheder og bragte mig i Førstningen ofte i alvorlig Forlegenhed. Det var let for Englænderen at gjenkjende Ordene, naar jeg udtalte dem som de skrives, men for mig at gjenkjende dem efter Lyden, der ofte er saa høist forskjellig fra Bogstaven, det fandt jeg alt andet end morsomt, allerhelst naar jeg fangedes i dumme Feiltagelser. Efter den første Uge var dog det værste hermed overstaaet. Fruentimmerne var det altid lettere at forstaa, da deres Stemme er skarpere og klarere for det uvante Øre. Mr. Papes Kone, som stod for Udsalget i Mandens Fraværelse, og som altid havde saa meget at snakke om, var mig til stor Hjælp med Ordenes Udtale, ikke blot fordi hun altid snakkede, men ogsaa fordi hun lagde an paa at udtale hvert Ord klart og bestemt. Baade hun og Manden vare meget venlige og kristeligsindede Folk; de bad mig komme med dem til Kirken, hvor jeg for første Gang fik høre den engelske Gudstjeneste. Mr. Pape gik ogsaa en Dag med mig til en af Byens store Almueskoler, hvor jeg fik Anledning til at anstille nogle Sammenligninger med Hensyn til Undervisningsvæsenet, hvilket jeg forresten ikke fandt stort anderledes end i de ældre Skoler i Bergen.

Den unge Søn af det bergenske Rederi, med hvis Skib jeg var kommen over, og som havde været den nærmeste Anledning til min Reise, skulde forblive ved et Handelskontor et Aars Tid, og da vort Skib efter sex Ugers Forløb blev seilfærdigt for Tilbagereisen, blev Spørgsmaalet for mig, om jeg skulde gaa tilbage med samme Skib eller vove at blive, til der gaves en anden Leilighed. Opholdet var dyrt, og jeg syntes min lille under den strengeste Sparsomhed opsparede Kapital blev temmelig haardt medtaget, ligesom mit sex

Maaneders Forlov maaske kunde udløbe, før jeg fik en ny Leilighed til at komme tilbage over Nordsøen; dengang var der nemlig ikke Dampskibsfart mellem de to Lande, som der nu er. Just som jeg en Dag ombord i vort Skib, som skulde afgaa næste Morgen, stod og omtalte denne Sag med vor Superkargo—en stolt, egennyttig Mand, hvis Velvilie jeg dog paa en Maade havde vundet ved at løbe en Mængde Ærinder for ham i Byen — kom en anden Bergens Kaptein, der seilede for samme Rederi, ombord og fortalte, at han netop var kommen op fra Shields med Jernbanen og ventede sit Skib opad Roveret, saasnart Flodtiden indtraf. Han ventede at blive henliggende i flere Uger, før han fik losset, og atter indtage en Ladning Stykgods, der almindelig medtager en hel Del Tid. Jeg vilde altsaa faa en fortræffelig Leilighed til at følge ham tilbage, hvorom jeg da ogsaa strax traf Overenskomst med ham. Det var en meget interessant, venskabelig og frisindet Mand, med hvem jeg senere kom til at staa i et fortroligt Forhold, og hvem jeg har at takke for adskillige Tjeneste. Opholdet i England blev saaledes forlænget til over tre Maaneder, og Mr. Papes skaffede mig en Timelærer, som kom og læste med mig en Time daglig for en meget ubetydelig Godtgjørelse.

En Handlende fra Kjøbenhavn ved Navn T. Hansen var bosat i Newcastle og var Kommissionær for næsten alle norske og danske Skippere, som ankom dertil. Paa den Tid, jeg var der, ankom et betydeligt Antal danske Jægter med Kornladninger, da Korntolden formedelst Mangel paa Brødstof var midlertidig bleven ophævet. Denne Kjøbmand Hansen havde en Søn, der ogsaa viste mig adskillig Velvilie under mit Ophold i Byen. Det var en godslig, selskabelig ung Mand, som forresten lod til at være en Loafer, der Intet vilde bestille uden at more sig. Naar og hvor han traf mig, sagde han: "I wish to drink a glass with you," og saa trakterede han, men altid kun med et Par smaa Vinglas.

Jeg havde altid fundet, at Sprogstudier var det, jeg lettest kom afsted med, og mit Engelsk begyndte derfor ved Udgangen af de tre Maaneder at blive saavidt respektabelt, at Mrs. Papes med stor Tilfredshed kunde sige mig, at jeg nu ikke mere behøvede at ryste med Hovedet og sige: "nichts verstehe." Forsaavidt havde Reisen altsaa ikke været forgjæves; dog var Frugten i andre Henseender af langt større Vigtighed for mig end Sprogkundskaben, der maaske vilde blive af liden praktisk Nytte. Det var nu først rigtig gaaet op for mig, at Verden paa en Maade laa aaben for mig; Blikket blev udvidet; det travle Liv i England, med den umaadelige Kontrast mellem Rigdom og Fattigdom, havde givet min Livsanskuelse en forandret Retning; det lille norske Kastevæsen med sine smaa Forargelser var trængt i Baggrunden ved Synet af de uhyre Fabrik- og Landmonopoler i England. Handelsaristokratiet begyndte her allerede at blive ligesaa mægtigt som Adelsaristokratiet. Ledsaget af Lykken kunde den dygtige og arbeidsomme Plebeier ved sine Handelsforetagender hæve sig op paa Pengearistokratiets Høider, lade sig vælge til Parlamentet osv. De Indtryk, jeg havde faaet, hvad jeg havde seet, hørt og erfaret paa min Englandsreise, gjorde mig mere haabefuld, lykkelig og tilfreds i min Stilling, end jeg nogensinde havde været. Jeg vilde med Troskab og Flid udtjene mine 7 Aar som Lærer og imidlertid forberede mig for Handelsstanden, saavidt Omstændighederne tillod.

Hjemreisen med den Skipper, som ovenfor er omtalt, frembød intet, som er værd Omtale. Med en drivende Vestenvind gik det i en rivende Fart over Nordsøen, og i et øsende Regn kom vi for fulde Seil ind gjennem Bergensleden efter 2½ Døgns Reise. Var det ikke for den store Told, som engelske Fabrik- og Manufakturvarer dengang var underkastet, vilde Fordelen have været enorm paa disse Varer; der foregik i de Dage ikke saa liden Smugling langs den norske Kyst, og Lodserne kunde nok fortælle om mangen Otteæring, hvori Havstrilen afhenter Ladninger af kostbart Silketøi, Juveler o. desl. fra Siden af de fra England kommende Skibe, medens disse ligge bak i dette Øiemed. Disse Folk ere naturligvis medskyldige i Smugleriet, og kan derfor ikke angive uden selv at blive straffet. Regnveir og Storm er selvfølgelig det gunstigste Veir for saadanne Operationer, da der under disse Omstændigheder kun er faa Folk ude og færdes.

Da der endnu var et Par Maaneder tilbage af den Tid, jeg kunde være borte fra Skolen, tilbragte jeg disse i Bergen, hvor jeg altid befandt mig bedre end nogensteds ellers. Jeg havde nu vundet flere Venner her, hos hvem Opholdet intet kostede mig, og til Gjengjæld læste jeg af og til lidt med Børnene i Huset. Enkelte Oplysningsvenner gav mig Adgang til deres Privatbibliotheker (noget andet offentligt Bibliothek end Leiebibliotheket havdes dengang ikke) og laante mig beredvillig de Bøger, jeg ønskede at læse. Læsning og Selvstudium var egentlig det, jeg denne Gang havde foresat mig at anvende min Tid til i Bergen; thi jeg formaaede ikke at kjøbe mange Bøger, og naar jeg kom tilbage i mit Distrikt, var der ingen jeg kunde laane af. Foruden en Fortsættelse af Læseøvelser i Tydsk og Engelsk, var det især Historie og Geografi samt en Del Reisebeskrivelser, som nu mest optog min Tid, og jeg erindrer ikke, at nogen andre to Maaneder af mit Liv har gaaet hurtigere eller mere lykkelig end disse. Paa Hjemreisen meldte jeg mig atter hos Præsten; han betragtede min Englandsreise fra et fornuftigt Standpunkt, udtalte sig særdeles tilfreds med mit Foretagende og tilføiede, at han kunde ønske ret mange af Lærerne vilde foretage sig noget lignende. Ved en Visitation i Hovedsognets faste Skole, som Provsten holdt en kort Tid derefter, var jeg ogsaa kommen tilstede for at se og høre, hvorledes det gik til i vor faste Skole. Da Personelkapellanen forestillede mig og fortalte, at jeg havde været i England o.s.v., behagede det ogsaa Provsten at udtale sig meget bifaldende, og han underholdt sig med mig et Kvarterstid, uden at jeg mærkede noget til de mørke Skyer, som under min Religionsexamen var trukket op over hans Aasyn. Ved Hjemkomsten besøgte jeg min gamle Moder og flere af mine Søskende. Moder var alt andet end tilfreds med mit eventyrlige Liv — saaledes kaldte hun mit Ophold i Bergen, min Englandsreise, ja endog mine Ombudsreiser som Præstegjældets Vaccinatør. Mine Søskende, som alle vare ældre end jeg og vare komne i Jordveie i Bygden, protesterede ret alvorligt mod den ubesindige Brug, jeg gjorde af mine Penge. De beklagede sig inderlig over, at jeg ikke benyttede den herlige Anledning, jeg havde til at spare sammen Penge nok til at kjøbe en Jordvei, og spaaede mig Betlerstaven som en uundgaaelig Følge af min Læsegalskab. En af mine Brødre havde faaet fat paa en norsk Sproglære, som tilhørte mig; af denne forelæste han mig: "Jeg elsker, jeg elskede, jeg har elsket, jeg skal elske" osv. og udbrød derpaa triumferende: "Det Menneske, som kan lægge Penge ud for saadant meningsløst Fjas, maa være gal." Det nyttede kun lidet, at jeg indvendte, at han vistnok ikke i en norsk Sproglære vilde gjenfinde sine Katekismus-Satser, men at den derfor kunde være nyttig til sit Brug. Ligesaalidt som en Plov duede til at harve med eller en Harv til af pløie med, kunde en Grammatik være en Religionsbog og omvendt. Jeg mindede om, at man jo fra min Barndom af paa det strengeste havde straffet mit Hang til Læsning, at jeg trods al Modstand havde gjennemført mine Forsætter saa godt som muligt, og jeg syntes, at Resultatet dog var langt bedre, end de havde spaaet mig, og jeg vilde nødig opgive min Tro paa, at det ogsaa i Fremtiden vilde gaa bedre end man spaaede. Saavel min Moder som mine Søskende elskede mig dog inderlig og deres Raad var oprigtig ment. De vare loyale Folk i Bygden og overholdt strengt de gamle Fædreneskikke og de nedarvede Vedtægter, medens jeg ved min Omgang med Bøger og med Mænd af den herskende Klasse saavelsom med Fremmede havde tabt meget af det gamle til vante; mange Fordomme vare afslebne og Livsanskuelsen i betydelig Mon forandret. Denne Forandring aabenbarede sig end tydeligere i Omgangen med Folket i mit Skoledistrikt, og det bedrøvede mig ofte at finde en tiltagende Uoverensstemmelse med de Enkelte, som for det meste før havde været passive Modstandere. I Skolen arbeidede jeg atter med fornyet Kraft og vandt fuld Anerkjendelse af mine Foresatte saavelsom en ret opmuntrende Paaskjønnelse hos Flertallet af Forældrene i Distriktet. Skolekommissionen havde udsat en liden Præmiebelønning for den bedste Omgangsskole i Præstegjældet. Der var 15 Distrikter foruden Fastskolen, og da mit Distrikt i lokal Henseende var mindre heldigt stillet, havde jeg ikke tænkt paa at komme i Betragtning ved Uddelingen. Da Personelkapellanen var den eneste, som besøgte alle Skolerne, blev man enig om, at hans Anbefaling skulde gjøre Udslaget, og han betænkte sig ikke et Øieblik paa at erklære, at der efter hans Mening ikke kunde være nogen Tvivl om, hvem Præmien rettelig tilkom. Hans Grunde bleve i Korthed udviklede og enstemmigt tiltraadte, og den næste Søndag overrakte han mig Præmiebelønningen i Kirken i Menighedens Nærværelse med nogle Bemærkninger, som for mig visselig vare meget smigrende. Jeg havde altsaa her høstet nogle Laurbær, som jeg slet ikke havde drømt om — i Grunden havde hele min Tanke og Stræben i den senere Tid været saa fuldstændig absorberet af mine Gjøremaal og de nye skiftende Scener, at den personlige Ærekjærhed, hvoraf jeg udentvivl havde min Andel, var traadt ganske i Baggrunden.

IX.
Forsøg paa at oprette et Læseselskab.

I et Tidsskrift, hvis Navn jeg nu har glemt, fandt jeg offentliggjort en Katalog over Bøger, som Forfatteren ansaa mest passende for Almuebibliotheker. Dette vakte den Tanke hos mig at gjøre Forsøg med Oprettelsen af et Læseselskab i vort Sogn. Læseselskaber og Sogneselskaber existerede allerede i en Del Præstegjæld, men hos os var der endnu ingen saadan Indretning, og jeg havde mangengang inderlig følt Mangelen deraf. Nu blev det til en klar og stærk Overbevisning hos mig, at et velvalgt omend lidet Sognebibliothek vilde være et af de virksomste Midler til Folkeoplysningens Fremme, og jeg lagde derfor strax Haand paa Værket med al den Varme og Utaalmodighed, hvormed jeg i denne unge Alder tog fat paa enhver Ting, som interesserede mig. Der gaves i vort Sogn nogle mere oplyste, fordomsfrie og fremadstræbende Mænd, som stedse havde staaet Last og Brast med mig i de Kampe, som det gamle og nye næsten til alle Tider fører mod hinanden. Disse gik strax med Liv og Sjæl ind paa min Plan; de fornødne Statuter blev udarbeidet, og en Indbydelse til et Læseselskab udstedt. Hvert Medlem skulde ved Indtrædelsen betale 3 Spd. og derefter en aarlig Kontingent af 1 Spd., hvilket vi regnede paa i nogle Aar at give os en respektabel lille Bogsamling, forudsat at vi fik det paaregnede Antal Medlemmer, og herpaa var det selvfølgelig Sagens Udfald beroede. Der tegnede sig virkelig flere, end vi havde turdet regne paa, og Foreningen talte snart 30 Medlemmer. Til det første Indkjøb havde vi altsaa henimod 100 Spd. En Komite af 5 Medlemmer blev valgt til at udarbeide en Liste over de Bøger, som først skulde kjøbes. Saavidt jeg nu erindrer, var det Henr. Wergeland, som havde udarbeidet den for Sognebibliotheker bestemte Katalog, jeg havde fundet, og fra denne gjorde nu Komiteen sit Udvalg, og det blev mig overdraget at reise til Bergen og besørge Indkjøbet. Fra nogle gamle Brevskaber, som endnu findes blandt mine Papirer, anfører jeg her Navnene paa nogle af de Bøger, der fandtes i den første Samling, som blev kjøbt: Sverdrups Magazin, 4 Bind; Norges offentlige Ret; Priis's Haugekunst; Platous Geografi; Primons Lexikon; Det vigtigste af Naturlæren; Filosofi for ulærde; Jurks Naturhistorie; Neumans Haandbog; Paludans Raad for syge; Husdyrenes Behandling; Abildgaards Heste- og Kvægavl; Boyes Regnebog; Holst's juridiske Haandbog; Odeens Regnebog; Blatz om Havekunsten; Viborg om Svineavlen; Willaume om Mennesket; Newton for Ungdommen; Kunsten at blive rig og lykkelig; Falch om Fiskeri; Hus- og Reiselæge; Hirschfeldt om Frugttræer; Dalgas Lærebog i Agerbruget; Mallings store og gode Handlinger; Naturlæren og Naturhistorien; Haandbog for Omgangsskoler; Munthes Fædrelands Historie; Platous Verdenshistorie; Odelsmands Tanker; Almanakmanden, osv., osv. Jeg har her nævnt saa mange af vore Bøger for at kunne vise, hvor vanskeligt det var paa den Tid og i den Egn, hvor jeg var hjemme, at kunne tilfredsstille Almuemanden; thi dette Udvalg af Bøger, som jeg hovedsagelig fik Skylden for, bragte mig saa mange Ubehageligheder, at jeg aldrig kan glemme det. Jeg havde vistnok ikke selv noget personligt Kjendskab til alle disse Bøger, men det faldt mig dog aldrig ind, at der i saadanne Bøger skulde findes noget anstødeligt for Religion eller Kirke, Moral eller Sædelighed, og dog blev Læseselskabet, paa Grund af dets Bøger, overøst med de groveste Beskyldninger for Vantro og Ugudelighed af dem, som havde modarbeidet Foretagendet, saa at endog nogle Medlemmer bleve forskrækkede og intet mere vilde have med Sagen at gjøre. Saavidt jeg nu kan erindre, var det den sidstnævnte Bog, der er et Forsøg paa at forklare de astronomiske Beregninger i vore Almanakker og gjøre de første Grunde af Astronomien forstaaelige for Almuemanden, som først vakte Mistanke og Modstand. Deri fandt man fremsat og forklaret den Lære, at Solen ikke gik rundt om Jorden, men at det var Jordens daglige Bevægelse om sin Axe, som frembragte Solens tilsyneladende Gang omkring Jorden, samt at det var Jordens aarlige Bevægelse i en oval Kreds, som frembragte Aarstidernes Afvexling — ikke Solens Flytten mod Syd eller Nord, som man hidtil almindelig havde troet. Denne Bog, mente man, vilde altsaa gjøre Bibelens Ord til Løgn, hvor det hedder, at Gud paa Josuas Bøn lod Solen staa stille paa Himlen en hel Dag for at give ham Tid til at fuldende sine Fienders Nederlag i et Feltslag, som da netop stod paa. Den indeholdt altsaa en kjættersk og sjælefordærvende Lære, og de, som hørte til Læseselskabet, maatte være vantro Hunde og Tyrker, som det ikke var ret at taale i Samfundet. Da nu først den overtroiske Mistanke var vakt, varede det ikke længe, før man fandt et eller andet, som var galt i næsten hver eneste Bog, og overhovedet var det jo galt at læse i verdslige Bøger.

Læsning skulde kun anvendes paa Gudsord, og det var derfor en skrækkelig Gudsbespottelse at læse om Hestens Sygdomme og Svinets Behandling— det var altsammen "Historiebøker" og løgnagtige Fabler, man havde faaet for sine Penge, og de, som læste saadanne Bøger, maatte være Hedninger, thi der fandtes ikke et Gudsord i dem.

Denne Gang havde jeg altsaa slemt forregnet mig; at komme med Forklaringer nyttede ikke og Forargelsen var saa stor, at Præsten heller ikke turde tage mig i Forsvar. Jeg havde jo heller ikke raadført mig med ham, om hvilke Bøger vi burde vælge, og kunde saaledes ikke vente, at han vilde gjøre sig upopulær hos Almuen, af hvem han fik sit Offer og Tiende, allermindst ved at forsvare Bøger, som han maaske selv ikke havde anseet passende til Folkelæsning. Hvad Medlemmerne angaar, da var der omkring Halvparten af dem, som vaklede og begyndte at tale om at maatte faa sine Penge tilbage, da de ikke ønskede at eie nogen Andel i saadanne Bøger eller være bekjendt for at høre med i en Forening, der hyldede slige Anskuelser. Den anden Halvdel, der bestod af mere oplyste og fordomsfrie Mænd i en yngre Alder, sluttede sig om mig med den faste Bestemmelse, ikke at lade sig kujonere af en saa urimelig Fanatisme. For de vaklende Medlemmer paaviste de det latterlige i deres Færd og bad dem forklare, hvorfor og hvorledes det kunde være større Synd at læse om Husdyrenes Behandling, om Træplantning, Havedyrkning o.s.v. end at tale derom, og det gjorde de dog ofte. Hvad Jordens og Solens Bevægelse angik, da var det jo lige let for den Almægtige at lade den ene som den anden staa stille, om han saa fandt for godt, og at man vel gjorde bedst i ikke at ængste sig over Guds Forsyns Hemmeligheder. Desuden var der jo stor Uenighed mellem Theologerne selv angaaende dette Bibelsted, og det maatte derfor synes bedst for Lægfolk ikke at hænge sig fast i disse vanskelige Steder, som blot vilde foraarsage Bekymring og Splid, men heller lade Kirkens beskikkede Authoriteter bestemme over dem. Ialfald burde man give lidt Tid, læse disse Bøger selv og se, hvad der virkelig lærtes i dem, se hvad det egentlig var de handlede om, og ikke lade sig forskrække af Folk, som man jo vidste modsatte sig al Kundskab og Oplysning. Den, som da efter en saadan fuldstændig og upartisk Prøvelse vedblev sit Forsæt at ville træde ud, skulde faa sin indbetalte Kontingent tilbage. Det endelige Udfald blev, at kun nogle enkelte meldte sig ud, mindre paa Grund af deres Overtro end fordi deres Læseøvelse og Forstandsudvikling var saa indskrænket, at de ikke kunde læse og end mindre forstaa de fleste af Bøgerne, og derfor kun fandt saare liden Interesse i dem. Men medens saadanne traadte ud, kom Andre med større Læseøvelse og mindre indsnørede Tanker og meldte sig ind som Medlemmer, saa at Foretagendet egentlig ikke faldt igjennem, men blev dog meget lammet og indskrænket i sin Virksomhed. Og selv min egen Gjerning i Skolen blev derved stillet i en Skygge, som paa flere Steder gjorde det koldt og uhyggeligt, og da dette netop var blandt dem, jeg skulde søge at vinde for Oplysningens Sag—de karske have nemlig ikke Lægedom behov, men de som have ondt—følte jeg saameget smerteligere det uheldige i min Stilling. Præsterne var oplyste Mænd, den ene af dem kunde jeg endog kalde frisindet, og mellem sig indbyrdes og med sine Standsbrødre lo de ofte over Almuens Fordomsfuldhed; men de vare forsigtige, kloge, konservative Mænd, der mente, at man ikke for en Ides Skyld burde skabe sig Fiender blandt dem, man skulde nyde godt af, og at det desuden gik fort nok med de nye Reformer, som maaske kunde føre derhen, hvor man ikke vilde. Vore Modstandere bestyrkedes derfor meget i sin Iver, da de fandt, at Præsten, der hidtil altid havde bistaaet mig i alle Skoleanliggender, nu ikke gav mig videre Bifald. Et Par Aars Tid efter udkom fra Kirke- og Undervisningsdepartementet et Reglement med Hensyn til Sognebibliotheker, hvori Sognepræsten i hvert Præstegjeld skulde bestemme, hvilke Bøger man skulde faa Lov til at anskaffe sig i Læseselskaberne. Herved vaktes for første Gang min Opmærksomhed for Regjeringens Politik—en Sag jeg hidtil ikke havde tænkt stort paa. Jeg saa nu, at man paa høiere Steder ikke ønskede at lade det gaa hurtig med Folkeoplysningen, men at Smulerne maatte uddeles langsomt og spredes med varsom Haand over et langt Tidsrum for at undgaa revolutionære Tendentser; at saaledes som Regjeringens Politik var, saaledes maatte ogsaa Embedsstanden udover det hele Land være. Jeg for min Del var kommen for langt, og saa var flere af mine unge Venner i vort Præstegjeld; thi i de senere Aar havde flere af de yngre Skolelærere saavel som andre, der agtede at blive Lærere, begyndt at komme til mig for at faa Undervisning, og der var paa en Maade fremstaaet et Slags spontant Lærerseminarium, som lovede vigtige Resultater. Det var muligt, at jeg her var kommen udenfor min anviste Virkekreds. Enkelte trofaste Venner i den herskende Stand lod mig forstaa, at hvis jeg ikke var forsigtig, kunde jeg let faa en Modbør, der vilde blive farligere end Folkefordommene. Et Brev, som jeg havde skrevet til en Ven angaaende adskillige offentlige Spørgsmaal, og hvori jeg tildels paapegede de Hindringer, Kastevæsenet lagde iveien for Folkeoplysningen, var ved Modtagerens Uagtsomhed kommet i urette Hænder. Da jeg en Dag paa Thingstedet ventede i Fogdens Kontor, hvor jeg skulde oppebære mit Vaccinationsgebyr, aabnede jeg en Bog, som laa i Vinduet for at se i den. Blandt Ligemænd kunde dette ikke være noget Anstød mod Etiketten; tvertimod er det jo noget sædvanligt, at man viser den ventende den Høflighed at give ham en Avis eller Bog at fordrive Tiden med, naar man ikke kan underholde ham med Samtale. Men her var det ikke Ligemænd, og den tilstedeværende Kontorist blev meget indigneret over min Impertinence, og spurgte i en opbragt Tone, hvad jeg gjorde. Det var ikke nogen Bog for Bønder (det var en dansk Roman, hvis Titel jeg har glemt). Mine foresatte havde vist mig for megen Godhed, jeg var bleven uforskammet og lønnede mine Velgjørere med Utak, man havde nu fundet, at jeg var bleven Vinkelskriver og man skulde nok vide at sætte en Stopper for mine Bedrifter blandt Almuen. Før jeg kunde svare eller udbede mig nogen Forklaring over denne Tiltale af et Menneske, som jeg ikke engang kjendte, kom Fogden og strax expederede min Forretning, uden at mæle et Ord, og det var først en Tid senere jeg fik vide, at mit Brev havde været Gjenstand for Hr. Fogdens Opmærksomhed.

X.
Handelsforetagender.

Alle disse Ting i Forening med den Beslutning jeg, som tidligere anført, havde fattet under Englandsreisen, bestemte mig nu til at tage Afsked, saasnart min Tjenestetid var udløben. I Virkeligheden havde jeg allerede ved min Hjemkomst fra England kjøbt Halvparten i en større Hardangerjægt og havt Andel i nogle Handelsforetagender, uden dog hidtil selv at have anvendt noget af min Tid dermed. Havde det ikke været for den frastødende Kulde, for ikke at kalde det med noget haardere Navn, hvormed jeg mødtes baade fra oven og fra neden i min Virksomhed for Folkeoplysningens Fremme, er det dog meget sandsynligt, at jeg var forbleven ved Lærerfaget, hvortil jeg af Naturen nærmest syntes bestemt. Nu derimod var der ingen Tvivl tilbage hos mig om, hvad jeg burde gjøre. Jeg havde nemlig endnu langt fra ikke gaaet længe nok i Livets Skole, jeg havde endnu ikke paa langt nær gjennemgaaet de Prøvelser, den Modgang og de Lidelser, som udfordres til at frembringe den Visdom og Maadehold, uden hvilke en fyrig Ungdomsnatur aldrig ret ved, hvad der bedst tjener den. Den modnere Erfaring viste mig senere, at jeg her havde spændt Buen for haardt. Hvorfor ikke være taalmodig og temporisere? Hvorfor ikke slaa af Noget hist og her af nogle Biting for dog at redde Hovedsagen? Rom blev ikke bygget paa en Dag. Naar man kunde anvende Aarhundreder paa at fuldføre en eneste Kirkebygning til Herrens Pris, hvorfor ikke være tilfreds med at lægge Sten til Sten i Folkeoplysningens herlige Bygning uden at ængstes over, at det gik saa langsomt? Det er dog en Bygning, som der stadig maa bygges paa fra Slægt til Slægt, uden at man kan sige, at den er færdig. Men det ligger ikke i det unge Hjertes Natur at søge Trøst mod Utak og Miskjendelse i sine gode Hensigter og redelige Forsætter; det tilhører den modnere Alder. Jeg havde dog mange hengivne og trofaste Venner, som oprigtig beklagede det afgørende Skridt, jeg nu skulde tage, og forsikrede mig, at jeg vilde komme til at fortryde det. Jeg havde selv ofte en bange Anelse herom, naar jeg saa tilbage paa de Aar, jeg her havde tilbragt. Jeg havde dog havt det saa godt, og det var bleven mig forundt at virke med større Held i mit simple Kald end mine Forgjængere. Børnene havde altid elsket, agtet og adlydt mig; mine jevnaldrende havde alle holdt af mig og glædet sig i min Omgang, Undervisning og Raad. De Venskabets Baand, som her vare knyttede, skulde nu atter overskjæres og jeg skulde igjen ud blandt Fremmede for at bryde en ny Bane. Men det sentimentale havde ikke stort Herredømme over mig, og Utak og Miskjendelse var dog den Mynt, man helst vilde betale med i den Stilling jeg havde, medens Handelens og Søfartens skiftende Scener og Storme lovede en langt mere uindskrænket Tumleplads for en Aand, som aldrig var tilfreds uden en rastløs Bevægelse.

Paa den Tid, her omtales, vare de saakaldte Hardangerjægter komne i stærkt Brug. Enkelte driftige og foretagsomme Mænd havde i kort Tid samlet Formuer ved de rige Fiskerier, som da gik for sig langs Norges Vestkyst baade Vinter og Sommer. Med en Fætter, som havde nogen Erfaring i Faget, besluttede jeg at prøve Lykken som Jægtefører. Jeg agter ikke her at give nogen udførlig Beretning om de tre travle og begivenhedsrige Aar, jeg tilbragte i denne Forretning. De Erfaringer, jeg gjorde, kan ikke have nogen stor almindelig Interesse, og det er maaske nok at sige, at hvad Lykken det ene Aar rundhaandet gav, tog den som oftest det næste Aar tilbage. Undertiden eiede jeg et Par Tusind Daler og saa igjen næsten ingenting, og da Pengefortjeneste i Handelsveien altid er Hovedsagen, syntes der at være lange Udsigter med at naa det tilsigtede Maal. Tanken om Udvandring til Amerika gjorde sig derfor atter stærkt gjældende hos mig. Jeg solgte derfor, hvad rørlig Eiendom jeg havde, og naar alt Regnskab var afgjort, havde jeg med alt mit Slid og Slæb ikke kunnet spare sammen saa meget som et Tusind Daler. Hvad enten det nu er det blinde Tilfælde eller den uundgaaelige Skjæbne, som gjør, at det ene Menneske neppe kan røre ved en Forretning, uden at Lykken begunstiger ham, kan et andet Menneske med al sin Flid og Omtanke aldrig vinde Lykkens Gunst. Hermed være det nu som det vil. Udfaldet blev, at jeg Vaaren 1843 reiste til Amerika.

XI.
Livet i Amerika.

Om denne Reise er der tidligere berettet Noget i denne lille Bog, og det skal ikke her gjentages. Ogsaa om Nybyggerlivet i Wisconsin er der tidligere berettet, saa at det ikke her ansees nødvendigt at tilføie mere. Om det lidet, jeg formaaede at udrette mellem Nybyggerne i det saakaldte Yorkville Settlement, kan jeg fatte mig i Korthed. Folkeoplysningen var, som man vil have seet, min Kjæphest. Som forhenværende Lærer interesserede jeg mig levende for Oplysningsvæsenet, havde en aktiv Andel i Oprettelsen af en engelsk Skole for Distriktet, virkede for Oprettelsen af et Skolebibliothek, Debatselskaber og Sangforeninger. Jeg skrev en Ansøgning til Post-Departementet i Washington om Aabningen af en Postrute gjennem Settlementet. Forsynet med talrige Underskrifter og en Anbefaling fra Wisconsins Legislatur sendtes Ansøgningen til Washington, hvor den strax blev bevilget og Postruten etableret. Det er nu snart 30 Aar, siden Postofficet "North Cape" oprettedes, og K. Adland, som endnu sidder i Embedet, blev ansat som Postmester. Dette Postkontor ligger i Midten af Settlementet og har udøvet en uberegnelig Indflydelse til Oplysning og Fremskridt i Naboskabet. Var ikke denne Postrute bleven aabnet netop da det skede, vilde den 3 Maaneder senere være bleven henlagt ad en anden Vei, og Folket i Settlementet vilde faaet fra 6 til 10 Mile at gaa til Posthuset. Man kan vanskelig beregne, hvad Virkning dette vilde have paa Brevvexling og Avislæsning. Det var altid med Tilfredshed, at jeg saa den stadigt stigende Intelligents og Udvikling i alt det, som var godt og nyttigt blandt de Norske paa dette Sted, og det glædede mig at vide, at det var faldet i min Lod at gjøre de første Skridt i denne Retning. Paa et andet Sted i denne Bog er omtalt min Andel i Udgivelsen af den første norske Avis i Amerika og skal ikke her gjentages.

I Aaret 1860 var jeg Medlem af Legislaturen, og som saadan faldt det atter i min Lod at gjøre mit Naboskab en Tjeneste. Der laa nemlig i Townet Norway en Strækning Swampland paa 2,500 Acres, hvilket tilhørte det saakaldte Drainingsfond og eiedes af Staten. Om at give dette Land til Town of Norway indleverede jeg et Lovforslag, udarbeidet med stor Omhu af en af Statens bedste lovkyndige. Denne Bill blev, efter en haard Kamp, antaget af begge Huse og blev Lov. Dette Land blev da solgt til de omboende Farmere for en lav Pris og de indkomne Penge anvendte til dets Udgrøftning. Istedetfor hidtil at have været en Kilde til malariske Febere og andre Sygdomme for den omboende Befolkning, blev det nu til en god Indtægtskilde som et rigt Hø- og Pastureland, og den nævnte Lov maa ansees for at have været til ikke saa liden Nytte for Naboskabet.

Det havde længe været paa Tale blandt mine Venner i Chicago, at jeg burde komme der og gjøre et nyt Forsøg med en norsk Avis; men da jeg selv havde gjort dyre Erfaringer og tillige seet, hvor uheldigt det havde gaaet andre, kunde jeg ikke give dem noget opmuntrende Svar. Endelig i Sommeren 1865 kom Hr. John Anderson ud til min Farm i Racine County, da han paa et Besøg hos sin Kones Forældre befandt sig i Racine. Han var kommen til Chicago med sine Forældre i en meget ung Alder og havde lært Bogtrykkerkunsten ved Chicago Tribune, og mine Venner havde anbefalet ham til mig som vel skikket til at bestyre Trykkeriet. Der blev dog dengang intet bestemt afgjort, da jeg endnu havde Betænkeligheder ved at indlade mig paa det vaagelige Foretagende. Tidlig om Vaaren det næste Aar kom han atter derud og bragte Anbefalingsbrev med sig fra Iver Lawson, hvori der fremholdtes Tanken om en liden Pengeunderstøttelse, hvis dette skulde blive nøvendigt, samt Forsikring om, at han ansaa Hr. Anderson kompetent som Bogtrykker og Forretningsfører. Derved overvandtes mine Skrupler, og Resultatet blev, at det første Nummer af "Skandinaven" udkom den 1ste Juni 1866. Hr. Marcus Thrane havde et Par Maaneder tidligere begyndt sin "Norske Amerikaner" i Chicago. Desuden havde vi de to ledende norske Aviser i Wisconsin, nemlig "Emigranten" i Madison og "Fædrelandet" i La Crosse. Alle troede derfor, at vort Foretagende var haabløst og vilde ende med Nederlag for "Skandinaven". Heri blev man dog skuffet; thi "Skandinaven" fandt uventet Støtte hos Folket, og da Hr. Thrane overgav sin Subskriptionsliste til "Skandinaven" mod en liden Godtgjørelse, vandt "Skandinaven" hurtig en stor Udbredelse og dens Fremtid blev betrygget. Mit Arbeide som Redaktør af "Skandinaven" ligger os altfor nær til her at trænge nogen nærmere Omtale. Som gammel Abolitionist var jeg altid en ivrig Forfægter af det republikanske Partis Grundsætninger, saalænge jeg forestod Redaktionen, og hvor meget eller hvor lidet dette havde at gjøre med Bladets heldige Fremgang hos Folket, ved jeg ikke. Sandsynligt er det, at en dygtig Forretningsførelse og en sparsom Bestyrelse af Trykkeriet reddede Bladet fra den Skjæbne, man havde forudsagt.

Mit Forsvar for den amerikanske Commonskole udgjorde, bortseet fra den politiske Virksomhed, maaske Hovedmomentet i mit Redaktionsarbeide og ledte til den uventede Hædersbevisning, at en af Chicagos Folkeskoler blev opkaldt efter mig. Den langvarige Diskussion om Slaveriet og Commonskolen tiltrak sig en almindelig udbredt Opmærksomhed og tjente stærkt til Bladets Udbredelse overalt, hvor de Norske boede.

I 1880 blev jeg paa Forslag af Redaktør [Ferdinand A.] Husher udnævnt som en af Wisconsins Electors paa den republikanske Ticket. Dette var en Hædersbevisning, som formodentlig skulde være Løn for en lang og tro Partitjeneste, og jeg negter ikke, at Udnævnelsen kunde have sit Værd som saadan; men seet fra en Arbeiders Standpunkt, der skal brødføde sig med haardt Arbeide, er det Pengeværdien han mest ser paa. For den Dag, Electorerne tilbragte i Madison ved Valghandlingen, fik de $2.50, medens Opholdet i Hotellet kostede dem $3.00 — altsaa et Tab af 50 Cents. Det er gjerne saa, at naar et Embede har Pengeværdi, er der Tusinder, som søger det, og det er vanskeligt at faa. Det er den almindelige Erfaring, jeg har gjort i politiske Anliggender, og jeg formoder, at dette var Grunden til, at denne Hæderspost blev givet mig, uden at jeg havde bedet derom. Jeg er ikke utaknemmelig for den Velvilie, mine Landsmænd viste mig i Konventionen ved deres enige Optræden for mig. Men naar det senere fortaltes i mit Naboskab, at nu havde jeg faaet et Embede, som med engang vilde gjøre mig til en Rigmand, beroede dette, som af ovenanførte vil sees, paa en Misforstaaelse af Sagen.

Hvad der senere tildrog sig i Washington og tillige kom tilsyne paa en saa bedrøvelig Maade i deres Kamp angaaende Byttet, har sat mig i stor Betænkelighed overfor Partipolitiken og givet mig en vis Afsky for den. Jeg har derfor raadet mine Landsmænd til større Uafhængighed og Alsidighed i deres politiske Virksomhed. Præsident Garfields Mord, det afskyelige Embedsjageri i Washington, Blaines Intriger mod Roscoe Conkling, hans Raab til Garfield paa Backbone, hvoraf fulgte Conklings Nederlag, Tabet af New York for Republikanerne og Clevelands Valg — alt dette aabnede mine Øine for Partipolitikens Fordærvelse og den Fare, som fra det blinde Partiraseri truede Landet, og jeg kom til den fulde og faste Overbevisning, at de store republikanske Majoriteter havde bragt hensynsløse Politikere til Fronten, og at det var blevet en Nødvendighed at bruge Bremsen for at holde dem i Tømme. Partierne er til for at holde hinanden i Tømme, og dette kunne de kun gjøre, naar deres Stemmetal er nogenlunde lige. En Smule Uafhængighed hos Vælgerne er derfor paa rette Sted — ja den er egentlig Valghandlingens Kjærne. Det samme gjælder ogsaa, naar vore Landsmænd søger Udnævnelser. Naar en Konvention tilsidesætter vor Nationalitet og saa at sige spytter os i Ansigtet, bør vi ikke skrige og skraale som et dængt Barn, men slaa igjen som myndige Mænd ved Valgurnen. Det er det eneste Vaaben, som bider paa Politikerne, og de, som bruger det, faar sit Ønske frem næste Gang; thi man skal jo have Stemmeflerhed for sin Ticket.

Biography.

Knud Langeland (October 27, 1813 – February 8, 1888)

Knud Langeland.

"Langeland's life and activities," the newspaper *Skandinaven* observed in his 1888 obituary, "must be considered among the most meaningful of immigrated Norwegians." Knud Langeland was born in the municipality of Samnanger east of the city of Bergen October 27, 1813 as the youngest of ten siblings, born to Knud Pedersen Langeland and Magdela Monsdatter Langeland. By all accounts, Langeland descended from a gifted family of farmers, his father being an enlightened and literate man. He died in 1827 when Knud was only thirteen years old.

Knud engaged in farm work to assist his mother, but as his biographers write, hungered for books and education. When the farm was sold after a few years, the young Knud was left to "seek his own fortune." He suffered the social injustice of his day. He pursued his own education, learning German by comparing a German-language Bible with the Norwegian biblical translation. In Bergen he continued his studies under the guidance of a student; his efforts to extend his knowledge were ridiculed by members of his family. After passing examinations, he was appointed itinerant schoolteacher and precentor in a community close to his birthplace. Knud considered the memories from this time of his life among his most joyful.

In addition to his teaching during the winter months, he found employment as public vaccinator of children in summer. During these years, Knud spent nearly six months in England, acquiring skills that later eased his adjustment to American society. His decision to emigrate related to his failed business ventures after he in 1841 resigned from public teaching. He became smitten with the America fever, and emigrated from Bergen in spring 1843 on the brig *Lucy Marie*. Older siblings with their families, a brother, Mons Knudsen Aadland, born 1793, and a sister, Magdela Knudsdatter Langeland, born 1800, had embarked for America on the *Ægir* in April 1837, the first emigrant ship from Bergen. After having surmounted initial difficulties, they encouraged Knud to join them in America. It was indeed a pioneer venture.

Yorkville Prairie in Racine County, Wisconsin, became Langeland's first home in America. His restless pursuit of knowledge and insight, moved him to participate in political party agitation and debates, and he already in 1844 joined a small, early group of abolitionists. It was again the bitter memories of social inequality and class distinction from his old homeland, as well as his strong sense of freedom, inspired by the poet Henrik Wergeland and an incipient Norwegian labor movement, that motivated his political engagement and protest against human slavery in the new land.

In 1845 Langeland settled on a claim in the southern part of Columbia County and is credited with being one of the four founders of the Norwegian Spring Grove settlement. He sold his claim and returned to his farm in Racine County the following year, where he gave his support to all initiatives that promoted the prosperity of the area. On April 10, 1849, he married the younger Anna Jensdatter Hatlestad (January 12, 1831 – July 16, 1908), who had emigrated from Skjold, crossing the Atlantic on board the *Norden* from Stavanger in May 1846 together with her brother Ole Jensen Hatlestad and parents Jens Olsen and Anne Olsdatter Hatlestad. The family they started in time numbered eight children.

Langeland described America as "the Land of Newspapers." He himself became one of the striking figures in the history of the Norwegian American press. The desire for a separate Norwegian newspaper arose, Langeland wrote, among "the more enlightened emigrated Norwegian peasants." During the 1840s Wisconsin became the main region of Norwegian settlement, at mid-century housing a Norwegian population of 9,467; Illinois, with a growing Norwegian urban colony in Chicago, had 2,067 Norwegians. In late fall 1849 Langeland together with his brother-in-law Ole Hatlestad purchased the weekly *Nordlyset*, which had been launched July 29, 1847 in the Muskego settlement to serve the Norwegian community, with a postal address at Norway, Racine County. They moved the newspaper to Racine and in June 1850 changed the name to *Democraten* and finally published it in Janesville. The last issue was dated in October 1851. Norwegian immigrants were not yet ready to support a Norwegian-language press. Politically the newspapers had affiliated with Free Soil Party's policy of free public lands and intense antislavery stance.

In 1856 Langeland for a time edited the weekly *Den Norske Amerikaner* (The Norwegian American) in Madison, Wisconsin, but his strong antislavery stance made him resign when the paper gave its support to the Democratic presidential candidate James Buchanan. Langeland's involvement in politics led to his election to the state assembly in 1860. Thereafter Langeland spent a number of years on his farm, content with having his opinion pieces printed in a newspaper like *Emigranten*, until he in 1866 was again induced to enter journalism, this time as editor of *Skandinaven*, launched in Chicago June 1 of that year. His editorship of *Skandinaven* from its start nearly continuously until 1881 gained him his greatest fame. He only parted company with *Skandinaven* for a few months in 1872 as co-publisher and editor of the weekly *Amerika*. It merged with *Skandinaven* and Langeland returned to its editorial office. It became an organ for the ordinary person and enjoyed a powerful position among Norwegian Americans; it for a time had the status of being the largest Norwegian-language newspaper, not only in America, but in the entire world.

Skandinaven was consistently Republican, and political candidates eagerly sought the newspaper's support. Langeland encouraged his compatriots to join the party that was founded on the eternal truth of equality before the law for all citizens of the land without regard to religion, place of birth, or color of skin. In 1880 the Republicans recognized his services by nominating him for presidential elector, and, being elected, he cast his vote for James A. Garfield.

Langeland expressed a clear anticlerical position against the high-church Norwegian Synod, and during the Civil War years and later strongly objected to the Synod clergy's teaching on slavery as being theologically justified –

"not in and by itself a sin." Langeland spoke for the laity in the Synod, which like Norwegian Americans in general abhorred slavery.

The low-church Eielsens Synod had early on made an antislavery resolution, and *Skandinaven* had great sympathy for the low-church movement and was thought of as its organ. Langeland entered into controversy with the Synod on a number of issues, and as long-time editor of the newspaper *Decorah-Posten*, Johannes Wist, wrote, his "ingrained ill-will toward Norwegian authority figures made him give special attention to Norwegian theologians in this country, who in his eyes represented the same mindset as the government officials in [his birthplace] Samnanger."

His defense of the American public school system against the Norwegian Synod pastors, who saw it as an inherent threat to Lutheranism and the Norwegian language, caused a controversy well documented in *Skandinaven*'s columns. Langeland editorially challenged the Synod clergy; he emphasized that the common school encouraged democracy, indirectly taught religious tolerance, and promoted patriotism and love of freedom. His defense of the common school led to the distinction of having one of Chicago's elementary schools named after him. In conclusion, historian Arlow Andersen's assessment of Langeland is fitting: "He transcended what might have been an unfortunate immigrant provincialism and, in the process, retained that which was durable in his cultural and religious heritage."

Knud Langeland died in his home in Milwaukee February 8, 1888, after a long illness, and is buried at Forest Home Cemetery in Milwaukee.

Sources/Kilder.

Arlow W. Andersen, "Knud Langeland: Pioneer Editor," in *Norwegian-American Studies and Records* (Northfield, MN, 1944), 122-38; Arlow W. Andersen, *The Immigrant Takes His Stand: The Norwegian-American Press, 1847-1872* (Northfield, MN, 1953); Arlow W. Andersen, *Rough Road to Glory: The Norwegian-American Press Speaks Out on Public Affairs, 1875 to 1925* (Philadelphia, 1990); Leola Nelson Bergmann, *Americans from Norway* (Philadelphia, 1950); George T. Flom, *A History of Norwegian Immigration to the United States* (Iowa City, IA, 1909); Jean Skogerboe Hansen, "A History of the John Anderson Publishing Company of Chicago, Illinois" (Master's thesis, University of Chicago, 1972); Knud Langeland, *Nordmændene i Amerika. Nogle Optegnelser om Den Norske Udvandring til Amerika* (Chicago, 1888); Odd S. Lovoll, *Norwegian Newspapers in America: Connecting Norway and the New Land* (St. Paul, MN, 2010); O. N. Nelson, comp. and ed., *History of the Scandinavians and Successful Scandinavians in the United States* (Minneapolis, 1900); Johannes B. Wist, *Norsk-Amerikanernes Festskrift 1914* (Decorah, IA, 1914); *Emigranten*, October 24, 1859, October 7, 1861; *Norden*, August 16, 1882; *Skandinaven*, January 18, February 1, 15, 1888.

Biografi.

Knud Langeland (27. oktober 1813 – 8. februar 1888)

"Langelands Liv og Virksomhed", bemerket avisen *Skandinaven* i hans nekrolog i 1888, "maa regnes blandt de mest betydningsfulde af indvandrede Nordmænds". Knud Langeland var født i Samnanger kommune øst for Bergen 27. oktober 1813 som den yngste av Knud Pedersen Langeland og Magdela Monsdatter Langelands ti barn. Etter alt å dømme, kom Langeland fra en begavet bondeslekt; hans far var en opplyst og belest mann. Han døde i 1827 da Knud var bare 13 år gammel.

Knud Langeland drev gårdsarbeid for å hjelpe sin mor, men som hans biografer skriver, hungret han etter bøker og lærdom. Da gårdsbruket ble solgt etter noen få år, måtte den unge Knud "prøve Lykken paa egen Haand". Han led under tidens sosiale urettferdighet. Han søkte utdannelse gjennom selvstudium, og han lærte seg tysk ved å sammenligne en tyskspråklig bibel med den norske bibeloversettelsen. I Bergen fortsatte han sine studier veiledet av en student; hans anstrengelser på å utvide sin kunnskap ble latterliggjort av noen av hans familiemedlemmer. Etter fullført ble han ansatt som omgangsskolelærer og klokker i en bygd nær hans hjemsted. Knud betraktet minnene fra denne tiden blant de lykkeligste i hans liv.

I tillegg til undervisning i vintermånedene, fikk han ansettelse som offentlig vaksinatør av barn om sommeren. I disse årene tilbrakte Knud nesten seks måneder i England og skaffet seg ferdigheter som lettet hans tilpasning til det amerikanske samfunnet. Hans avgjørelse om å utvandre er knyttet til hans feilslåtte forretningstiltak etter at han i 1841 sa opp sin lærerstilling. Han ble smittet av amerikafeberen og utvandret fra Bergen våren 1843 på utvandrerskipet *Lucy Marie*. Eldre søsken sammen med deres familier, en bror, Mons Knudsen Aadland, født 1793, og en søster, Magdela Knudsdatter Langeland, født 1800, hadde innskipet seg for overfarten til Amerika på *Ægir* i april 1837, det første utvandrerskipet fra Bergen. Etter at de hadde overvunnet de første vanskelighetene, rådet de Knud til å komme til Amerika. Det var sannelig et dristig pionérforetak.

Yorkville Prairie i Racine *county*, Wisconsin, ble Langelands første hjem i Amerika. Hans rastløse streben etter kunnskap og opplysning beveget ham til å delta i politisk agitasjon og debatt, og så tidlig som 1844 sluttet han seg til en liten og tidlig abolisjonistgruppe. Det var de bitre minner fra den sosiale urettferd og klasseforskjell fra gamlelandet, i tillegg til hans sterke frihetsfølelse, inspirert av dikteren Henrik Wergeland og den gryende norske arbeiderbevegelse, som motiverte hans politiske engasjement og protest mot menneskeslaveri i det nye landet.

I 1845 slo Langeland ned på et *claim* - nybyggerbruk - i den sørlige del av Columbia *county* og ble ansett som en av de fire grunnleggerne av det norske Spring Grove settlementet. Han solgte bruket året etter og flyttet tilbake til sin farm i Racine *county*, hvor han støttet alle tiltak som fremmet velstanden i området. 10. april 1849 ekteviet han den yngre Anna Jensdatter Hatlestad (12. januar 1831 – 16. juli 1908), som utvandret fra Skjold og krysset Atlantern ombord på *Norden* fra Stavanger i 1846 sammen med en yngre bror Ole Jensen Hatlestad og sine foreldre Jens Olsen og Anne Olsdatter Hatlestad. Deres familie talte med tiden åtte barn.

Langeland beskrev Amerika som "Avisernes Land". Han selv ble en av de framstående skikkelser i historien til den norskamerikanske presse. Ønsket om en egen norskamerikansk avis ble til, skrev Langeland, blant "de mere oplyste af de udvandrede norske Bønder". I 1840-årene ble Wisconsin hovedområdet for norsk settlement. I 1850 huset staten en norsk befolkning på 9 467; Illinois, med en voksende norsk urban koloni i Chicago, hadde 2 067 nordmenn. Senhøstes 1849 kjøpte Langeland sammen med sin svoger Ole Hatlestad ukebladet *Nordlyset*, som var blitt lansert 29. juli 1847 i Muskego-settlementet for å stå til tjeneste for det norske samfunnet, med postaladresse i Norway, Racine *county*. De flyttet avisen til Racine og i juni 1850 forandret navnet til *Democraten* og til slutt ga den ut i Janesville. Det siste nummer er datert i oktober 1851. Norske innvandrere var ikke enda rede til å gi sin støtte til en norskamerikansk presse. Politisk hadde avisen sluttet seg til free soil-partiets politiske program om fritt offentlig land og intense antislaveristandpunkt.

I 1856 redigerte Langeland en tid ukebladet *Den Norske Amerikaner* i Madison, Wisconsin, men hans sterke antislaveristandpunkt overbeviste ham om å trekke seg fra stillingen da avisen ga sin støtte til den demokratiske presidentkandidaten James Buchanan. Langelands deltakelse i politikk førte til hans valg til statens lovgivende forsamling i 1860. Etter den tid oppholdt han seg en del år på sin farm, og nøyde seg med innlegg i en avis som *Emigranten*, til han i 1866 ble overtalt til å vende tilbake til journalistikk, denne gang som redaktør i *Skandinaven*, lansert i Chicago 1. juni det året. Hans redaktørstilling i *Skandinaven* fra dens begynnelse nesten kontinuerlig fram til 1881 skaffet ham hans største berømmelse. Han skilte lag med *Skandi-*

naven bare noen få måneder i 1872 som medeier og redaktør i ukebladet *Amerika*. Det fusjonerte med *Skandinaven* og Langeland returnerte til redaktørkontoret. *Skandinaven* ble en avis for den vanlige person og hadde en sterk posisjon blant norskamerikanere; i en tid hadde den status som den største norskspråklige avis, ikke bare i Amerika, men i hele verden.

Skandinaven var konsekvent republikansk og politiske kandidater søkte ivrig avisens støtte. Langeland oppfordret sine landsmenn til å slutte seg til partiet som var grunnet på den evige sanning om likhet under loven for alle borgere i landet uten hensyn til religiøs tro, fødested eller hudfarge. I 1880 anerkjente republikanerne hans tjenester og nominerte ham til president-valgmann, og, da han ble valgt, ga han sin stemme til James A. Garfield.

Langeland ga uttrykk for en tydelig antiklerikal innstilling mot den høykirkelige Norske Synode, og under borgerkrigen og senere protesterte han mot Synodepresteskapets lære om at slaveri var teologisk berettiget – "ikke en Synd i og for sig". Langeland talte for legfolk i Synoden, som i likhet med norskammerikanere flest avskydde slaveri.

Den lavkirkelige Eielsens synode hadde tidlig vedtatt en resolusjon mot slaveri, og *Skandinaven* hadde stor sympati for den lavkirkelige bevegelsen og ble betraktet som dens organ. Langeland engasjerte seg i kontrovers med Synoden i et antall saker, og som langtidsredaktør i *Decorah-Posten*, Johannes Wist, skrev "at han med sin indgrodde uvilje mot norske øvrighetspersoner særlig la sin elsk paa de norske teologer herover, der i hans øine representerte samme aandsretning som embedsmændene i [hans fødested] Samnanger".

Hans forsvar av det amerikanske offentlige slolestellet mot Den norske Synodes prester, som betraktet det som en inherent trussel mot den lutherske tro og det norske språk, førte til en kontrovers som er godt dokumentert i *Skandinavens* spalter. Langeland utfordret Synodepresteskapet redaksjonelt; han framhevet at *common school* ansporet demokrati, indirekte lærte religiøs toleranse og fremmet patriotisme og kjærlighet til frihet. Hans forsvar av *common school* førte til hedersbevisningen å få en av Chicagos grunnskoler oppkalt etter seg. Som konklusjon er historiker Arlow Andersens bedømmelse passende: "Han transcenderte det som kunne ha blitt en uheldig innvandrerprovinsialisme og i denne prosessen beholdt det som var varig i hans kulturelle og religiøse arv".

Knud Langeland døde i sitt hjem i Milwaukee 8. februar 1888 etter en lang sykdom og er bisatt på gravplassen Forest Home Cemetery i Milwaukee.

Odd Sverre Lovoll
Professor Emeritus of History, St. Olaf College

Index

"aa" and "æ" indexed with "a" and "ø" indexed with "o"